From Exile to Diaspora

From Exile to Diaspora

Versions of the Filipino Experience in the United States

E. San Juan, Jr.

WestviewPress
A Division of HarperCollins*Publishers*

Chapter 3 is a revised version of "In Search of Filipino Writing," in David Palumbo-Liu, ed., *The Ethnic Canon* (Minneapolis: University of Minnesota Press, 1995). Reprinted with permission. Chapter 5 is a revised version of "From National Allegory to the Performance of the Joyful Subject: On Philip Vera Cruz," *AmerAsia Journal* 21.3 (1995–1996). Reprinted with permission. Chapter 7 is a revised version of "Fragments from an Exile's Journal," *AmerAsia Journal* (forthcoming). Reprinted with permission. The author also thanks R. Zamora Linmark for permission to reprint excerpts from his poem in *Rolling the R's*; the UCLA Asian American Studies Center for permission to reprint excerpts from Al Robles's poems in *Rappin' with Ten Thousand Carabaos in the Dark*; and Nick Carbo for permission to reprint excerpts from his poem "Running Amok."

Published in 1998 in the United States of America by Westview Press, 5500 Central Avenue, Boulder, Colorado 80301-2877, and in the United Kingdom by Westview Press, 12 Hid's Copse Road, Cumnor Hill, Oxford OX2 9JJ

Library of Congress Cataloging-in-Publication Data
San Juan, E. (Epifanio), 1938–
   From exile to diaspora : versions of the Filipino experience in the United States / E. San Juan, Jr.
    p. cm.
   Includes bibliographical references (p.   ) and index.
   ISBN 0-8133-3169-2 (hardcover)
   1. Filipino Americans—Ethnic identity.   2. Filipino Americans—Cultural assimilation.   3. American literature—Filipino American authors.   I. Title.
E184.F4S26 1998
305.89'921073—dc21
                                                          97-43234
                                                            CIP

10   9   8   7   6   5   4   3   2   1

*To the memory of thousands of martyrs to
the cause of popular democracy and national liberation,
among them Gene Viernes, Silme Domingo,
Maria Lorena Barros, Magtanggol Roque,
Rolando Olalia, Macliing Dulag, Bobby de la Paz,
Emmanuel Lacaba, Edgar Jopson,
and nameless others*

Contents

Acknowledgments

An accidental but heuristic coincidence underlies the publication of this book: 1998 marks the centenary of the founding of the first Philippine Republic and also the intervention of the United States with the outbreak of the Spanish-American War. After the Filipino-American War of 1898–1902 and the defeat of the Filipino revolutionary forces, the Philippines became a colonial possession of the United States, with its people subjugated and "Americanized" for almost a century.

This is the context in which Filipinos—neither aliens nor citizens but "nationals"—appeared first in Hawaii, then in California, Washington state, and throughout the North American continent. One can say that the interruption of the struggle for national independence and popular sovereignty is what inaugurates the beginning of the narrative of Filipino lives in the United States. It is a narrative still unfolding, replete with countless episodes, reversals, ellipses, flashbacks and flash-forwards, unpredictable climaxes, and repetitions, seemingly without any denouement. It is a narrative of unity and contradiction. In this collection of essays, I attempt to present versions of this narrative to provoke an interrogation of the conventional wisdom and a critique of the global system of capital. It is a system whose triumph over its challengers (either of socialist or "Third World" inspiration) is being celebrated without any awareness of its origin in the domination and genocide of people of color, including the million Filipinos who died at the turn of the century resisting imperial power.

On the threshold of the twenty-first century, I take this opportunity to dedicate this book to the memory of Filipinos, in the Philippines and in the diaspora, who sacrificed their lives for the freedom, dignity, and happiness of present and future generations. The struggle for those ideals is still continuing today.

I am grateful to the following colleagues and friends for their unstinting help and cooperation: James Bennett, Alan Wald, Sam Noumoff, Arif Dirlik, Robert Dombroski, Bruce Franklin, Tim Libretti, Roger Bresnahan, Jim Zwick, Michael Lowy, Elmer and Elenita Ordoñez, Soledad Reyes, Joseph Lim, and Emmanuel T. Santos. Thanks also to Dr. Enrique de la Cruz of the University of California

(Los Angeles) Asian American Studies Center for organizing the Round Table Discussion with students at UCLA in February 1995; Russell Leong, editor of *AmerAsia Journal*; Professor Evelyn Hu De-Hart, chair of the Department of Ethnic Studies, University of Colorado; Professor Paul Wong, former Director of Comparative American Cultures Program at Washington State University; Dr. Karen Gould, Dean of the College of Arts and Letters, Old Dominion University; Professor Michael Martin, Chair of the Department of Ethnic Studies, Bowling Green State University; and to many students, among them Jeffrey Arellano Cabusao and the Oberlin College group, Theo Gonzales, Augusto Espiritu, Zeus Leonardo, and others who are my critics and comrades in the "long march." For insights, corrections, advice, and protracted conversation on the topics of this book, I am eternally indebted to Karin Aguilar–San Juan, Delia Aguilar, and Eric San Juan.

Finally, I wish to thank the editors and publishers of the following journals and books in which the essays here first appeared in rough, early versions: *AmerAsia Journal, Mediations, Philippine Studies, Diaspora, The State of Asian America* (edited by Karin Aguilar–San Juan), *American Literary History, Racial Formations/Critical Transformations* (Humanities Press), *The Ethnic Canon* (edited by David Palumbo Liu), *Journal of Ethnic Studies, Prisoners of Image* (New York City Alternative Museum), and *Kultura*.

                                                    E. San Juan, Jr.

Introduction

In the discipline of cultural studies today, the discovery of the body—
its pain, boredom, rapture, the virtual inexhaustibility of its finitude—
may signal a shift away from the despotism of the sign that has so far
prevailed in the discourses of the academy and the "social corps"
(Meillassoux 1993) of the propertied classes. But, in a milieu of reactionary backlash, a greater danger lurks behind this momentous
change. Are we returning to a newly discovered substratum of truth,
the ultimate referent that can no longer be deconstructed? Faces, eye
shapes, skin colors, hair textures, and so on—all these resurrect
clichés, banal stereotypes, the platitudes and blandishments of average "common sense." Such concentration on surfaces and appearances
eventually triggers explosions of catastrophic magnitude, as in Los
Angeles in May 1992. Meanwhile, the "specter" of essentialism returns, its transcendental metaphysics and closure as seductive as
ever—a paradoxical turn of events in the present triumphalist reign of
the universal commodity in the fabled "free" marketplace of ideas.

Everyone in our individualist and fragmented world is suspicious of
generalizations. Skepticism of abstractions prevails. We are urged to
attend to the lived circumstantialities of everyday life, to the concrete
"thickness" of experience. Bodies register their centrality when victims of racial violence hit the headlines. We are then forced to analyze
society and locate bodies in a complex network of ideas, values,
norms. Everything becomes problematized, requiring the testing of
theory by practice. But fetishism of the body by the practitioners of
"identity politics" tends to obscure its articulation with invisible social categories, among them class, gender, nationality, and of course
"race." What results is the disciplinary and prophylactic anatomizing
of bodies named "Rodney King," "Vincent Chin," and so on. And
when this valorized and construed body turns out to be inhabited by a
EuroAmerican *mentalité*, sole proprietor of a transcendent "Reason,"
then we are back to the status quo of normative ruling-class paradigms that legitimize the colonization of Other bodies and of course
their worldwide commodification.

1

Amid the ruins of the affluent society, where then is the embodied psyche of the informed citizen? To be sure, it has not escaped definition by class, gender, race, sexuality, and so on. "Social relations penetrate the body, structure its psychic 'central fire'; psychic structure is social structure alive in the heart of the body" (Thrift 1996, 85). Colette Guillaumin (1995) has penetratingly described how women's bodies have been appropriated on multifarious levels by the worldwide regime of patriarchal capital. Granted these generalities, whose bodies in which times and places are we speaking about? What particular embodiments, what specific incarnations, are we engaged with? What configurations of geopolitical space can we point to that can map and reinscribe bodies (marked "Oriental" or exotic) other than the unmarked Western ones? As a fellow Asian once remarked, "All I asking for is my body."

Let me focus on singular bodies here in a unique historical conjuncture. I refer to bodies coming into U.S. territory from the southeast Asian islands called the Philippines, a former U.S. possession but now regarded formally as a sovereign nation-state—one current of the burgeoning and unprecedented Filipino diaspora, a phenomenon analogous not to the Jewish but to the African and Chinese dispersal around the world. I offer here only "versions" of this complex ongoing experience, hoping to capture the nuances of a predicament constituted by multifaceted contradictions.

According to the 1990 official census, Filipino bodies now total 1,406,770, next in number to the Chinese, with the Japanese, Indians, and Koreans following behind (U.S. Bureau of the Census 1993). By the year 2000, the Filipino body count will approach 3 million, making it the largest Asian American populace (Filipinos are now the majority Asians in California). These figures do not of course include the undocumented, overstaying Filipinos (typically those who entered as tourists, students, and so on), numbering in the millions. Nor do the figures include the more than 30,000 Filipinos serving in the U.S. Navy, a number exceeding the total manpower of the Philippine Navy itself—an anomalous phenomenon of Filipino citizens in search of vertical mobility functioning as mercenaries for the former colonial master, a telltale sign that scrambles time and space, making everything complicitous. In any case, what do these numbers signify for the Filipino "presence" in the register of U.S. civil discourse that polarizes persons into either citizen or enemy (Alexander 1992)?

Any number of guidebooks for the perplexed do-gooder will index the difficulties of locating Filipinos in the geopolitical and historical map of the United States. Who are these persons called "Filipinos"? What are the signs disclosing them? One of the more circumspect books is Theodore Gochenour's *Considering Filipinos* (1990). Although Gochenour is one of the very few who recognize the profoundly racialized and subjugated culture of Filipinos, he is still unable to avoid the lure of searching for "the essential Filipino." After a survey of Philippine history, geography, customs, religions, and languages, Gochenour relies on functionalist methodology to interpret selected batches of information that posit an object of knowledge: the Filipino people. Such an explanatory framework privileges value-laden practices—here we meet the hackneyed rubrics *pakikisama* (getting along with others), *hiya* (propriety or shame), and *utang na loob* (internal indebtedness)—that in effect hypostatize the Filipino in an abstract, timeless schematization designed to fix the Filipino "national character" for purposes of state policies. Culturalism of this type detaches beliefs and actions from the context of dynamic social relations, thus reifying them (Dirlik 1997). Of course, Gochenour is not alone in this taxonomic enterprise. In their popular guidebook in the series *Culture Shock* (1985), Alfredo and Grace Roces repeat the "party line." With various examples, they elaborate the formula of the "*hiya-amor-propio* syndrome," coupled with the *compadrazgo* system and the *barangay* or village kinship, as the key to unlock what under Western surveillance is deemed the enigmatic and well-nigh inscrutable "lovely Filipino."

Revisions of orthodoxy have occurred, to be sure, but their impact has not yet been fully assessed. Although the conscientious ethnographer knows how the sedimentation of history has altered the configuration of the Filipino "psyche," or more precisely its repertoire of predispositions and *habitus* (to use Bourdieu's 1986), the import of such changes has not been taken into account even in the sophisticated textbooks written by U.S. experts on the discipline of "Filipinology" like David Steinberg, Theodore Friend, Peter Stanley, Glenn May, and others. Shying away from fixities, generalizations, and stereotypes, we end up ironically with a conundrum, perhaps a postmodern riddle. As Gochenour puts it: "There is a general sense of being neither this nor that, of sharing something of the Pacific islands, of being heavily influenced by Spanish and American cultures, and of perceiving only a remote historical relationship with the major civilizations of Asia. If asked what the people of the Philippines are, the Filipino answer may well be, 'We are ourselves'" (1990, 42). "Ourselves" here signifies a sociopolitical construct inscribed by uneven historical pressures and determinations.

As simple as it may seem, this business of identifying and validating "ourselves" is a formidable challenge. For the question of identity is, I submit, not a matter of isolating a given substance or quality, an inimitable essence; rather, it is a matter of referencing a grid of multivariable relations, a constellation of movements, trajectories, interactions—games of positioning, if you like, with life-or-death stakes. This complexity, however, is translated into postmodern flux and mutability. Consider, for example, the case of the Hawaii-born Filipina film star Tia Carrere: She is better known as Jade Soong or Venus Poon, Chinese personae in TV productions (Hamamoto 1994, 14). Less slippery in identity, or so we think, are Filipino activists like Joanne Bunuan (featured in the *New York Times Magazine*,), whose union organizing for the AFL-CIO disturbs the cobwebs of memory shrouding the Manongs (literally, "elders," referring to the farmworkers of the first three decades of the twentieth century), the generation of Philip Vera Cruz, Pablo Manlapit, Chris Mensalvas, and others (Belkin 1996). In documentary films like *A Dollar a Day, Ten Cents a Dance*, or *In No One's Shadow*, the Filipino is transfixed in a few stereotyped images: Once indentured hands, middle-class Filipinos are alleged to be on the way to "model minority" success. Have we really moved out of the shrouded margin into the limelight of core substantiveness? Because the hegemonic regime of representation still labors in the shadow of corporate power, misrecognition persists and impostors abound.

Despite our climate of multiculturalism, we are reputed to be burdened by cultural nostalgia and nationalist ethos, preserving our foreignness (Buell 1994). Even though we disavow ethnic revivalism and any claim to "primordial" authenticity, the difficulties of negotiating the ambiguities of overlapping, interfused cultural spaces cannot be wished away. But I also disclaim being a creature of "in-between" spaces, liminality, border crossings, hybridity—which is easier said than done. The reason for this, as I have elaborated elsewhere (1996c), is the finesse and ferocity of the colonial violence we have suffered under U.S. white supremacist power, a heritage filled with contradictions and paradoxes that needs scrupulous inventory to be surpassed. Postcoloniality enunciated in an anti-imperialist, revolutionary direction is embedded in this heritage.

It seems almost an unavoidable if somewhat comic necessity now, at least in the academic world, for someone who appears to be from a minority enclave to be labeled a "postcolonial" scholar or expert—unless you happen to be from East Timor; Corsica; Kurdistan; or, nearer U.S. shores, Puerto Rico, in which case your postality is in danger of evaporating or of being exposed as a fraud. My mailing address is no longer Manila, Philippines—for about half a century a bona fide colony of the United States and once administered under the Bureau of Indian Affairs, the Philippine Islands was granted formal independence in 1946.

The year 1998 marks the centennial of the first Philippine Republic, born from the fires of the 1896 revolution against Spain. In search of a springboard to the China market, the United States suppressed this embryonic Philippine Republic in the Filipino-American War of 1898–1902, killing a million resisting Filipinos and converting the rest into what William Howard Taft called "little brown brothers." It was an aborted revolution. During World War II, Filipinos under the U.S. flag died fighting against the Japanese. Independence was given soon after—but under duress: The Philippine Constitution had to be amended to give U.S. citizens parity in exploiting the country's natural and human resources. Original or primitive accumulation seems to have seized the country, repeating the age of booty capitalism in the sixteenth century. Throughout the Cold War epoch, the Philippines remained a virtual possession, a neocolony if you will, with over a dozen U.S. military installations, dependent militarily, economically, and culturally on the rulers in Washington. Despite the removal of the military bases, however, most Filipinos have been so profoundly "Americanized" that the claim of an autonomous and distinctive identity sounds like plea bargaining after summary conviction. We might have to go back and spend more time in the neocolonial prison to reeducate ourselves and earn "points" for parole and eventual release.

Most Americans who have visited the Philippines since 1945 confirm the trait of dependency: Filipino society is a nearly successful replica of the United States—except that its citizens are mostly dark skinned, poor, Roman Catholic in faith, and also speak a variety of American English. As for this last difference, Arjun Appadurai (1994), a postcolonial scholar, thinks it is negligible on the testimony of the world traveler Pico Iyer, who swears that Filipinos can sing American songs better than Americans themselves. How is this feat possible? Can we believe a mimicry or facsimile is better than the original—unless the original itself has lost its foundational, originary virtue and become a simulacrum? Can Filipinos, unbeknownst to themselves, be better Americans than Americans? Are we now, by that token, postcolonized and cast into what Aijaz Ahmad (1995) calls "the infinite regress of heterogeneity"? Is the Filipino experience of subjugation by and resistance to U.S. imperialism then a case of postcoloniality analogous to the experience of the Canadians and Australians, the Indians and Jamaicans, as the authors of *The Empire Writes Back* (Ashcroft et al. 1989) claim?

Today, we need a consensus to embark on a cognitive-ethical mapping of United States–Philippines relations that goes beyond the issues of postcolonial discourse, subaltern representation, and ethnic heterogeneity. The trope of "borderlands," now legitimized in canonical discourse, has become a ludic bait or alibi for opportunism. Like-

wise, "identity politics" has proved an accessory to evangelical pluralism, at best a locus of instability to be transformed into a habitat for
opposition and resistance. We need to redeploy the categories of nation, peoplehood, class struggle, sexuality, and gender to redefine the
specificity of the Filipino presence in the world arena. We need to delineate the Filipino role in the ongoing critique and revision of social
contracts in the international public sphere: as a force either for pre-
serving/maintaining the "New World Order" of market priorities or
for accelerating the process of radical democratic transformation.
What deserves imperative attention is the priority of popular empowerment and the primacy of justice as premises for building a democratic praxis of communicative interaction, that is, a dialogue of
equals. Forsaking chameleonic role playing and the masks of the savvy
trickster who can signify anything the master wants, we begin to engage in recovering our long and durable history of revolt against colonial oppression. Identity, I contend, is born from our responsibility to
the past, no longer a nightmare but a resource of hope, and from our
accountability to the present. Self-identification in freedom, then, is a
future always in the process of ceaseless renegotiation, from the destruction of one permanence and the construction of a new one. The
question of agency is thus "defined in terms of political commitment"
(Harvey 1996, 107).

Our future as a diasporic community is not so enigmatic as the previous reflections may suggest. Both separatism and assimilation are
not warranted by the field of possibilities already surveyed. By all
reckoning beyond the obsolescent facts in textbooks, Filipinos are
rapidly becoming (if they are not already in the official records) the
majority in the Asian American population of over 10 million. In 40
years, the Filipinos will expand to 4 million if present trends continue
(Gonzales 1993, 95). Because of this demographic change and the advent of a new generation of unevenly conscienticized Filipinos, it is
perhaps the opportune time to assert our relative autonomy from the
sweep of the categorizing rubric of "Asian American" even as we continue to unite with other people of color in tactical coalitions to assert
conjunctural political demands.

There is a specific reason why the Filipino contingent in the United
States (even though the majority are still unable to distinguish us
from Asian "look-alikes") needs to confront its own singular destiny
as a "transported" (in more ways than one), displaced, and disintegrated people. That reason is of course the fact that the Philippines
was a colony of the United States for over half a century and persists
up to now as a neocolony of the nation-state in whose territory we
find ourselves domiciled, investigated, and circumscribed. The reality

of U.S. colonial subjugation and its profound enduring effects—something most people cannot even begin to fathom, let alone acknowledge the existence of—distinguish the Filipino nationality from the Chinese, Japanese, Koreans, and other Asian cohorts. We are still suffering the trauma from the incalculable damage inflicted by the forward march of white supremacy. To understand what this means is already to resolve halfway the predicament and crisis of dislocation, self-hatred, pathological servility, exclusion, and alienation—tremendous spiritual and physical ordeals that people of color are forced to undergo when Western settlers and powers fight to divide the world into spheres of domination for the sake of capital accumulation and populations are expediently shuffled around in the global chessboard of warring and collusive interests (Van der Pijl 1997). This modern version of the Babylonian captivity cries out for a deliverance more attuned to human needs than the enunciation of a new amphibious identity, more decisive in remolding structures than a virtuoso shift in subject positions.

The irony is that although longing for home, Filipinos now "belong" to the whole world, in a manner of speaking. Formerly redundant liabilities, they become assets, "human capital," when they transplant themselves. This crisis of deracination and unsettlement (permanent or temporary) afflicting a whole society becomes pronounced in the phenomenon of the "brain drain," a factor that explains the continuing underdevelopment of the South or "Third World." It is not a joke to say that the Philippines, an economic basket case during the last decade of Marcos's despotic rule, produces every year thousands of doctors, nurses, scientists, and engineers for the world market. As exchangeable commodities, many of them immediately head for the United States—note that there are several million "warm body exports" now inhabiting the Middle East and Europe—whereas in the Philippines, where 80 percent of the people are poor and 30 percent of the children malnourished, most towns and villages lack decent medical and health care (not to mention other vital social services) to sustain a tolerable quality of life for their citizens (Aguilar 1997). For the new settlers, this sorry plight is now erased from memory, translated into a safe language, or set aside for retrieval on occasions when a need arises to justify why they left the no-longer-hospitable homeland.

Memory gives way to the omnipresent struggle for existence. Understandably enough, most Filipinos are busy earning enough to survive, to "make it," and at the same time support relatives and extended kin in the Philippines. As much as possible, these petty bourgeois "expatriates" (an honorific term for economic refugees) want nothing to do with what goes on politically in their country of origin (or even in the United States, for that matter) even though practically all the ordinary folk you encounter in the shopping malls and other public sites cannot but connect them to those islands—are they still "our" colonies in the Caribbean? How many Filipinos have we not heard confessing to their U.S. hosts that "My country [of origin] is shit!" and that they are so happy and proud finally to be sworn citizens of the United States? Although they have renounced the natal land associated with a mixture of pain, shame, and fitful bliss, these apologetic and resentful Pinays/Pinoys are not fully accepted by their white neighbors and so they drift in the limbo of what Frantz Fanon, in *The Wretched of the Earth* (1968), designates as the "occult zone" of subhumans who crave a welcoming habitat. This is the unrelenting pathos of the Filipino diaspora.

Pietas now yields to pragmatic compromises. As is to be expected, most middle-stratum Filipinos have dutifully internalized the individualist ethos of bureaucratic industrial society. They have absorbed the ABC of corporate utilitarianism from the media and other ideological apparatuses in the Philippines and reproduced here in the doxa, the received and commonsensical practices of suburban existence. Although some still mechanically perform the rituals of the patriarchal extended family, many have now transformed themselves into living exemplars of the cult of neosocial Darwinism in the belief that they are conforming to the mores of their adopted country and are making themselves "true" Americans, "the genuine stateside articles." The symptoms of colonial dispossession seem to linger, prolonged and aggravated by the exigencies of adaptation and their entailed self-deceptions.

Even after formal independence in 1946, the Philippines continued to be subject to U.S. extraterritorial rights and prerogatives, especially during the Cold War confrontations in Korea and Vietnam. We know that during hospital strikes in major U.S. cities planeloads of nurses from the Philippines were ordered in by the cost-cutting management to function as "scabs," a title which their sisters surely do not deserve. (It might be useful to note here that not so long ago, 50,000 Filipino nurses remitted over $100 million annually, more than the earnings from Philippine gold exports, and that the $6 billion remittance of Middle East workers and domestics in Canada, Japan, Hong Kong, and elsewhere, is the number one dollar earner that makes up for the local elite's foreign debt.) In one major case, in 1946, 7,000 Filipino workers and their families were recruited by the Hawaii Sugar Planters Association to break "The Great Sugar Workers Strike" (Catholic Institute 1989). On discovering that they were being used to suppress their class brothers and sisters, these workers then joined the strikers organized by the International Longshoremen's and Warehousemen's Union (ILWU).

If we are beginning to be "like" them, to echo R. Zamora Linmark's (1995) play on the idiom, will they then like us?

Resemblance, to be sure, does not guarantee access to opportunities or fair treatment. Despite the fact that a larger proportion of recent Filipino immigrants possess superior technical and professional skills, we still find a pattern of consistent downgrading and underemployment of highly trained professionals. How is this to be explained or justified? Pharmacists, lawyers, teachers, dentists, engineers, and medical technicians who have logged years of experience are often forced to engage in low-paid sales, clerical, and wage labor.

In the racially stratified or ethnically segmented labor market of the United States, as well as in the rest of the world, Filipinos occupy the lower strata, primarily in service occupations such as food, health, cleaning, and so on. Because of this, Filipino men earn only about two-thirds of the average income of white men. Despite these problems of discrimination in the labor market, underemployment, and chronic unemployment, Filipinos as a group (for various reasons not entirely cultural) have not developed entrepreneurial skills for small ethnic enterprises such as those undertaken by Koreans and Indians in the big cities. Our resources are our bodies. We are still the subjects of discipline, not yet of desire. We market labor power, not consumer goods, and so participate in the plight of commodity fetishes exposed and subject to the perversities of power.

Beyond the obvious economic causality, how can we explain this persisting subjugation of Filipino bodies and psyches? We perceive so many "manacled minds" impoverished by learned self-denigration and beset by tribal passions (what is now fashionably labeled "kin altruism"), concerned only with the welfare of their clans if not their own creature comforts. Labeled and endlessly classified and studied, we remain enigmas "always already" misrecognized. But, frankly speaking, are we that exceptional? We share commonalities and elective affinities with the scapegoats of the past (Chinese and Japanese workers) and of the present (undocumented aliens from the violated and superexploited regions of Latin America). Clearly, the vestiges of historical violence and amnesia resonate in our bodies and minds.

We still find evidence of the routine attitude of EuroAmericans to Filipinos as good only at manual work in the fields—those images of Filipino workers in California and Hawaii plantations still predominate in the consciousness of the EuroAmerican majority. In the past, Filipinos were considered petty merchandise listed next to "fertilizer" or "manure" by farm proprietors. Today, the demand for Filipino nurses and domestics—Overseas Contract Workers avidly promoted by the Philippine government, from Marcos to Corazon Aquino and

Fidel Ramos—may betoken for certain technocrats in the bureaucracy an improvement in our international status as supplier of cheap labor and other resources to the industrialized metropoles. This may accord with the logic of "comparative advantage"—to our lasting disadvantage (Miles 1986).

In the global capitalist dispensation being installed today, Filipino bodies indeed tend to find their proper niches, as before. At this juncture, a few rhetorical questions can orient our review of the Filipino experience in the United States. Why has the Filipino community languished so long in the "internal colony" (Stone 1996)? Why is it that unlike other racial minorities Filipinos are unable to resolve the crisis of expatriation and uprooting, of alienation and disenfranchisement, through strong and enduring commitment to promoting the larger good of a differentiated but coherent community? Why is it that this community is virtually nonexistent and, if manifest, at best disintegrated and inutile? Why is it that Filipinos in the diaspora do not feel or understand their subjugation as a distinct people, a nationality deprived of autonomy? Attempts have been made in the past to mobilize Filipinos for expedient causes, under opportunistic leaderships. One recalls that a few Filipinos who followed the notorious Hilario Moncado and joined his Filipino Federation of America (founded in 1925 in Los Angeles) opposed the unionization efforts of Filipinos in Hawaii (San Buenaventura 1996). This is arguably one more proof that pursuing liberation via ethnic pride alone, divorced from the ideal of popular sovereignty, would be otiose if not suicidal. [1]

Various U.S. experts have ventured opinions to explain the continuing "invisibility" or "forgottenness" of the Filipinos in the United States and in the same breath sought to diagnose the causes of underdevelopment in the homeland (Hart 1982). Theodore Friend, for one, blames the historic legacy of Spain fostered by Marcos and Aquino, a legacy that plagues Latin American countries as evidenced in such markers of dysfunctionality as "autocracy, gross corruption, bloated debt, a deprofessionalized military, private armies, death squads" (1989, 4). Remarking on Aquino's charisma as "Mother of Sorrows," unable to clean up "the patronage ridden" civil service and "the anarchy of ruling families" that define the patrimonial polity, Friend urges Filipinos to "shake free of Hispanic tradition" (4). But, if one may interject, what happened to the period of U.S. tutelage, from 1898 to 1946 and thereafter? Why omit as if by happenstance the asymmetrical power relations between "the bastion of the Free World" and its erstwhile territorial possession? It is revealing that nowhere does Friend even mention U.S. violence or U.S. disciplinary regimes, in particular the U.S. manipulation of the feudal and comprador elite in the colonial conquest and domination of the Philippines for almost a century! An incredible attack of amnesia? This willed forgetfulness is also the message of Stanley Karnow (1989) in his lengthy, self-righteous apologia for U.S. imperialism, *In Our Image* (San Juan 1992b).

Another distinguished scholar, the historian Peter Stanley, does mention U.S. colonial plunder but only to praise it as "the relatively libertarian character of U.S. rule" over Taft's "little brown brothers." The much-touted U.S. legacy of schools, roads, public health programs, artesian wells, democratic politicians, and "the most gregariously informal, backslapping imperialist rulers known to history" serves to explain, for Stanley, why Filipinos cherish a "deferential friendship" for Americans. By all indications, this brief for U.S. "exceptionalism"—namely, the United States never became an imperial power—cannot thrive except by praising the "civilizing mission" of U.S. military interventions all over the globe. It may not be overpatronizing then for Stanley and his colleagues to suggest that Filipinos in the United States who come from different regions of the islands form fraternal groups based on localities of origin because they find it "difficult to conceive of each other as sharing a national identity."

What our U.S. tutors seem to be telling us is this: If the sleep of Reason breeds monsters, uneven development begets mongrels. U.S. government experts, Peace Corps administrators, philanthropic pundits, and well-meaning commentators who claim to cherish "directness, sincerity, efficiency, and quality," confess that they are bewildered by the paradoxes and illogicalities of Filipino culture. This culminates in their own predicament about playing roles other than what they consider their natural or normal U.S. "self." Confusion and resentment follow. A recent travelogue, *God's Dust* by Ian Buruma (1989), turns the table around. Abetted by Filipino intellectuals who dilate on the power of residual superstitious beliefs, Filipino upper-class hybrid culture, the upsurge of immigration to the United States, and scenes of local chaos and corruption, Buruma can dismiss insouciantly the entire nation as afflicted with frivolity spiced with vulgarity, cynicism, and fraud. Buruma condemns Filipino nationalism as "the paranoid envy of the backward provincial for the metropole, an envy especially acute in the Philippines, where American products, values, and dreams have been held up as superior for almost a century" (1989, 84). Instant knowledge—the Filipino is "thoroughly colonial" sandwiched between "the legacy of Spanish Catholicism and secondhand Americana . . . America is like a birthmark on the Filipino identity—no matter how hard you rub, it won't come off" (1989, 85)—is cheap and easy to come by. After all, the tourist-dilettante, with a conscience already pawned to corporate sponsors, is not answerable to anyone.

History, then, has stigmatized us. Although the diagnosis offered by Friend and replicated by others is flawed by a positivist, functionalist bias in blaming the victims for the inadequacy of their culture, it nevertheless prompts us to reflect on strategies of containment and cooptation that prevent our collective awakening and on ways of overcoming them. It is never too late to recapitulate the themes of colonial subjugation and conscientization rehearsed by Frantz Fanon, Amilcar Cabral, Paulo Freire, Renato Constantino, and others. Our subaltern conscience prompts the following intervention addressed to the Other, the alter/native: We (if I may adopt a ventriloquial stance) lack any real identification of ourselves as belonging to a nation because that nation of all classes and constituencies in the Philippines remains nonexistent. A sovereign Philippines, that achieved embodiment of the national-popular will, has not yet come into being, has in fact been aborted and suppressed by U.S. military power when it was being born during the revolution of 1896–1898, a culmination of three centuries of popular uprisings against Spanish tyranny. That much is already taken for granted and therefore overlooked. We do not have as of now a popular-democratic nation; it is still the object of class struggle, still in the process of being created as the matrix and site of authentic sharing and participation—that privileged quasi-utopian space is still in the process of emergence through a manifold complex of antagonisms, coalitions, and compromises. That body of the nation is still going through the agony of birth. What we call the Philippines today, a geopolitical space where state power is controlled by a comprador-oligarchic elite whose interests center on the preservation of an unjust and oppressive status quo, is for all practical purposes still a dependent, subordinated formation. It is virtually an appendage of the U. S. corporate power elite, notwithstanding substantial gains in decolonization during the past twenty years climaxing in the Philippine Senate's decision in 1992 to remove the U.S. military bases and abrogate nonreciprocal treaties with the former master.

Perhaps we in the diaspora do not belong anywhere, as yet, because we have not yet exercised the freedom to choose from a range of alternatives and possibilities. Filipino immigrants from the beginning up to the fifties were perceived as a social problem (for example, see Rabaya 1971). The Filipinologist H. Brett Melendy (1980) problematizes Filipino ethnogenesis on account of the natives' "cultural backgrounds and value systems" that pivot around the family and indigenous kinship structure.[2] Melendy blames the Filipinos for their sojourner mentality, not the racializing apparatuses of the U.S. state or the hierarchic institutions of civil society. Like other scholars, Melendy asserts that Filipinos' peculiar cultural traits warranted their exclusion and exploitation and hence their abject status. The ethnic norms and standard of values of these poor victims have somehow escaped destruction by U.S. colonial force—they in fact maintain that system of dependency that, although increasingly challenged, still manages to extract surplus value and obeisance—amid the surface Westernization and mock modernization of the whole society. Our ethics of self-mastery just seems fortuitously to elude Melendy and other experts in quest of the quintessential Filipino.[3]

This perspective partly explains the political nullity of Filipinos who, formally interpellated as citizens, are unable to unite and construct their community in symbolic rituals of autonomy and integrity, to represent it as a coherent, resourceful, sustainable locus of meaning and value. Earlier efforts have failed, in part only because, as I said earlier, we cannot ignore the structures of racial differentiation and hierarchizing that historically constitute the elite hegemony and civic consensus of U.S. society, as well as the assimilationist strategies of the U.S. racial state and its various political techniques of co-optation and disarticulation. These mechanisms have confined people of color to perpetual subalternity. If they cannot represent themselves, surely they will be represented by others, as Marx once said of the French small-holding peasantry of 1848 (Fischer 1996, 83). Culture or ethnic identity cannot therefore be separated from questions of power and property relations, from the coercive instrumentality of the state and the disciplinary institutions of civil society.

This is the predicament we, Filipinos scattered in the territory of the United States, face as we enter the threshold of a new century. Let us reverse for once the traditional significations. The face and bodies of the Other (from the dominant optic), as Alphonso Lingis contends, "are simultaneously signifiers for indicative and informative significations and traces of the signifying hollow, which is emptied out in vocative and imperative moves" (1994, 199). Our faces and bodies then constitute an ineluctable appeal, displacing the subjunctive mood with injunctions and summons. We are indeed a problematizing force, not a "problem"; we symbolize an open question, disturbers of the peace in more ways than one. We are not like the majority, so can they like us? Instead of attending to "them," settlers whose morale depends on the perpetual invocation of the "yellow horde" and "brown monkey," we need this time to attend to the imperative of the popular/united front, the desideratum of solidarity. Here begins our redemption from servitude. As we are often reminded, "Humankind sets itself only such problems as it can solve" (Ball 1991, 141). In the crisis of dislocation and demoralization that we continue to experience in a racist polity, how can we reconstitute a single unified community that can generate a discourse of autonomy, critique, and trans-valuation via mobilizing a praxis of collective resistance? In other words, how can we unleash the power and joy of bodies as the "expression of a possible world," the Other as the structure and horizon of possibilities (Deleuze 1993, 60)?

Sometime in 1989, I sent a letter to the *Philippine News* in San Francisco posing questions that elaborate possible stages of our communal self-transformation and, I hope, open up a space for critical exchange. I resurrect part of this letter here:

> What really distinguishes the Filipino community here in its historical formation? How is it tied to the history of the Philippines as a colony of Western powers? What specific elements of immigrant history, the suffering and resistance of various contingents (not "waves" blown willy-nilly), should we foreground and invest in that will unify and mobilize Filipinos for substantive collective goals? What political and moral education should we undertake to develop and heighten the consciousness of a distinct Filipino identity and ethicopolitical presence in the United States? What series of struggles should we engage in to forge a dynamic and cohesive identity, struggles that will actualize the substance of democratic human rights? Finally, on what political and ethical principles (superior and alternative to the bureaucratic individualism of the free market that informs and motivates the hegemonic ideology of racial pluralism) should we ground the agency of this Filipino community? In other words, what social goods corresponding to what concrete social needs should we articulate as the fundamental goal or end of our community within the larger global formation of competing nation-states?

Lest I be misconstrued, I hasten to assure readers that I do not envision a *Realpolitik* of rivalry with other embattled ethnic and racial groups. On the contrary, we need dialogue and mutual aid. People of color cannot accede to the divide-and-conquer policy of the hegemonic bloc to remedy historic injustices and redress everyday grievances. We need a principled critique of the system and organized united front resistance. This is not just a matter of instrumentalizing the members of the community to gain material resources and advantages necessary to survive and reproduce the next generation. It is not a juridical matter of entitlement for either situated or unencumbered selves. It is not just a question of the cultural norms (which the structural-functionalist doctrinaire insist is the decisive criterion of successful performance) required to make us fully participate in the political process, a question of what do I want and with whom shall I cooperate to acquire what I want. Let us try to overcome utilitarian cretinism, the short-range prudential calculation of means-ends. The question of what we are going to do cannot be answered unless we respond to a prior question: In what narrative or narratives that are now unfolding in contemporary world history shall we participate? Is it a narrative of assimilation and integration, or a narrative of emancipation and national self-determination? Is there a universalizing or transcendent multiracial narrative, a genuinely ecumenical and cosmopolitan narrative that subsumes and insures our self-empowering if long-delayed liberation as an autonomous community?

We return then to the fact of bodies and the politics of representation, of knowledge circumscribed by power and the necessity of objective determinations. No doubt we make our own history but only under certain determinate conditions, within definite objective parameters (Meillassoux 1993). No matter how they try, Filipinos cannot be Americans as long as the common American identity is racially and unilaterally defined.[4] We might learn from the dilemma of others. Speaking of the displaced subaltern intellectuals like himself (a Jamaican in Britain), Stuart Hall (1996) describes them as "familiar strangers." We can be provisionally "familiar strangers" to both the Philippines and the United States, knowing both places but not wholly of either place. Hall calls this "the diasporic experience, far away enough to experience the sense of exile and loss, close enough to understand the enigma of an always-postponed 'arrival'" (1996, 490). We are, to put it in the best terms, both inside and outside, a partisan of the two historical trajectories I discuss in Chapter 6. This transvalues the archetypal late-modern condition that used to be called exile, deracination, homelessness. Hall argues that this is paradigmatically the contemporary diasporic experience shared by millions of people:

> Since migration has turned out to be the world-historical event of late modernity, the classic postmodern experience turns out to be the diasporic experience. . . . I think cultural identity is not fixed, it's always hybrid. But this is precisely because it comes out of very specific historical formations, out of very specific histories and cultural repertoires of enunciation, that it can constitute a "positionality," which we call, provisionally, identity. It's not just anything. So each of those identity-stories is inscribed in the positions we take up and identify with, and we have to live this ensemble of identity-positions in all its specificities. (1996, 490, 502)

What Hall envisages is a new conceptualization of ethnicity that acknowledges the places of history, language, and culture in the construction of subjectivity and agency. Representation of identity as a group thus becomes possible within the framework of languages and codes enabled by particular histories and lived experiences. This sense of ethnic identity not equivalent to race, imperialism, or the nation-state can operate only within a cultural politics that engages rather

than suppresses difference cognized as conditional and conjunctural—
that is, on the recognition that "we all speak from a particular place,
out of a particular history, out of a particular experience, a particular
culture, without being contained by that position" (Hall 1996, 447).
Such militant particularism, however, needs to be qualified by a "political possibilism" and principled realism unique to the Marxian socialist tradition.

What I would propose from this new perspective, beyond the formu-
las of liberal multiculturalism and pacified ethnic diversity, is a politics of counterhegemonic struggle. This is, in the ultimate analysis, a
struggle between imperial-transnational powers and insurgent subalterns around the world. For Filipinos kindled by the desire to correct
the misrepresentations of the past, we need a popular-democratic politics of contestation to dispute the dominant logic of representation,
the scenarios of hegemonic interpellation that constitute subjectivity,
identity, and agency, inflected by class, race, gender, sexuality, and so
on. A good example of this is the way Filipino gays have intervened in
the current official representation of AIDS to the community (see
Manalansan 1995). What I want to stress is the way this new politics
then brings into play the immense diversity and differentiation of the
historical and cultural experience of Filipinos—from the Manongs of
the twenties and thirties to the "brown" yuppies of the eighties and
nineties—so as to put an end, once and for all, to the grand racist rationale that all Filipinos look alike and should go back where they came
from. This will combine in a flexible way the war of maneuver (class
politics in the raw) in the Philippines with the war of position in the
United States, an interrogation of identification and otherness, cognizant of the play of fear and desire in the ambivalent process of identification, of identity formation (the internalization of the self as
Other, a dialogic alterity in the making). In this new horizon of the
politics of recognition and contestation immanent within global
class/nation antagonisms, I envision the Filipino community shaping
its own identity through solidarity with all the oppressed and exploited as a responsible autonomous force committed to distributive
justice, to genuine self-determination, to socialist democracy. Opposing a common enemy, this struggle necessarily traverses space and
crosses state boundaries, joining the diaspora with brothers and sisters
in the islands in Southeast Asia and reconstructing the homeland as
habitat for a segment of the human species.

In the meantime, what is to be done? I can offer only topics for discussion and thought experiments to arm the spirit, perhaps to recover
that fabled Orphic "soul" of the ethnos deciphered from the stigmata
of bodies scattered in the hell of late-capitalist reification. What "we"

(to use a figurative site of enunciation) need to do, the agenda for constituting the Filipino community as an agent of historic change in a racist society, cannot of course be prescribed by one individual. The mapping and execution of such a project—this book is an integral part of it—can only be the product of a collective effort by everyone who claims to be a "Filipino"—a category still in the process of becoming, of revaluation and redefinition—in the midst of engaging in actual, concrete struggles, in conjunction with the efforts of other people of color in the United States and worldwide, to rid society of the material conditions that beget and reproduce class, gender, national, and racial oppression. The future in the twenty-first century is there for us to shape—if we dare to imagine and struggle for a world in which each group is recognized for its own singular worth and dignity, equal to all the others, contributing its significant share to the realization of humanity's potential. Our exile and diaspora, our vernacular modernity, will not be wasted, finding here at last the dignity, justice, and fulfillment of homecoming.

1

Alias "Flips," "Pinoys," "Brown Monkeys . . . "

From the Boondocks to the "Belly of the Beast"

I hope that the Americans will understand that the present state of culture of the Filipino people shall not put up with subjugation by force as a permanent condition. The Filipinos may be vanquished now and again, but as long as they are denied every kind of right, there will not be lasting peace. . . . Today the Filipinos share in the life of other nations and they have tasted, even if only for a short time and in an incomplete manner, the joys of an independent life.

Apolinario Mabini

If there is no permanent condition in nature, how much less there ought to be in the life of peoples, beings endowed with mobility and energy.

Jose Rizal

No uprising fails. Each one is a step in the right direction.

Salud Algabre

In a ploy to co-opt the nationalist resistance after the bitterly fought Filipino-American War of 1898–1902, William Howard Taft invented the slogan "Philippines for Filipinos" and in the process congratulated his "little brown brothers" for their cooperation (Wolff 1961). Some of the "brothers" complied (they became the elite), many more resisted (stigmatized as *bandidos*, indigenous freedom fighters), and still others fled—to Hawaii and the West Coast of the United States. Coming from the "great white father," Taft's call for independence was obviously suspected of being a bait, a trap. It took many more lives, and many more bodies transported to the metropolitan shores, for the Philippines to achieve its independence. Meanwhile, as the poet Maria Fatima Lim puts it, the Filipino got rid of the European devil only to embrace "the sixfoot santa claus," the natives dreaming "of a pure white christmas/in our land of constant summer and lent" (Lim-Wilson 1984, 44). In the process of such transformations, a new species called "Filipino-Americans," one of the hyphenated variety, emerged.

It was not so long ago that Filipino villages sheltered the guerillas of the beleaguered first Philippine Republic. Fresh from routing Native Americans, Cubans, and Puerto Ricans, the U.S. expeditionary legion proceeded to annihilate over a million Filipino insurgents in that little-known episode of the Filipino-American War (1898–1902), the "first Vietnam." It was, from the viewpoint of a participant, "a hot game of killing niggers." In the jingoist atmosphere of the fin de siècle, the U.S. public's idea of Filipinos as (in Samuel Gompers's words) "a semi-barbaric population, almost primitive in their habits and customs " (1908, 17) found visual confirmation in a putative scientific/cultural event. I am referring to the 1904 St. Louis World's Fair (modeled after the 1893 Chicago Columbian Exposition) where, together with Geronimo and the African "pygmy" Ota Benga, tribal "specimens" from the Igorot, Negrito, and Moro communities were displayed. Exhibits from "Darkest Africa" to "Mysterious Asia" jostled with the Filipino "savages" converted "by American methods into civilized workers (Robinson 1994)." This exhibition perhaps cleared up the pundit's doubt whether the "Philippines" referred to islands or canned goods.

Shades of American Indians in the court of Louis XIV? Not quite. We are now in the stage of finance and monopoly capitalism (Brewer 1990). A carnival of commodification and an ethos of mass consumption of images and illusions predominate. That now-historic exposition may be said to have fleshed out, in a pseudo-scientific bazaar of spectacles, the rhetoric of William McKinley, Henry Cabot Lodge, Theodore Roosevelt, and the howling chauvinists of "manifest destiny" who then felt obligated to defend the mandate of Anglo-Saxon imperial supremacy across the continental frontier. The vision of white imperial technology was successfully staged as it conquered the barbarians via the panopticon of progress spiced with magical gadgets and circus delights. What was achieved there was the reconfirmation of racial hierarchy (already established with the suppression of the American Indian and the segregation of Africans and Mexicans) that legitimized the U.S. national identity and global civilizing mission.

Over half a century of U.S. tutelage has made many Filipinos entrenched fanatics of the American "Dream of Success." Over 40,000 Filipinos (not counting the TNTs, or *tago nang tago*, literally, "always hiding," whose visas have expired) since 1976 immigrate to the U.S. annually. Many accept low-income jobs even though they are well-trained professionals (dentists, engineers, lawyers, and other "brain drain" cadres). This repeats a gesture of sacrifice made by their predecessors, often described by the misleading trope of "waves," or serialized cohorts, that conceal the dependent/neocolonized status of the islands and evoke connotations of a natural happening, cyclical outbreaks, uncontrollable circumstances. The theory of push/pull factors in immigration only reproduces the myth of equality among nations and states.

In most textbooks dealing with ethnic "minorities," the dominant paradigm used in appraising the economic, cultural, and political condition of Filipinos is that of "acculturation/cultural assimilation." Its programmatic aim is to judge how Others (colonized or enslaved people of color) adapt or fit into the hierarchical class/status system. For example, Pauline Agbayani-Siewert and Linda Revilla (1995) ascribe such problems as youth gangs and low educational achievement to weak ethnic identity. Thus, when Filipinos in Hawaii lived in segregated, isolated homes and celebrated "rites of passage" with multiple godparents, they enjoyed strong ethnicity. With their dispersal, Filipino ethnicity presumably weakened. In the case of the "identity movement" in the sixties and second-generation Filipino Americans, ethnicity becomes a matter of personal or group decision. This logic of acculturation generates the most inane tautologies, such as Filipino Americans "who identified themselves as 'very Americanized' tended to have political orientations that were more assimilationist in nature" (Agbayani-Siewert and Revilla 1995, 154), whereas Filipinos who valued family togetherness and respect for elders—alleged to be "traditional Filipino values" (see also Pido 1986)—displayed strong ethnicity. Paradoxically, despite the emphasis on the prevalence of Filipino traditional beliefs and family structure—even claiming that authority in the family is "not patriarchal, but more egalitarian," our experts conclude that "Filipino Americans do not organize as a cohesive population around political, economic, or ethnic issues as do other Asian groups" (Agbayani-Siewert and Revilla 1995, 164). Not only is that assertion historically and empirically false, but it betrays the pernicious effect of structural-functional reductionism. This is compounded by purveying myths about gender equality in the Filipino family (see Aguilar 1988, 1995). We need to liberate ourselves from the doxa of utilitarian pragmatism, from habits of subservience to a normative order legitimized by sociological theories that sanction inequality, racism, and injustice. The fulfillment of such an agenda has been long overdue.

One of the first tasks of a decolonizing Filipino critical social science is to repudiate the putative rationality of such an apologia for the status quo. We need to replace it with a conscientious historical-materialist analysis. I have in mind exploratory inquiries like Bruce Occeña's synoptic overview, "The Filipino Nationality in the U.S." (1985).[1]

Except for patent economistic inadequacies, Occeña's attempt to delineate the historical, social, and political contours of the Filipino in the United States as a distinct nationality can be considered a salutary point of departure.[2] Occeña should be credited for his insistence on grounding the specific oppression of the different segments of Filipino immigrants in their race, class, and nationality determinants (for background data, see Catholic Institute 1989). Not only are Filipinos distinguished from other Asians by their collective experience at home of U.S. imperial oppression, but each episode of Filipino migration manifests distinctive characteristics rooted in the unequal relations of power between the Philippines and the United States. According to Occeña, two basic conditions have decisively affected the development of a unique Filipino nationality in the United States: first, the continuing oppression of the Filipino nation by U.S. imperialism, and, second, the fact that as a group, "Filipinos have been integrated into U.S. society on the bases of inequality and subjected to discrimination due both to their race and nationality" (31).[3]

What follows is a broad outline of the sociopolitical tendencies of three contingents of migration needed to clarify the heterogeneous character of Filipino nationality. The first contingent (1906–1946) covers 150,000 workers concentrated in Hawaii and California, mostly bachelor sojourners—crippled "birds of passage," as it were—forced by poverty, ill health, and demoralization to settle permanently; the second (1946–1964) comprised 30,000 war veterans and their families whose mentality is generally conservative because of relative privileges. And the third (numbering about 630,000 from 1965 to 1984) encompasses the most dense, complexly stratified group, due to the fact that these persons moved at a time when all sectors of Philippine society were undergoing cataclysmic changes. Members of this latest influx harbor nationalist sentiments that help focus their consciousness on multifaceted struggles at home and keep alive their hope of returning when and if their life chances improve. (Although some will stay because of their children, the gradual elimination of welfare and medical benefits for the elderly might "persuade" many to return to the Philippines.) Given the collapse of distances by the greater scope and frequency of modern communications and travel, linguistic, cultural, and social links of the Filipino diaspora to the islands have been reinforced sufficiently to influence the dynamics of community politics and culture in the United States. Consequently, we now have a situation "quite different from the previous period when the Filipino community was in the process of evolving a conspicuously distinct subculture which was principally a reflection of their experiences in U.S. society and alien in many ways to the national culture of the Philippines itself" (Occeña 1985, 38).[4]

Contradictory networks of thought and feeling traverse this last substantial segment of the community, problematizing the evolution of a monolithic "Filipino American" sensibility not fissured by ambivalence, opportunism, and schizoid loyalties (Cariño et al 1990). The methodological principle of "one divides into two" can be applied here. Recent immigrants are composed of (1) urban professional strata exhibiting a self-centered concern for mobility and status via consumerism; and (2) a progressive majority who occupy the lower echelons of the working class exposed to the worst forms of class, racial, and national oppression. Occeña posits the prospect that "the life options of many of these Filipino-Americans are grim—the 'poverty draft' will push them into the front lines of the U.S. war machine or the life of low paid service workers. Consequently, this emerging generation promises to be the most thoroughly proletarianized section of the third wave" (41) and thus ripe for mobilization.

Although I think the last inference is mechanical and does not allow for the impact of changing political alignments, ideological mutations, and other contingencies in the "New World Order" of late "disorganized" capitalism, Occeña's emphasis on the unifying pressure of racial and national marginalization serves to rectify the narcosis of an "identity" politics that posits a mystifying "Filipino American" essence for reactionary ends. This critical-realist diagnosis of U.S. society shatters all the totems and icons of "model minority" success propagated by *Filipinas*, the *Philippine News*, and hustlers of the pornographic Asian Imaginary (Moy 1996).

My main reservation regarding Occeña's inquiry concerns its naively economistic bias. Defining the majority of the "third wave" as "concentrated in the lower strata of the U.S. working class" does not automatically endow them with a proletarianized consciousness. Occeña also neglects, if not downplays, the forces of gender and sexuality. It might be instructive to note that 60 percent of this new batch of immigrants is female and also endowed with a more sophisticated awareness of gender politics, if not of feminist thinking (Beltran and De Dios 1992; Evasco et al. 1990). Moreover, Occeña (like most experts on Filipino ethnicity) still clings to a static and monolithic conception of the extended family as constitutive of the social and political dynamics of the Filipino diaspora today. In addition, a focus on the overlay and articulation of the key sociological features of the three contingents in the extended family networks should modify the schematic partitioning of this survey and intimate a more dynamic, interactive milieu within which Filipino heterogeneity can be further enhanced and profiled. In the context of new developments, it is salutary to decenter the orthodox paradigm of "waves" and "push-pull" factors that obfuscate asymmetrical power relations and obscure movements of resistance.

It becomes clear now why, given these deterritorializing circuits of exchange between (from our revisionist optic) the fertilizing margin and parasitic center, the use of the rubric "Filipino American" can be sectarian and thus susceptible to hegemonic disarticulation. Should we then bracket "American" (not reducible to heart or mind) in this moment of analysis, mimicking the antimiscegenation law of the twenties and thirties? Because of its co-optative and incorporative effect, the use of "American" should therefore be phased out in line with the 1974 California state practice of assigning a separate category for "Filipino." This move interrogates the consensus of "white supremacy" that informs the multiculturalist core of what is designated "American."

Let us follow the itinerary of Filipinos who came before the hyphenation of our collective ethos. There are two groups often mistaken by many to be the first Filipino immigrants: the government scholars called *pensionados* and the "Manillamen." The *pensionados* (nicknamed "fountain-pen boys") from 1903 to 1910 were chosen and financed by the U.S. colonial administration. It was part of the conciliatory "Filipinization" scheme of U.S. Governor General William Howard Taft and his ilk. Models of colonial disciplinary "success," these graduates (about 183 in 1907) in engineering, education, and agriculture returned to the islands to occupy positions in business and in government. They were neither sojourners nor precursors of "brain drain" immigrants.

Nor were the fugitives from Spanish galleons (the galleon trade from Acapulco to Manila thrived from 1593 to 1815) and pirate ships immigrants in the proper construal of the term. Those adventurous souls moved on from Mexico and the Caribbean to what became the states of California, Texas, and Louisiana. In 1763, the "Manillamen," native sailors from Spanish ships, settled as fishermen or hunters in the now-legendary fishing village of St. Malo, Louisiana, at the mouth of the Mississippi (see Chapter 7). In 1870, they founded a benevolent association, La Union Filipina, in New Orleans. St Malo was destroyed by a hurricane in 1893, with most of its inhabitants allegedly killed. Later, in 1897, a Filipino seaman by the name of Quintin de la Cruz established a fishing port, Manila Village, forty miles south of New Orleans in Barataria Bay (Mangiafico 1988). By 1933, the Filipinos there numbered 1,500, engaged for their livelihood in fishing for shrimps and trout and hunting muskrats for fur. Once exoticized by Lafcadio Hearn (1883) and other journalists, these Filipinos have now become objects of an antiquarian cult parasitic on their having arrived earlier, really "first off the boats," than the recruited field hands destined for what became dystopic Hawaiian havens.

Filipinos appeared in U.S. territory by grace of the racialized exclusion of the Chinese (the infamous 1882 Act) and the selective barring of the Japanese (1908 Gentlemen's Agreement). With the acquisition of the Philippines and Puerto Rico, the planters in Hawaii and on the West Coast found a solution to their need for cheap and easily replenishable manpower. The first group of Filipinos in 1906 comprised recruited peasants hired by the Hawaiian Sugar Planters Association to work in the sugar plantations. Between 1909 and 1931, 112,820 Filipinos were working in Hawaii (Mangiafico 1988). Although their plight has been reviewed so many times, a mere citation of facts always questions the divide between truth and fantasy. From 1920 to 1929, Filipino males numbered 65,618 compared to 5,286 women—less than seven "Pinays" for every one hundred men; in the 1930s the ratio was 23 to 1. They were segregated from other ethnic groups and allowed only such recreation as gambling, prostitution, and ritual festivals in their community (see the testimonies in Vallangca 1977). They were victims of racist laws and discriminatory practices. They were hoodwinked by inflated advertisements of wealth supposed to be acquired through honest manual labor, but soon enough they learned the reality of the marketplace: "Filipinos and dogs not allowed."

In 1911, Pablo Manlapit and his coworkers organized the Filipino Federation of Labor. Experiencing the truth of exploitation in a regime of possessive/acquisitive individualism, Filipinos joined the Japanese plantation workers in fierce strikes in the twenties and up to the forties. At Hanapepe, Kauai, in April 1924, sixteen Filipino strikers were massacred by the state defending the interests of agribusiness. Visiting the "Plantation Village" at Waipahu, Hawaii, March 1995, I was reminded of how the International Longshoremen's and Warehousemen's Union (ILWU) was born when, in the multiracial strike of 1949,

6,000 workers from the Philippines who were deceived into playing the role of scabs all decided to join the union and thus foiled the planters' schemes. Right from the start, the Filipino as militant striker seized the headlines.

But it was during the Depression that Filipinos assumed the role of lynching target, the scapegoat position. As Carey McWilliams wrote, "To be a Filipino in California is to belong to a blood brotherhood, a freemasonry of the ostracized" (1964, 241). One instance is the January 1930 killing of a Filipino and the beating of scores in Watsonville, California, by a mob of 500 white vigilantes.

A background review may be appropriate here. After the initial exodus to Hawaii, Filipinos began to settle in California around 1919. After the Immigration Act of 1924, which prohibited entry of inhabitants from the "barred zone" (from East Asia to the Middle East), thus excluding Chinese and Japanese labor, Filipinos were catapulted to the rank of the dominant migrant labor force in the Central Valley of California. Released from their three-year contract, many farmhands came from Hawaii. As usual, they were accused of keeping wages low and taking jobs away from whites. On October 24, 1929, in the town of Exeter, a mob of 300 white men attacked a ranch where Filipinos were living—an incident preceded by one in Yakima, Washington, in 1928, and then followed by others in California: Watsonville in 1930, Salinas in 1934, and Lake County in 1939 (see Crouchett 1982; Takaki 1989; Chan 1991).

The incidents in Watsonville, California, epitomize the containment strategy of the hegemonic dispensation. On January 7–10, 1930, the North Monterey County Chamber of Commerce met to discuss the "Filipino problem" and resolved that the "half-breeds" should be sent home so that "white people who have inherited this country for themselves and their offspring might live" (Bogardus 1976, 53). The struggle for *Lebensraum*, living space, occupied center stage in the moral panic that seized the white community. On this basis, Justice of the Peace D. W. Rohrback of Pajaro Valley predicted that the situation would lead to either "the exclusion of the Filipino or the deterioration of the white race" in California. Rohrback pronounced the Filipinos "but ten years removed from the bolo and breechcloth" (Bogardus, 1976, 53), able to tolerate subsistence wages enough to provide low-standard housing and meager food. He was only echoing the prejudices of the turn-of-the-century Establishment. In the adjoining town of Watsonville, anti-Filipino demonstrations exploded and raged for four days. On January 22, the rioting vigilantes beat up forty-six Filipinos and killed Fermin Tobera. After a short trial, six white youths pleaded guilty to the attack but received sentences of only probation or a few days in jail. After the inquest, "It was decided that the person who had fired the fatal shot was unknown" (Bogardus 1976, 56). On February 2, designated as "humiliation day," Tobera was given a state funeral in the Philippines.

The miasma of the Watsonville incident has now evaporated from public memory, but its déjà vu aura lingers. It seems from hindsight a minor repeat of Yankee soldiers conducting a systematic slaughter of Filipino peasant families in insurgent villages in Samar, Batangas, and other provinces at the turn of the century. One witness of the Filipino collective ordeal in the thirties was Carlos Bulosan whose testimony, in *America Is in the Heart* ([1946] 1973), speaks for all the dispossessed and disinherited: "The mockery of it all is that Filipinos are taught to regard Americans as our equals. Adhering to American ideals, living American life, these are contributory to our feelings of equality. The terrible truth in America shatters the Filipino's dreams of fraternity" (1995, 173).

It might be instructive to recall that about 175,000 Filipinos in the thirties were officially designated "nationals," wards under U.S. "tutelage." They were neither aliens nor eligible for citizenship because they were neither Caucasian nor Negro. Even before their initiation into modernity, Filipinos seem to have already metamorphosed into postmodern hybrids (Burma 1954). With the passage of the Tydings-McDuffie Act on March 24, 1934, which promised to grant independence to the islands in ten years, all Filipinos suddenly became aliens. They were "birds of passage" trapped in the temporary haven of a "promised" land. With the enactment of the Filipino Repatriation Act in 1935, 2,200 Filipinos returned home. Immigration thereafter was restricted to fifty persons a year. Earlier Asians and other people of color were denied the right of naturalization (a 1790 statute restricted naturalization to "free white persons"). They were forbidden to marry Caucasians; the *Roldan v. Los Angeles County* court case in 1933 confirmed this antimiscegenation bias when the California legislature included Malays among "Negroes, mulattos, and Mongolians," who were prohibited from marrying whites; this lasted until 1948 when the antimiscegenation laws were ruled unconstitutional. More than a few judges and legislators succumbed to the labyrinthine logic that categorized Filipinos as "Mongolian" (Foster 1994). Filipinos were also proscribed from owning land or receiving federal assistance in finding jobs and housing. In 1940, they were subjected to another humiliation: All Filipinos had to register and be fingerprinted like ordinary criminals, even though thousands were already serving in the military.

What seems incredible even for modern skeptics is the story of Maria Ofalsa, an exemplum for all her sisters. She arrived in 1926 and two years later was hospitalized "from overwork and exhaustion"; her family suffered years of overt and covert prejudice, harassment, and eviction, all of which they quietly endured. Finally, after getting her citizenship in 1952, this target of unrelenting racism advised her compatriots: "When you come here to the U.S. remember this is not our country, so you try to be nice and don't lose your temper and try to be friendly and don't put on a sour face" (Johnson 1988, 25). That pathos of subalternity can scarcely be matched although it is still replicated by recent paragons like Governor Benjamin Cayetano of Hawaii who refuse to be called "Filipino American" (Gaborro 1997). Frankly I do not know whether, without any ecclesiastical imprimatur, Ofalsa should be canonized or beatified.

Contemporaries of Maria Ofalsa like Manuel Buaken and Carlos Bulosan probably lost their temper then. Buaken wrote in 1940: "Where is the heart of America? I am one of the many thousands of young men born under the American Flag, raised as loyal idealistic Americans under your promise of equality for all. . . . Once here we are met by exploiters, shunted into slums, greeted by gamblers and prostitutes, taught only the worst in your civilization" (411). Bulosan summed up his experiences in the decade before World War II: "I came to know afterward that in many ways it was a crime to be a Filipino in California" (1995, 173). Given this wayward and tortuous itinerary, the Filipino adventure mocks the archetypal myth of a hero's quest and transformation, a reductive formula of assimilation into a multiculturalist fantasy island (see, for example, Meñez 1986–1987) bereft of circumstantial particularity.

The historical record amply shows that Filipinos, faced with rampant paralegal violence in Watsonville, California, and in other places in the late twenties and thirties, did not act "nicely" when they initiated militant actions like those by the 30,000-strong Filipino Labor Union in 1933 (Dewitt 1978) or those by the Agricultural Workers Organizing Committee in 1959 that culminated in the historic grape strike of 1965 and the subsequent founding of the United Farm Workers of America. The epochal interethnic union struggles of Filipinos and Japanese workers in Hawaii in 1920 and 1924 also deserve tribute and commemoration. Philip Vera Cruz, a distinguished veteran union leader, declared in the sixties: "I think the only way to change things is to break up the corporations and weaken the enemy. . . . Agribusiness is built on the exploitation of farm workers. . . . It's the same struggle all over the world, many fronts of the same struggle" (1992, 125).

Disillusionment, however, gave way to the birth of another ideal, one enshrined in textbooks that glorify the liberation of the Philippines by General Douglas MacArthur. The valiant resistance fought by Filipinos side by side with Americans in Bataan and Corregidor during World War II has inscribed the image of the Filipino freedom fighter practicing racial solidarity in the annals of U.S.-Philippine relations. MacArthur and Magsaysay became, for the chroniclers of "special relations" between subaltern and colonizer, the two symbols linking the two races—an emblem of persistent dependency and patronage.[5] This exorbitant mythmaking (aggravated by Stanley Karnow's 1989 apologia for U.S. imperialism, *In Our Image*) has prompted some U.S. commentators to claim that the colonial experience is "like a birthmark on the Filipino identity," difficult to rub off. Provoked, "born-again" Filipinos demur and insist that they, as "citizens of the world," can be whatever they want to be. Meanwhile, Flor Contemplacion, Sarah Balabagan, and thousands more around the world are hanged, beaten, starved, raped, and killed—without too much complaint from the Americanized elite.

With formal independence granted in 1946, and the coordinated resistance of Filipino workers in the United States in the late forties and fifties—in particular among Alaskan cannery workers—to racist violence and persecution, a new sensibility emerged among second-generation Filipinos (Vallangca 1987; Espiritu 1995). Most of those who came of age in the great civil rights struggles of the sixties and the antiwar movement of the early seventies began to articulate the Filipino protest against racial and national oppression in sympathy with the resurgent anti-imperialist movement in the Philippines against the U.S.-Marcos dictatorship (Churchill 1995). Many Filipinos born in the United States matured during the "Great Transformation" of the sixties and began to connect with the heroic ordeals of the Manongs in such mass coalitions as around the International Hotel in San Francisco and around other programs to address still-unredressed grievances. A whole history is still to be written about this not-yet-forgotten itinerary of conscientization and mass agitation. When the eighties arrived, the impulse of opposition and critique ebbed with the rise of neoconservatism and other forms of atavistic response to capitalist crisis.

Today, this cognitive mapping seems like the genealogy of a nostalgia. For, indeed, the "dream of fraternity" instantiated in the battlefields of World War II has not been cited as reason enough to cause an improvement in the situation of at least 9,000 stewards in the U.S. Navy in the sixties. They occupied the position of menial servants who not only serviced the warships but also staffed the kitchen force of the White House and other official residences. In the sixties, Filipinos as nurses and doctors became visible as they serviced whole hospitals, with the newly imported nurses sometimes serving as scabs or performing work shunned by white employees. During this period, the case of two Filipina nurses (Filipinas Narciso and Leonora Perez) accused of killing patients in a veterans hospital in Michigan became a sensational story, reinforcing the old impression of Filipinos as "devious," "inscrutable" troublemakers, and so on. In spite of their acquittal, the stigma of wrongdoing still contaminates the sites where Filipinos congregate. Meanwhile, the generation of Filipino farmworkers in California that spearheaded union organizing in the thirties and forties finally merged their patient endeavors with the more numerous Chicanos in 1965, with Cesar Chavez eclipsing the figures of the veteran organizers Larry Itliong and Philip Vera Cruz in the formation of the United Farm Workers of America (see Chapter 5).

With the exposure of the Marcos regime's corruption and complicity with U.S. imperial aggression in Indochina, the Filipino acquired rebel status: Political exiles like Benigno Aquino, husband of President Corazon Aquino, and other dissidents (not exactly anticommunist emigrés idolized by Establishment neoliberals) graced the front pages of the metropolitan dailies. They were juxtaposed with photos of New People's Army guerillas and Moro National Liberation Front partisans, the latter resurrecting in the popular memory their heroic ancestors who up to the Commonwealth period (1935–1945) defied "Gringo" intruders led by Leonard Wood and John Pershing, veterans of the wars to exterminate the American Indians and pacify Latino recalcitrants. Together with the Igorots of exposition fame (now recorded in Marlon Fuentes's videofilm *Bontoc Eulogy*), thousands of Moro combatants, joined by a coalition of aboriginal groups in the Mindanaw Lumad, are presently mounting attacks on oppressive institutions underwritten by transnational business, the International Monetary Fund/World Bank, and other multilateral financial consortiums (Rodil 1993).

One hopes that the February 1986 insurrection has erased in the majoritarian consciousness any lingering vestige of the 1904 St. Louis Exposition. For the postyuppie generation, the term "Filipino" might evoke images of the striking militants of the Hawaiian cane fields (one of whom returned to the Philippines to lead the Tayug rural uprising in the late twenties), the Huk guerillas of World War II, the ILWU activists Chris Mensalvas and Ernesto Mangaong who resisted McCarthyist witch-hunting and won (Vera 1994), or the anti–martial law activists of the seventies. We hope that the ritual symbolism of "people power" popularized after Aquino's assassination has partly replaced the derogatory stereotypes of "gooks" and "flips" swinging their yo-yos with the scenario of thousands of progressive youth, urban workers, women, and Filipinos from all walks of life surrounding U.S.-made tanks and U.S.-subsidized soldiers in the streets of Metro

Manila. The unprecedented 1986 insurrection, treading closely in the wake of those gory details of Aquino's cadaver bloodying the tarmac of the Manila International Airport, should be viewed as the climax of decades of resistance by militant activists who in turn were inspired by the nationalist renaissance in the fifties led by Claro Recto and Lorenzo Tanada and the radical anti-imperialism of the seventies and eighties.

The resurgence of national-democratic protests in the eighties prompted Filipinos in the United States to reconnect once more with the homeland. Collective roots became the key to reaching our destination. I cite an unusual letter of confession printed in the *Hartford Courant*:

> I was born a Filipino. That may seem like an easy statement to make, but even as I write it, I am amazed at the embarrassment I used to feel. Ever since my parents brought me to the United States, I had been ashamed of who I am, and ashamed of my nation. . . .
>
> I was ashamed [as my brother was] of being different. When friends at school said it was disgusting to see my mother serve fish with the head still intact, or for my father to eat rice with his hands, or to learn that stewed dogs and goats were some examples of Filipino delicacies, I took their side. I accused my own of being unsanitary in their eating habits. . . . When Marcos flaunted his tyranny and declared martial law in 1972, . . . I accused Filipinos of lacking the guts to fight for themselves . . . But everything changed for me when that man [Aquino] I had laughed at landed in my homeland and died on the airport tarmac.
>
> For the first time, I accused myself of not having enough faith in, and hope for, my own people. In the past, I felt that I had no right to be proud of my people. Now, with the cruel Marcos regime tottering, I have finally awakened. Filipinos all over the world need the strength that comes with pride, now more than ever. (Beraquit 1983, 4)

Such "pride" surely needs more than one victim to avoid sentimentality. It is clear that this Filipina teenager has not heard of the April 1924 strike of 31,000 Filipinos in Hawaii or all the numerous acts of resistance from the twenties up to the campaign to save the San Francisco International Hotel in the sixties that have colored (what an appropriate if paradoxical term!) the biased perception of Filipinos. Yet, the past is there for each generation of Filipinos to rediscover and draw lessons from. This will include the fact that as "nonwhites" (until 1946) Filipinos were refused service in restaurants, barbershops, swimming pools, and movie theaters and were prohibited from marrying Caucasians because, as one California state prosecutor said, Malays are prone to "homicidal mania" called "running amuck." The figure of the amok, however, cuts both ways, as derogatory ideologeme for the potboiler *Ghosts of Manila* (1994) by James Hamilton-Paterson and as emancipatory trope in Nick Carbo's laconic poem "Running Amok": "During the Filipino-American War/from 1900 to 1902, the Colt .45 pistol/was refined to kill crazed/Moro fighters who ran amok/and would not stop attacking" the Yankee conquistadors (1995, 28).

Confusion about the racial category to which Filipinos should be assigned has run rampant in the mind of the white imperial elite ever since the subjugation of the Philippines at the turn of the century. Despite the media barrage of information, the ordinary citizen in suburbia can not say whether the Malay is a Mongolian; whether the Filipino is an African, Chinese, Japanese, or what. Even today, because of the shape of my eyes and nose, I am mistaken for being a Japanese or Chinese at the university, in the desolate malls of New England, along small-town streets of the Midwest and the South, almost everywhere. And when I tell the curious observer I am from the Philippines (an original, as they say, "born in the islands"), indeed, the image of an island in the Caribbean immediately flashes in their minds, especially because my name (and those of most Filipinos) is Spanish in origin. But wait—who are you that you cannot recognize who I am?

At first, there was the invasion of uncouth "jungle folk" and "primitive island folk" that replaced the "yellow peril." In *Moby Dick* (1851), Melville purveyed the Orientalist motif of the subtly diabolic aborigines of Manila, "paid spies and secret confidential agents on the water of the devil, their Lord." A problem and menace, the half-breeds assumed the guise of Asiatic Niggers, sex fiends, then "brown-skinned Apaches." If it is of any consolation for would-be settlers, one can say that we are no longer strangers to U.S. immigration officials. For when Jose Rizal (later canonized as the national hero) arrived in San Francisco in transit to Europe in 1888, he (together with 643 Chinese coolies) was promptly quarantined and fumigated by customs officials on the pretext that he was a carrier of typhoid, cholera, leprosy, and other "yellow perils." Meanwhile, 700 bales of precious Chinese silk were unloaded from the ship without fumigation. Writing in his journal years later, Rizal mused that "America is the land par excellence of freedom, but only for the whites." In 1908, a Hawaiian farm owner ordered his usual supplies, listing after "fertiliser" the item "Filipinos" (see letter dated May 5, 1908, by H. Hackfield and Company sent to George Wilcox of the Grove Farm Plantation, Hawaii, cited in Takaki 1987, 4). Witness also: "It must be realized that the Filipino is just the same as the manure that we put on the land—just the same" (from an interview with a secretary of an agricultural association in 1930, cited in Takaki 1989, 324). Today, the most valuable commodities from the islands are no longer hemp, sugar, or coconuts, but mail-order brides followed by Overseas Contract Workers (domestic help, "hospitality" girls, semi-skilled labor). Our status as part of the proverbial "model minority"—ironic unsettling terms, indeed—needs emergency rectification.

Soon, before the end of this century, there will be more than 2 million Filipinos in the United States, a leap from 774,652 in 1980 (of whom two-thirds were born in the Philippines). It is the fastest-growing community of former colonial subjects (many of course still colonized without the slightest suspicion or unease), centered on the West Coast, in Chicago, New Jersey–New York, and of course Hawaii and Alaska. Are Filipinos really the "forgotten" Asians? Not quite, as long as mass media, the Internet, and everyday conversation feed off the inexhaustible scandals of the Marcos dynasty, Mount Pinatubo's fireworks, and the danger of a communist "takeover" in the Philippines, or some equivalent calamity hobbling business operations. Kidlat Tahimik interposes: Who invented the yo-yo and the moon buggy? (Feria 1988). Unforgettable Filipinos, indeed! Behold millions of domestics, brides for sale, bar entertainers, versatile nurses and other commodified professionals heading for Europe, North America, and elsewhere, mixing with average citizens, politicians, crooks, and fugitive adventurers of all sorts.

Indeed, how can the much-ballyhooed image of Corazon Aquino overshadowing the Marcos aura be so easily forgotten? Smiling pink round face, gold-rimmed designer spectacles adding intellectual veneer to Aquino's winsome look as she props her chin, poised proudly to look at readers of *Time, Newsweek, Ms.*, the *New York Times:* This electronic fantasy, now slightly frayed, after February 1986 dominated the world's consciousness for some time. Aquino has displaced the tawdry Iron Butterfly, Imelda Marcos, in the pantheon of the mass media even as the scandal of billions of dollars looted from the Philippine treasury, the parade of court indictments, underworld shenanigans, and so forth continue to define the Filipino stereotype for the U.S. public. In the October 1986 article on Aquino in *Ms.*, a Filipina propagandist for the new regime (by not-so-deft quotes) tried to convince the public that Tita (Auntie) Cory, by virtue of being a woman, will save 56 million Filipinos from being crushed "between the gun [military brutality] and the crucifix [religious sexism]." After less than a thousand days of Aquino's regime, the image of the Filipino in the international media is still a cross between the stereotypes of the Mexican bandit and the wily "inscrutable Oriental."

We still see in sporadic news items the Filipino running "amok" in contested villages in the Philippines. Much more publicized are the "warm body export" of Filipino workers in the Middle East; the availability of Filipinas as mail-order brides; ubiquitous prostitutes around former military bases; "hospitality girls" in Tokyo, Bangkok, Cyprus, and elsewhere. Of late, the *Oxford English Dictionary* was reported as poised to define "Filipina" as "domestic"—it turned out to be in truth only a rumor. Meanwhile, in Hong Kong, dolls of Filipino women dressed as maids, complete with passport and labor contract, compete as toys in the department stores (Escoda 1989). This is the latest stage in the ongoing metamorphosis of our brothers and sisters: the Filipina not as chic tourist nor wannabe Loida Nicolas-Lewis but as transnational worker; not Goethe's world citizen but a nomadic proletariat and petty consumer in the global village of megamalls.

The phenomenon of the Marcos interlude in Philippine history has in fact generated a new semantics of racial categorization that expands it to cover the whole Third World: Marcos joins the ranks of the infamous and quasi-legendary Duvaliers, Somozas, Shah of Iran, and other "not quite civilized" despots to reinforce once again the myth of the West as the virtuous, enlightened *homo sapiens* civilizing the benighted natives. Unfortunately, the highly touted avant garde films of Kidlat Tahimik (Eric de Guia) like *The Perfumed Nightmare, Turumba, Who Invented the Yo-yo and the Moon-Buggy?* have not succeeded in displacing the Hollywood/Madison Avenue stereotypes of Filipinos as lowly denizens occupying the boundary line between China and Latin America, an enigmatic zone that seems to defy neat racist labeling. Bulosan and other Filipino American writers remain excluded from most textbooks, whereas the late enigmatic exile Jose Garcia Villa (not to be confused as before with Pancho Villa, the Mexican revolutionary), who befriended e. e. cummings and other hegemonic intellectuals, languished in an obscure corner of Greenwich Village for almost half a century.

With the advent of a melancholy "New World Order," what is in store for Filipinos? Are we now cyborgs, borderland creatures fit for portentous "auguries of innocence or experience"? At this conjuncture, I want to quote a passage from one of Bulosan's letters (written in the forties) to recapture and perhaps recuperate the force of the Filipinos' submerged history. This mode of speculation remains emblematic of the way Filipinos (and perhaps other voyagers from the Third World) articulate the moral and ideological core of their predicament as exiles, immigrants, expatriates, or refugees—not quite "world citizens," as the European Enlightenment dreamed of their peripatetic entrepreneurs. Bulosan outlines the scheme of his project in the subjunctive mode:

> I have been wanting to do something of great significance to the future of the islands. I will probably start one of the most important books in my life soon, maybe sometime next week. . . . It concerns racial lies: the rela-

tions between Pinoys and white Americans. Here it is: Suddenly in the night a Filipino houseboy kills a friend and in his attempt to escape from the law he stumbles into his dark room and bumps against the wall. When he wakes up he is confronted by a veiled image in the darkness who reveals to him that he has become white. It is true, of course, that he has become a white man. But the image tells him he will remain a white man so long as he will not fall in love with a white woman! And that is the tragedy because he has already fallen in love with a white woman. Get that? So long as he will not fall in love with a white woman! Then, according to the warning of the image, he would become a Filipino again, ugly, illiterate, monster-like, and vicious.

This is a parable, of course, an American parable. Some elements in America gave us a gift of speech, education, money, but they also wanted to take away our heart. They give you money but deny your humanity. (1995, 177)

This dilemma has of course been rehearsed a million times, over and over in the waking experiences, dreams, and nightmares of millions of blacks, Latinos, Native Americans, and Asian Pacific Islanders. Repetition breeds truth, as Nietzsche once warned us; but how can we finally break this cycle and construct our identity on the edge of difference? Not to make a mystique of the Other, of difference itself as a virtue, but to identify our desire for recognition via the gaze of the Other?

We have had the testimonies of other Third World comrades: Fanon's *Black Skin, White Masks*, George Jackson's *Soledad Brother*, the activists in La Raza Unida, the American Indian Movement, and now the agitation for Hawaiian sovereignty. I think it is naive if not pathetically confusing for Filipinos born in the United States to identify "my native homeland," "the land of my life and my death," with the hegemonic state or government of the white corporate power bloc (see Cordova 1984, 4) while at the same time claiming pride in their ethnicity. This is disingenuous opportunism if not naive wish fulfillment. While the Philippines still occupies subaltern status under U.S. hegemony, one cannot have it both ways; absent substantive parity, the hyphen between Filipino and American cannot be translated as a dialogue of peers or allies. This is the lesson learned by the Manongs; by Pablo Manlapit, Chris Mensalvas, and Ernesto Mangaong; by the veterans who fought the Japanese aggressors in defense of U.S. territorial possessions; by young men recruited into the U.S. Navy; by Silme Domingo and Gene Viernes, murdered by a heritage of subservience and mendacity—how much more sacrifice is needed to uphold the right of self-determination, the right to affirm one's dignity and humanity?

For the Filipino circumscribed by a territorial state jurisdiction, I venture to suggest a horizon, a project, an aspiration: to liberate the homeland from imperial-racial domination and free our minds from the white supremacist manacles forged about a hundred years ago and still being reforged in the alienating and commodifying practices of everyday life in this belly of the moribund beast, the postmodern descendant of Moby Dick. This of course is not just a Filipino project but that of everyone whose humanity remains locked in the prison of nationality, race, gender, class, and so on. We may re-pose our previous questions: Who will rescue the aboriginal "tribes" from that prison of the St. Louis Exposition? The poet Al Robles hurls the challenge to the "mongo heart & isda mind" of Filipinos in "Rappin' with Ten Thousand Carabaos in the Dark":

> *Ah, Pilipinos*
> *if you only knew how brown you are*
> *you would slide down*
> *from the highest*
> *mountain top*
> *you would whip out your lava tongue*
> *& burn up all that white shit*
> *that's keeping your people down.* (1996, 113)

What is at stake in this deadly "game" is not just our psyches but also our bodies and those of our children. Can the mass media, art, and museums, as well as our discourse of the tolerant, pluralist society welcoming "the toiling millions" purge themselves of the poison of racism under the aegis of neoliberal democracy and predatory "free enterprise"? That is the urgent question we need to address ourselves to—who are these shadowy, fantasized selves hovering around us?—as we face the close of the twentieth century and the genesis of the twenty-first.

2

From Identity Politics to Transformative Critique

The Predicament of the Asian American Writer
in Late Capitalism

With the presumed collapse of the transcendental grounds for universal standards of norms and values, proponents of the postmodernist "revolution" in cultural studies in Europe and North America have celebrated *différance*, marginality, nomadic and decentered identities, indeterminacy, simulacra and the sublime, undecidability, ironic dissemination, textuality, and so forth. A multiplicity of power plays and language games supposedly abound. The intertextuality of power, desire, and interest begets strategies of positionalities. So take your pick. Instead of the totalizing master narratives of Enlightenment progress, postmodernist thinkers valorize the local, the heterogeneous, the contingent and conjunctural. Is it still meaningful to speak of truth? Are we still permitted to address issues of class, gender, and race?

What are the implications of this postmodernist "transvaluation" of paradigms for literary studies in general and minority/ethnic writing in particular? One salutary repercussion has been the questioning of the Eurocentric canonical archive by feminists, peoples of color, dissenters inside and outside. The poststructuralist critique of the self-identical Subject (by convention white, bourgeois, patriarch) has inspired a perspectivalist revision of various disciplinary approaches in history, comparative aesthetics, and others. To cite three inaugural examples: Houston Baker's text-specific inventory of the black vernacular "blues" tradition presented in *Blues, Ideology and Afro-American Literature* (1984), Arnold Krupat's foregrounding of oral tribal allegory in American Indian autobiographies enabled by a "materially situated historicism" in *The Voice in the Margin* (1989), and Ramon Saldivar's dialectical assessment of the Chicano narrative as an "oppositional articulation" of the gaps and silences in U.S. literary history, a thesis vigorously argued in *Chicano Narrative* (1990). Premised on the notion that everything is sociodiscursively constructed, these initiatives so far have not been paralleled by Asian American intellectuals. Who indeed will speak for this composite group?

One would suspect that the rubric "Asian American," itself an artificial hypostasis of unstable elements, would preemptively vitiate any unilateral program of systematization. In addition, Asian Americans being judged by media and government as a "model minority," some allegedly whiter than whites (see Thernstrom 1983, 252; Lee 1991), makes their marginality quite problematic. Perhaps more than other peoples of color, Asian Americans find themselves trapped in a classic postmodernist predicament: Essentialized by the official pluralism as formerly the "yellow peril" and now the "superminority," they nevertheless seek to reaffirm their complex internal differences in projects of hybrid and syncretic genealogy. Objectified by state-ordained juridical exclusions (Chinese, Japanese, and Filipinos share this historically unique commonality), they pursue particularistic agendas for economic and cultural autonomy. Given these antinomic forces at work, can Asian American writers collectively pursue a "molecular micropolitics" of marginality? What is at stake if a well-known authority on ethnic affairs like Ronald Takaki (whose 1989 book affords a point of departure for my metacommentary) tries to articulate the identity-in-difference of this fragmented and dispersed ensemble of ethnoi? (Grigulevich and Kozlov 1974, 17–44). How does a postmodernist politics of identity refract the innovative yet tradition-bound performances of the Chinese Maxine Hong Kingston and the Filipino Carlos Bulosan? Given the crisis of the postmodernist politics of identity, can we legitimately propose an oppositional "emergency" strategy of writing whose historic agency is still on trial as it were, on reprieve? My inquiry in this chapter begins with remarks on Asian American history's textuality as prelude to its possible aesthetic inscription.

In composing *Strangers from a Different Shore* (1989), in a period when the planet is beginning to be homogenized by a new pax EuroAmericana, a "New World Order" spawning (as I write) from the Persian Gulf, Ronald Takaki has performed for us the unprecedented task of unifying the rich, protean, intractable diversity of Asian lives in the United States without erasing the specificities, the ramifying genealogies, the incommensurable repertoire of idiosyncrasies of each constituent group. It is a postmodernist feat of reconciling incommensurables, to say the least. There are of course many discrete chronicles of each Asian community, mostly written by sympathetic EuroAmerican scholars, before Takaki's work. But what distinguishes Takaki's account, aside from his empathy with his subject and documentary trustworthiness, is its claim to represent the truth based on the prima facie experiences of individuals. At once, we are confronted with the crucial problem plaguing such claims to veracity or authenticity: Can these subalterns represent themselves (to paraphrase Gayatri Spivak 1988) as self-conscious members of a collectivity-for-itself? Or has Takaki mediated the immediacy of naive experience with a theory of representation that privileges the *homo economicus* as the founding subject of his discourse?[1]

No one should underestimate Takaki's achievement here as elsewhere in challenging the tenability of the received dogma (espoused by Nathan Glazer and other neoconservative pundits) that the European immigrant model of successful assimilation applies to peoples of color in the United States (see Takaki 1987). Europe's Others, hitherto excluded from the canonical tradition, are beginning to speak and *present* themselves so as to rectify the others' re-presentation of themselves. In this light, Takaki is to be credited above all for giving Asian Americans a synoptic view of their deracinated lives by making them (as protagonists who discover their roles and destinies in the process) perform the drama of their diverse singularities. This is stage managed within the framework of a chronological history of their ordeals in struggling to survive, adapt, and multiply in a hostile habitat, with their accompanying rage and grief and laughter. By a montage of personal testimony—anecdotes, letters, songs, telegrams, eyewitness reports, confessions, album photographs, quotidian fragments, clichés and banalities of everyday life—juxtaposed with statistics, official documents, reprise of punctual events, Takaki skillfully renders a complex intricate drama of Asians enacting and living their own history. We can perhaps find our own lives already anticipated, pantomimed, rounded off, and judged in one of his varied "talk stories"—a case of life imitating the art of history.

Granted the book's "truth effects," I enter a caveat. For all its massive accumulation of raw data and plausible images of numerous protagonists and actions spanning more than a century of wars and revolutions, Takaki's narrative leaves us wondering whether the collective life trajectory of Asian Americans imitates the European immigrant success story, spiced with quaint "Oriental" twists—which he clearly implies at the end. If so, it is just one thread of the national fabric, no more tormented or pacified than any other. If not, then this history is unique in some way that escapes the traditional emplotment of previous annals deriving from the master narrative of humankind's continuous material improvement, self-emancipation and technoadministrative mastery conceived by the philosophes of the European Enlightenment. Either way, there is no reason for Asian Americans to feel excluded from the grand March of Progress. Our puzzlement, however, is not clarified by the book's concluding chapter, which exposes the myth of the "model minority" in an eloquent argument, assuring us that Asians did not "let the course of their lives be determined completely by the 'necessity' of race and class" (473).

In the same breath, Takaki warns of a resurgent tide of racially motivated attacks against Asians manifested in the media; in campus harassments; in the 1982 murder of Vincent Chin, mistaken for a Japanese by unemployed Detroit autoworkers (and, I might add here, in the January 1989 massacre of Vietnamese and Cambodian schoolchildren in Stockton, California, by a man obsessed with hatred for southeast Asian refugees). During this same period, in contrast, the judicial victory of the Japanese concentration camp internees' demand for redress and reparations as well as the growing visibility of Asian American artists furnish convincing proof that what David Harvey calls the post-Fordist post-Keynesian system (1989, 173–78) still allows dreams to come true, that is, allows Asians the opportunity in particular "to help America accept and appreciate its diversity."

Calculating the losses and gains, Takaki prudentially opts for a meliorative closure. In retrospect, the telos of *Strangers from a Different Shore* can be thematized as the Asian immigrants' almost miraculous struggle for survival and recognition of their desperately-won middle-class status. What is sought is the redemption of individual sacrifices by way of conformity to the utilitarian, competitive ethos of a business society. Reversing the dismaying prospect of Asians forecast by an earlier survey, *American Racism* (1970) by Roger Daniels and Harry Kitano, Takaki offers a balance sheet for general consumption:

> Asian Americans are no longer victimized by legislation denying them naturalized citizenship and landownership. They have begun to exercise their political voices and have representatives in both houses of Congress as well as in state legislatures and on city councils. They enjoy much of the protection of civil rights laws that outlaw racial discrimination in employment as well as housing and that provide for affirmative action for racial minorities. They have greater freedom than did the earlier immigrants to embrace their own "diversity"—their own cultures as well as their own distinctive physical characteristics, such as their complexion and the shape of their eyes. (473–74)

It now becomes clear that despite its encyclopedic scope and archival competence, Takaki's somewhat premature synthesis is a learned endeavor to deploy a strategy of containment. His rhetoric activates a mode of comic emplotment in which all problems are finally resolved through hard work and individual effort, inspired by past memories of clan solidarity and intuitive faith in a gradually improving future. What is this if not a refurbished version of the liberal ideology of market-centered, pluralist society in which all disparities in values and beliefs, nay, even the sharpest contradictions implicating race, class, and gender, can be harmonized within the prevailing structure of power relations?

This is not to say that such changes toward empowering disenfranchised nationalities are futile or deceptive. But what needs a more-than-gestural critique is the extent to which such reforms do not eliminate the rationale for the hierarchical, invidious categorizing of people by race (as well as by gender and class) and their subsequent deprivation. Lacking such self-reflection, unable to problematize his theoretical organon, what Takaki has superbly accomplished is the articulation of the hegemonic doctrine of acquisitive/possessive liberalism as the informing principle of Asian American lives. Whether this is an effect of postmodernist tropology or a symptom of "bad faith" investing the logic of elite populism, I am not quite sure.

My reservations are shared by other Asian American observers who detect an apologetic agenda in such liberal historiography. At best, Takaki's text operates by an ironic if not duplicitous strategy: To counter hegemonic Eurocentrism, which erases the Asian American presence, a positivist-empiricist valorization of "lived experience" is carried out within the master narrative of evolutionary, gradualist progress. The American "Dream of Success" is thereby ultimately vindicated. This is not to suggest that historians like Takaki have suddenly been afflicted with amnesia, forgetting that it is the totalizing state practice of this ideology of market liberalism that underlies, for one, the violent colonial domination of peoples of color and rape of the land of such decolonizing territories as the Philippines (my country of origin) and Puerto Rico in the aftermath of the Spanish-American War. It is the social practice of an expansive political economy that converts humans to exchangeable commodities (African chattel slavery in the South) and commodified labor power, thus requiring for its industrial takeoff a huge supply of free labor; hence the need for European immigrants, especially after the Civil War and the genocidal suppression of the American Indians. It is the expansion of this social formation that recruited Chinese coolies for railroad construction (the "fathers" poignantly described in Kingston's 1989 *China Men*); Japanese and Filipino labor (and Mexican braceros later) for agribusiness in Hawaii and California, for the canneries in Alaska. It is this same hegemonic worldview of free monopoly enterprise, also known as the "civilizing mission" of Eurocentric humanism, that forced the opening of the China market in the opium wars of the nineteenth century and the numerous military interventions in China and Indochina up to the Vietnam War and the coming of the "boat people." Of course, it is also the power/knowledge episteme of the modernization process in Kenya, South Korea, Mexico, Indonesia, Egypt, Grenada, and all the neocolonial or peripheral dependencies of the world system named by Immanuel Wallerstein as "historical capitalism"(1983, 13–43; see Amin 1989).

It is now generally acknowledged that we cannot understand the situation of Asian Americans in the United States today or in the past without a thorough comprehension of the global relations of power, the capitalist world system, that "pushed" populations from the colonies and dependencies and "pulled" them to terrain where a supply of cheap labor was needed. These relations of power broke up families, separating husbands from wives, parents from children; at present they motivate the "warm body export" of cheap labor from Thailand, the Philippines, and elsewhere. They legitimize the unregulated market for brides and hospitality girls, the free trade zones, and other postmodern schemes of capital accumulation in Third World countries. The discourse of the liberal free market underpins these power relations, constructing fluid georacial boundaries to guarantee the supply of cheap labor. Race acquires salience in this world system when, according to John Rex, "The language of racial difference . . . becomes the means whereby men allocate each other to different social and economic positions. . . . The exploitation of clearly marked groups in a variety of different ways is integral to capitalism. . . . Ethnic groups unite and act together because they have been subjected to distinct and differentiated types of exploitation" (1983, 406–7). The colonization and industrialization of the North American continent epitomize the asymmetrical power relations characteristic of this world system.

The sociocultural formation of global apartheid has been long in the making. In studies like Eric Wolf's *Europe and the People Without History* (1982) or Richard Barnet and Ronald Muller's *Global Reach* (1974), to mention only the elementary texts, one can see that the migration of peoples around the world, the displacement of refugees or the forced expulsion and exile of individuals and whole groups (the Palestinian diaspora is the most flagrant), have occurred not by choice or accident but by the complex interaction of political, economic, and social forces from the period of mercantile capitalism to colonialism from the sixteenth to the nineteenth century and imperialism in the twentieth century. This historical context, the self-reproduction of its mechanisms and the sedimentation of its effects, is what is occluded in Takaki's narrative (see Nakanishi 1976).

Racial antagonism has marked the process of U.S. ethnogenesis from the outset. Since the beginning of the U.S. social formation as Britain's colonial outpost, its evolution has been distinguished by the violent exclusion and subjugation of the American Indians and the subsequent differential incorporation of various racial groups. Takaki is sensitive to this process but assumes it is normal and inescapable, not an index to subsequent race relations in the metropolitan center. Historians like Eugene Genovese, Gabriel Kolko, Howard Zinn, and others have pointed out that U.S. society has been discriminative from the very beginning. Alexander Saxton points out Nathan Glazer's fundamental mistake in assuming that a policy of equal rights characterized U.S. history from its inception: "Already in the days of Jefferson and the 'sainted Jackson' (to use Walt Whitman's phrase) the nation had assumed the form of a racially exclusive democracy—democratic in the sense that it sought to provide equal opportunities for the pursuit of happiness by its white citizens through the enslavement of Afro-Americans, extermination of Indians, and territorial expansion largely at the expense of Mexicans and Indians" (1977, 145). By privileging ethnic (chiefly cultural superficialities) difference as a key sociological factor and ignoring what Michael Banton and Robert Miles call "racism"— the justification of unequal treatment of groups by deterministic ascription of negative characteristics to them (1984, 228; see also Banton 1987; Miles 1989)—U.S. disciplinary regimes subsumed the plight of peoples of color into the European immigrant model. Thus, they actualized a racial formation with ideological roots in Puritan doctrine and in Enlightenment humanist-scientific rationality.

The concept of racial formation I have in mind originates from the dialectical articulation of state policies, discriminatory practices in civil society, and popular resistance to them. With the rise of the civil rights movement in the sixties, a new historical consciousness precipitated an understanding of such phenomena as "internal colonialism" imposed by the state on subject populations (as cogently argued by Robert Blauner in *Racial Oppression in America* [1972]) and the segmentation of the labor market. By the eighties, with the renewed assault on civil rights by the particular brand of neoconservatism represented by the Reagan administration, it is necessary to reassess and correct our theoretical perspective to grasp the changed configuration of the U.S. racial state and racial politics; this is the signal accomplishment of Michael Omi and Howard Winant's (1986) study *Racial Formation in the United States from the 1960s to the 1980s* (see San Juan 1989b). Lacking a theory of the changing articulation of racial discourse in different historical stages and the mutations of "differential exclusion" in late capitalism (see Davis 1984), ethnic histories like Takaki's find themselves undermined by what Etienne Balibar (1991) refers to as the "theoretical racism" of liberal democracy (283–94). Meanwhile, the subjects interpellated by such discourses find themselves "decentered" by the seemingly gratuitous pathos of living through the accelerated cyclic boom and bust of a postmodern, schizoid, but still profit-centered economy.

As we live through the aftereffects of the "authoritarian populism" of the eighties, the neoconservative backlash against the "welfare state," the rollback of affirmative action programs affecting a wide range of social transfer payments that benefited disadvantaged sectors and the "underclass," and lately the media euphoria over the debacle of "actually existing socialism" in Eastern Europe, what is in store for Asian Americans at the threshold of the twenty-first century? One thing is predictable: Without an alternative or oppositional strategy that can challenge the logic of liberal possessive individualism and the seductive lure of consumerism (what W. F. Haug [1986] calls "commodity aesthetics"), I suspect that the only recourse is to revive versions of individualist metaphysics, the most popular of which is "identity politics," that is, the tendency to base one's politics on a sense of identity, internalizing or privatizing all issues and thus either voiding them of any meaning or trivializing them (see Fuss 1989, 97–112). From a strategic angle, this tactical move recuperates an autochthonous will, an indigenous Otherness, if you like.[2] But what is unfortunately lost in the process is the historical density of collective resistance and revolt, the texture of our involvement in our communities that Takaki attempted to capture, together with the necessary concrete knowledge of society and politics—the mutable and highly mediated field of discourses, practices, institutions—on which our sense of responsibility can be nurtured, on which strategies of parody, satire, and expressive disruption can be anchored. But are questions like "Who am I?" "Why am I writing and for whom?" irrelevant or counterproductive?

Questions of precisely this sort—interrogating the archaeology of a postmodernist, hyperreal auto-da-fé itself—were the ones grappled with by over a dozen Asian American intellectuals (writers, critics, social scientists) joined by a handful of African Americans and EuroAmericans in a three-day symposium, "Issues of Identity," held at Cornell University to which I was invited to participate in as a representative of the Filipino American "ethnic" category.

In my view, the event recapitulated the problems and lessons of the Asian American experience memorialized by Takaki. What transpired may be conceived of as a case study of the identity politics syndrome complicated by the usual group dynamics of local born/expatriate encounters traversing a range of sexual, ethical, and occupational discourses. Not only was identity reduced to the home garden variety of egos striking confessional postures, but the assorted group of writers (none of whom commanded the stature of Maxine Hong Kingston, whose absent presence evoked a peculiar ressentiment from some writers) found themselves privileged somehow as the fountainhead of answers to questions of Asian American personal/collective identity. This privileging of the artist's status, orchestrated by the Hong Kong–born impresario of the symposium, may have ruined any possibility of dialogue. When the critics (all based in such higher institutions of the empire as the universities of California, Michigan, Wisconsin; Cornell University; and so on), who were assigned to comment specifically on the solicited texts (mostly essays) of the six authors, presented their commentaries in the language of contemporary critical theory, most of the writers immediately reacted with disappointment, incomprehension, anger, disgust, futile rage. "Where are you coming from? Speak simply so common people can understand you!" (Such reactions were addressed to the reading of the comments, not to the written texts.) The event culminated in a quasi-Puritanical witch trial in which the personal motives of the critics were questioned. One Chinese American poet from Hawaii even derogated Kingston—"Why is she always quoted as an authority on our community?" It reached the point where I was attacked for using obscure, pedantic language; for laying down a political line, imposing a theory (the vulgar terrorist label to make someone superfluous is of course "Marxist"), and—to say the least—for not conforming to the unwittingly self-serving identity politics that, by some insidious operation of shame psychology, had by then become the all-purpose weapon of the embattled *ecrivains*. In fact, the writers' response subsided to the crudest debunking accusation that the critics only engaged in such activity for the sake of tenure, fat salaries, prestige, professional vanity, and so forth. How was all this warranted by the ritual of a seemingly cultivated, polite, formally structured academic exchange?

Let me venture an explanation. Apart from my criticism of liberal ideology such as that presiding over Takaki's popularizing effort and also the writers' self-serving justification of their function, what aroused the most intense hostility was my nuanced indictment of "multiculturalism," the writer's solution to the malaise of "cultural schizophrenia" and a pre-Lacanian hyphenated identity. A Filipino American writer inter alia observed that for her multiculturalism in the white media was "just mind-blowing": Witness those black rappers, Asian ethnic fashion and technology, Zen car commercials, and so forth. To this now hackneyed glorification of consumer society as the site of creative freedom, spontaneity—you can be whatever you want to be—and seemingly infinite libidinal gratification, I countered that the self-indulgence in this fabled cornucopia of simulacra, replicas, commodified spectacles—the pastiche offered by yuppie catalogues and antiseptic supermalls cloned from postmodernist Las Vegas—is a hallucinatory path that does not lead to discovering one's creative alterity. Rather, it leads to the suppression of the imagination's potential and unrelenting submission to the monolithic law of a racist dispensation. That cornucopia is really the emblem of what Henri Lefebvre describes as "the bureaucratic society of controlled consumption"(1968, 68–109). Asian American citizens who articulate their subjecthood, their subalternity, through multiculturalism (assimilation via acculturation lurks not far behind) betray an ignorance of the lopsided distribution of power and wealth in a racially stratified society. And so, in what might be a postmodern aporia, binary opposites turn out to be double binds (I am both American and Asian, and many other things)—virtually disabling ruses of complicity, self-incriminating games of co-optation.

Recent scholars have documented the growing mass appeal of a new racist practice based on the language of diverse cultures, lifestyles, personal tastes, and free choices, articulated with issues of class, gender, age, and so forth. What the advocates of multiculturalism are innocent of is the concept of hegemony (of which more later), which allows a latitude of diverse trends and tendencies in a putative laissez-faire market system provided these operate within the monadic framework of contractual arrangements and hierarchical property relations. Corporate hegemony precisely thrives on your freedom to shop—until your credit runs out and the right to be bankrupt is invoked. In lieu of moralizing, probably the best retort to this rather premature celebration of the postmodernist orgy of the Emersonian Self is from the manifesto of one of its high priests, Jean-Francois Lyotard:

> Eclecticism is the degree zero of contemporary general culture: one listens to reggae, watches a western, eats MacDonald's food for lunch and local cuisine for dinner, wears Paris perfume in Tokyo and "retro" clothes in Hong Kong; knowledge is a matter for TV games. It is easy to find a public for eclectic works. By becoming kitsch, art panders to the confusion which reigns in the "taste" of the patrons. Artists, gallery owners, critics, and public wallow together in the "anything goes," and the epoch is one of slackening. But this realism of the "anything goes" is in fact that of money; in the absence of aesthetic criteria, it remains possible and useful to assess the value of works of art according to the profits they yield. Such realism accommodates all tendencies, just as capital accommodates all "needs," providing that the tendencies and needs have purchasing power. (1984, 76)

My reservation then to the assumption by racial subjects of an autonomous identity envisaged by multiculturalism (which I would consider the guilty conscience or "bad faith" of petty suburban liberalism) concerns the orthodox conception of the dominant culture as simply comprising lifestyles that you can pick and wear anytime you please. That is just unfeasible since this hegemonic multiculture (practices, discourses), viewed from a historical materialist perspective, is precisely the enabling power of a system produced and reproduced by racial, gender, and class divisions. It coincides with a network of domination and subordination in civil society that prevents one from choosing any lifestyle or, for that matter, refusing alienated work to realize one's social potential, that is, the "species being" Marx postulates in his *1844 Economic and Philosophical Manuscripts* (1973). In this context, hegemony implies the reproduction of subordinate Others to confirm the hierarchy; but at the same time, sites of contestation open up where desire, phantasy, and the unconscious begin to erode hierarchy. Here is the blind spot that identity politics cannot apprehend, namely, that the contingencies of a hegemonic struggle can generate a variety of subject positions that are neither fixed nor shifting but capable of being articulated in various directions according to the play of political forces and the conjunctural alignment of multilayered determinants (see Williams 1977, 108–11; Hall 1986). Oblivious of this deeper analysis, the exponents of identity politics construe "identity" in an abstract formalist fashion: the consumer as prototype. But this politics conceals its essentialism in its claim of affirming universalizing, humanist goals—one writer expatriated from the Philippines and now domiciled in Greenwich Village, extolled her world citizenship as her credential of entitlement.

I believe this escape route of the "Unhappy Consciousness," this catharsis of a post-Stoic universalism, harbors a genealogy that can be traced all the way back to the Renaissance. One filiation is Goethe's vanguard internationalism, which despite its humanitarian intention exemplifies pure culinary (to borrow Brecht's term) liberalism, although one much ahead of its time. In his "Conversations with Eckermann," Goethe (1962) speculates about the advent of "world literature," multiculturalism on a planetary scale. After reading one Chinese novel, this archetypal European culture hero tries to impart his wisdom to us benighted denizens from Asia:

> The Chinese think, act, and feel almost exactly like ourselves; and we soon find that we are perfectly like them, except that all they do is more clear, more pure and decorous than with us. . . .
> National literature is now rather an unmeaning term; the epoch of World Literature is at hand, and every one must strive to hasten its approach. But, while we thus value what is foreign, we must not bind ourselves to anything in particular, and regard it as a model. We must not give this value to the Chinese, or the Serbian. . . . If we really want a pat-

tern, we must always return to the ancient Greeks, in whose works the beauty of mankind is constantly represented. All the rest we must look at only historically, appropriating to ourselves what is good, so far as it goes. (1962, 48)

And so the Faustian spirit of the Caucasian conscience marches on, with Aphrodite at its vanguard and the postmodern Spirit of Negation trailing behind. Nonetheless, it must be said that Goethe's internationalist good sense, in anticipating Hegel's "concrete universal," established the groundwork for conceiving Marx's "species being" and thenceforth Fanon's Third World partisanship and Che Guevarra's "New Socialist Person."

To return to the symposium: Aside from inadequate logistics and inexperienced planning, I think the provenance of whatever misrecognitions occurred—the Asian American psyche cannot plead to be exceptional—cannot just be personal and/or bureaucratic. Causality inheres in the political-symbolic economy of liberal exchange. It inhabits the paradoxical space that syncopates structural constraints and conjunctural opportunities: constraints due to the organizers allowing the writers to monopolize the center of attention and the attendant failure to establish an atmosphere of productive conflict by circulating all the texts and distributing occasions for speech in an egalitarian manner. Both failures consequently fostered an attitude of acknowledging differences sublimated in utterly homogenizing repertoires of communication, that is, in commonsense platitudes and pedantic trivia. In the process, novel conjunctural opportunities were missed: for example, my proposal that we distinguish carefully between experience (almost everyone uncritically endorsed the wonderful "chaos" from which writers drew inspiration—a gesture of "bad faith") and knowledge. "Knowledge," however, was immediately yoked to "theory" and denounced as dogmatic, mechanical, rigid, obscurantist, and so forth. The opportunity for answering why writers, tuned to a different level of discourse, could not understand the critics' idiom and theoretical formulations, was forfeited. Instead of an ambience of genuine national diversity due to uneven development of consciousnesses, ironically a leveling temper supervened in which hierarchy was covertly reinstituted: The writer was a prophet/oracle who speaks truth and purveys sacrosanct knowledge. Because these oracles needed informed readers and intelligent listeners who would confirm their truths, however, a profound anxiety haunted them. They craved the critics' attention and approval as though the critics could supply the psychoanalytic cure, thus confirming the fact that they could not find this cure in the mirror images of themselves performing their improvised, minstrel-like roles. And so Narcissus takes revenge in identity politics, albeit spiced with cyborgean pyrotechnics, which converts dialogue as a pretext for monologue.

Although the critics in general tried to follow the path of compromise, engaging in a liberal game of balancing negative and positive qualities discerned in their readings, the distinction between knowledge and experience, the necessity of which I argued for (inasmuch as this articulation between the two conditions the textualization of identity fought in the battlefields of disciplinary regimes) fell on deaf ears. I argued for the need to posit a wide spectrum of levels of understanding, appreciation, and judgment; for the need to criticize the assumptions of identity politics that functioned as the controlling paradigm in mainstream cultural comparative studies;[3] for the need to guard against anti-intellectualism or a relapse into the banal pragmatic-instrumentalist humanism that preaches that we are all the same, we can all partake of the wealth of the transnational boutiques, and so on. But all these were missed. A "rectification of names" was thus aborted.

In fairness, I should say that what the writers testified to was the enigmatic power of poststructuralist critical discourse, which, to some extent under certain conditions, can be mobilized in the service of an oppositional or alternative politics. Such power perhaps bewildered the writers and provoked defensive, panic symptoms. Rejecting the imputation of ill will or narrow self-serving intentions, the critics all tried to make the texts of the writers (no one, as far as I can recall, alluded to Sartre's *What Is Literature?* or Barthes and Foucault on the authorship function when the writers began to fondle their own texts like private consumption goods) release a virtue that can communicate with the high cultural productions of the Establishment elite, with the discourse of the canonical authors and their foundational critiques. Our project (if I may stress the positive) also aimed to unleash the potential reach of their texts by affording their reading a degree of intelligibility that would challenge and even displace the canonical texts of EuroAmerican hegemonic culture.[4] But, unarguably, the writers' reflex of self-justification took over and converted the symposium into a theater of naive and pathetic self-congratulation, with disagreements ironed out for the moment, "faces" saved, suspicions deflected—another day swallowed up in the *mise en abîme* of ghetto marginality and ethnic vainglory. Liberalism, identity politics, has conquered again. Unfortunately, the handful of outsiders in the scene may carry away with them the wrong impression that Asian American writers and intellectuals (compared to the astute African Americans and the resourceful Chicanos) have a long way to go in "the long march through the institutions," in forging consensus and solidarity through demonstrated respect for their differences. On the other hand, I think the symposium testifies to a recalcitrance and intractability ideal for a counterhegemonic drive against the panoptic, reifying thrust of a "New World Order" managed from Washington, D.C.

Still, the co-optative seductiveness of identity politics cannot be discounted. One way of circumventing it may be illustrated by the signifying practice of the Filipino American writer Carlos Bulosan (1913–1953). Cognizant of the risks of textualizing an illegible Filipino identity enveloped in a culture of silence, Bulosan wrote the only extant epic chronicle of Filipino migrant workers in the United States, *America Is in the Heart* ([1946] 1973; see San Juan 1972, 1979). In this quasi-autobiographical life history of a whole community, Bulosan invented a metamorphic persona, a self disintegrated by the competitive labor market of the West Coast and Hawaii. At the same time, this persona is also constituted by the itinerary of the seasonal labor hired by the farms and the ritualized forms of excess (Georges Bataille [1985] sees in excess, in transgression, the essence of the sacred, of sociality as such); in those moments, space dissolves into the time of annihilating boundaries together with the ethos of bourgeois decorum. In fiction like "Be American," "Story of a Letter," and "As Long as the Grass Shall Grow," Bulosan successfully projected the "I" of subalternity, a self dispersed and inscribed across the commodified space of the West Coast—its desire (use value) alienated in the exchange value of commodities expropriated from the time and energies of bodily life.

In the classic story "As Long as the Grass Shall Grow" (Bulosan 1983a), we witness the condensation of fragments of the protagonist's identity occurring in the same trajectory of its displacement. The passage through a racialized terrain bifurcates the character, displaces his naivete, only to reconstitute it as a metaphor for what has been lost: autonomy, security of home, organic happiness. The eighteen-year-old Filipino boy of this story lands in the United States to join a nomadic group of migrant workers hired to pick seasonal crops in the state of Washington. He is befriended by an Irish schoolteacher, Miss O'Reilly, who volunteers to teach him and the other workers how to read; her excursions to their bunkhouse provoke threats from racist elements in the town. In exchange for her labor and time, translated into the gift of the capacity to read, the workers give her peas and flowers symbolic of their communion with nature.

Forbidden to visit the workers—the patriarchs of the town consider the workers' learning how to read dangerous to the status quo, an attitude reminiscent of the antebellum South—Miss O'Reilly invites them to the schoolhouse instead. One evening, the protagonist begins demonstrating his writing skill: "Suddenly I wrote a poem about what I saw outside in the night [the silent sea and the wide clear sky]. Miss O'Reilly started laughing because my lines were all wrong and many of the words were misspelled and incorrectly used" (1995b, 80–81). The protagonist's "I" then goes through a series of interpellations and substitutions as the woman teacher reads the "Song of Solomon" from the Bible:

> I liked the rich language, the beautiful imagery, and the depth of the old man's passion for the girl and the vineyard.
> "This is the best poetry in the world," Miss O'Reilly said when she finished the chapter. "I would like you to remember it. There was a time when men loved deeply and were not afraid to love."
> I was touched by the songs. I thought of the pea vines on the hillside and silent blue sea not far away. And I said to myself: *Some day I will come back in memory to this place and time and write about you, Miss O'Reilly. How gratifying it will be to come back to you with a book in my hands about all that we are feeling here tonight!* (101)

Immediately after this, the boy is beaten up by racist thugs on his way home to the bunkhouse; regaining consciousness past midnight, he weeps and reflects: "Slowly I realized what had happened" (1995b, 82). Miss O'Reilly disappears; toward the end of the harvesting season, she reappears and tells the boy she is leaving for the big city. The workers celebrate her return with a farewell party lasting through the night, with the moon and stars above the sea and tall mountains surrounding them. Even as she reads the "Song of Solomon," however, the boy has already anticipated her disappearance (in the narrative diegesis) and staged her fictional resurrection here in this text. His "I" fuses narrator-participant and narrator-artist. The narrative voice synthesizes in the circuit of reading/listening to the subject of the text's enunciation and the speaking subject. This semiosis engenders a dialogic persona, not a monadic ego. Synchrony and diachrony, the paradigmatic and the syntagmatic axes, coalesce as memory is transported to the future to recuperate the present moment of narration. The "I" becomes a site for registering the present as resistance to forgetfulness, loss of pleasure, reification.

Dispersed and sublimated into the predicament of the Filipino community (about 120,036 strong in the mid-thirties; Gonzales 1993, 183), the "I" of Bulosan's story maps its own itinerary, its recursive passage. It maps a pre–World War II rural geography that urgently evokes the provincial landscape of the homeland (the Philippines, the only Asian colony of the United States, then about to be ravaged by the Japanese) and induces an uncanny vision, a moment when the repressed returns, when the maternal and educative function of Miss O'Reilly preempts the space once tabooed by racist violence. At this point, her figure, metonymically tied to the cyclic fruitfulness of the land, condenses into a metaphor of home: "One morning I found I had been away from home for twenty years. But where was home? I saw the grass of another spring growing on the hills and in the fields. And the thought came to me that I had had Miss O'Reilly with me all the time, there in the broad fields and verdant hills of America, my home" (104).

In all of Bulosan's fiction, the migrant folk's residual memory of the national liberation struggle of millions of Filipinos against Spanish colonialism and U.S. imperialism mediates the adolescent protagonist's rite of passage from the archaic ways of the feudal countryside to the modern site of metropolitan commodity fetishism, the brute facticity of the racist United States, where the labor of colored bodies is reduced to abstract exchange value (the cash nexus) and wasted away. The adventure of the youthful narrator, whose nascent self-awareness is fixated on traumatic experiences in childhood, suffers a displacement: U.S. business society is not the way it was presented in the colonial textbooks. In effect, the rational Cartesian ego inhabiting the utilitarian ethos of liberal society never really materializes in the Filipino worker's psyche shrouded with a nostalgic alterity, branded by an irrecuperable loss.

On the whole, intertextuality overdetermines the "I" of Bulosan's fiction. We see the stark contrast between the pastoral locus of the worker's origin and the alienated milieu of the labor camps in the West Coast; this hiatus decenters the native psyche for which a strategy of refusing self-definition by the racist order and its official, homogenizing monoglossia is the only hope of survival. Bulosan's art refuses identity politics as a refuge because the reality of life for an immigrant cannot be legitimized or rationalized by it. In its indigenous cunning, Bulosan's writing registers the ambiguity of freedom, of democratic opportunity in the United States by inventing the unrepresentable mutant "I" who exercises the sensibility of the pariah, the incorporate outcast, in discriminating between what is merely beguiling appearance and what is suffered daily by the worker's body.

Another strategy of creative disruption that can outflank the lure of identity politics, the lure of the romantic totem of the liberal imagination for writers who overvalorize its demiurgic capacity, is that mobilized by Maxine Hong Kingston in *The Woman Warrior* (1976) and *China Men* (1989). Suffice it to cite here the ludic, witty colloquium in the last chapter of *China Men* to illustrate Kingston's mode of problematizing racial identity in the United States. In "On Listening," the narrator questions a Filipino scholar (wandering from the Philippines to nowhere, Simmel's amphibious "stranger") who captivates her with the quite implausible report that Chinese mandarins came to the Philippines in March 1603 looking for the Gold Mountain, specifically a gold needle in a mountain, with a chained Chinese prisoner as guide. Kingston asks: "Gold needle? What for?" A Chinese American ventures the opinion that a Chinese monk also traveled to Mexico looking for the Gold Mountain. "Gold Mountain" is the mythical name given to the United States by the Chinese in China to symbolize familial aspirations for wealth, freedom, happiness, and so on. But in this playful exchange, the rubric "Gold Mountain" becomes detached from the aura of myth owing to the pressure of painful, dehumanizing experiences undergone by generations of sojourners and settlers from the 1860s on; it becomes a floating signifier, a charisma-laden mana, which then can be affixed to the Philippines, Mexico, Spain, or wherever the imagination or Eros cathects its adventurous utopian drive.

So the pursuit of truth is distracted, rechanneled, and left suspended as the coordinates of the mountain shift depending on the speaker's focalizing stance relative to the questioner, the fictive narrator of *China Men*. Cowboys in California claim to have watched mandarins floating in a "hot air balloon," index of technology and sci-fi fabulation. When the narrator returns to the Filipino scholar, the Chinese fortune seekers have already drained swamps; raised families; built homes, roads, railroads, cities—in other words, accomplished a civilizing task on their way to the Gold Mountain, where they then sifted dirt and rocks. But the upshot of this is that although "They found a gold needle . . . , they filled a basket with dirt to take with them back to China." To which Kingston replies: "Do you mean the Filipinos tricked them? . . . What were they doing in Spain?" (1989, 308). Places are reshuffled, confusion ensues; dirt, not the gold needle, is transported to China. The positions of speaker and listener are scrambled; signifiers lose their referents. The Filipino scholar wryly promises to distill the facts and mail them to Kingston: Truth/knowledge production aborts further exchange. In conclusion, Kingston says: "Good. Now I could watch the young men who listen" (1989, 308). The joke of reversing positions and demythologizing the Gold Mountain explodes the metaphysics of success, the work ethic, stereotyped images of the United States. We recall how, in the novel, the labor of generations of Chinese immigrants culminated in their being "Driven Out" (decreed by the 1882 Exclusion Act) and subsequently victimized in pogroms and lynchings. Veteran workers become fugitives, temporizing or permanent exiles in the belly of the metropolis. "On Listening" refuses the centralizing intelligence that would mediate discrepancies or reconcile opposites into a hypostatized moment of discovering the truth.

What Kingston executes very subtly in her anecdotal montage is the act of undercutting the formula of the American "Dream of Success" by presenting heterogeneous versions of what the Chinese did in pursuit of the Gold Mountain, versions none of which is privileged, so that the questions posed by the "I" who seeks an authoritative, official version never receives a definitive answer. Hence, the only recourse is to appreciate the virtue of listening, of being open to the possibilities created by our persevering struggles to subvert a monologic political economy. Kingston's maneuver of disrupting any answer that claims to be authoritative, whether it is the narcissistic speech of liberalism or the assimilationist speech of conservative populism ("E pluribus unum"), is one that, I suggest, can serve as a foil to the seduction of multiculturalism in our postmodern milieu. As Hazel Carby (1990) puts it, the politics of multicultural difference can effectively neutralize the response of a racialized subject, thus repressing criticism of a social order structured in dominance by race. The politics of difference is what underwrites ghettoization and apartheid in the pluralist United States.

Recently, in line with the deconstructionist trend in the discourse of the humanities and the recurrent if transitional vogue of revitalizing individualist "habits of the heart," the notion of inventing one's ethnic identity has been broached as an alternative to a modernized scheme of integration. One writer-participant in the Cornell University symposium, for example, mused about the supposed "multiple anchorages that ethnicity provides" amid the color-blind tolerance of the proverbial marketplace of ideas. This celebrates the form, not the substance, of bourgeois individualism retooled for a "postrevolutionary" era. But can one really invent one's identity as one wishes, given the constraints de jure and de facto enforced by the racial state? She confesses: "I can make myself up and this is the enticement, the exhilaration. . . . But only up to a point. And the point, the sticking point is my dark female body." Identity betrays its lack in the crucible of difference. Here is where I would finally foreground the phenotypical marker, the brand of the racial stigma, as the politically valorized signifier that cannot be denied in spite of the rules of formal juridical equality. The colored body and its tropes may be the uncanny sites where the repressed—history, desire, the body's needs—returns.

I would like to underscore here the nexus between the constraints on self-identification and the theoretical import of hegemony introduced earlier. In a field of forces where the liberal episteme is deeply entrenched, the key principle for the maintenance of a stable, self-reproducing hierarchical order of capital is hegemony, a concept first developed by Antonio Gramsci. Hegemony signifies the ascendancy of a historic bloc of forces able to win the voluntary consent of the ruled because the ruled accept their subordinate position for the sake of a degree of freedom that indulges certain libidinal drives, sutures fissured egos, fulfills fantasies, and so forth (Gramsci 1971, 206–76). In exchange for such limited gratification, the subalterns submit to the status quo on the condition that they have access to "individual freedoms," varied lifestyles, differential rewards, and so forth. In the context of the U.S. racial order, this arrangement is known as normative pluralism. A social system presided over by normative pluralism thrives precisely because it ignores the institutional differentiation of interests—we are all equal, each one can do her/his own thing. It also displaces onto quarantined terrain those incompatible, discrepant interests that in fact construct our individual and group positions synchronized to the hierarchical imperatives of the system. Everything is normal: I'm OK, you're OK.

It might be useful, in conclusion, to recapitulate certain propositions formulated earlier to highlight the contextual nature of what I would propose as an agenda for the committed imagination of peoples of color. This agenda would challenge pluralism as the discourse and practice of atomistic liberalism. This hegemonic pluralism operates most effectively in the guise of multiculturalism, alias ethnic diversity, within the parameters of a unifying national consensus that privileges one segment as the universal measure: the EuroAmerican elite. To secure its reproduction together with its basis in existing property relations, the hegemonic racial formation elides the conflictive relations of domination and subordination. It substitutes parallelism, synchrony or cohesion of interests. It negotiates the acceptance of a compromise, a homogeneous national l festyle (innocent of gender or class or racial antagonisms) into which other generalized cultures—Asian, Indian, Latino, African American—can be gradually assimilated. This liberal approach fails to recognize that the reality of U.S. institutional practices of racism is grounded on the unequal possession of wealth. Such inequality extends to the exercise of politicoeconomic control over resources and authority over institutions. Predicated on the uneven but combined development of political, economic, and ideological spheres of society, such inequality engenders forms of resistance to the power of the dominant social bloc and its ideology of plural identities.[5]

In this arena of struggle, what can be a realistic but also prophetic agenda for the subalterns, the borderline dissidents, the migrant insurgent intellects?[6] I acknowledge the concern that it may be exorbitant, even presumptuous, to draw any kind of guideline for "unacknowledged legislators." Whatever the risks, a heuristic call for organized initiatives may be broached to spark reflection and debate. And so,

taking inventory of the problems, misrecognitions, even "false consciousness" and alibis plaguing our ranks, I hazard the following "un-
timely" proposal:

What Asian American writers need to do as a fulfillment of their social responsibility is to pursue the "labor of the negative," that is, to
problematize the eccentric "and/or" of their immigrant, decolonizing
heritage and of their conjunctural embeddedness in the world system.
Such problematization would insist that their signifying practice
dovetail with the emergent strategies of resistance devised by all peoples of color to the U.S. racial state and its hegemonic instrumentali-
ties. Such linkage demands a radical critique of the politics of both di-
chotomous (private versus public) and unitary identity. It requires a
rigorous self-critique of one's vocation catalyzed by a staging of its internal contradictions, contradictions that surface when writer and
text are contextualized in specific times and places. In art, this may
assume the shape of what Bertolt Brecht calls allegorical distancing,
modalities of alienation crafted to trick and destroy the enemy: defamiliarizing the customary modes of expression, baring the devices of
ordinary commonsense behavior, exposing the artificiality of the con-
trivance behind the mystery, unveiling the stigmata behind the transcendental flag of the empire. It requires foregrounding the adversar-
ial, the contestatory, the interrogative. Demystify the normal order,
the shopper's everyday routine—"*C'est la vie!*" Defetishize the imperial self. In pursuing this duplicitous labor of the negative, we can perhaps forge in the process an Asian American vernacular that will in-
scribe our bifurcated or triangulated selves on emerging postnational
cosmopolitan texts—shades of Goethe's *Weltliteratur!*—with restora-
tive, galvanizing effect. In the womb of these vernaculars, we hope a
dialectics of the utopian power of the imagination and emancipatory
social praxis can materialize in, through, and beyond the boundaries of
race, class, and gender.[7]

But Where Did We Come From?
And Where Are We Going?

Although Filipinos are now the largest component of the "Asian
American" population in the United States—close to 3 million—in
the next few years, certainly before this century of wars and revolutions closes its account books, we—and I insert myself into this collective subject of enunciation—are still practically an erased, invisible, or silenced minority. We have been here a long time, but the early
tracks of our itinerary have vanished, have been expunged, rubbed out.

Our ethnic genealogy may be traced all the way back to the eighteenth century, when Filipino sailors, fugitives from the galleon trade between Mexico and the Philippines, found their way to what is now California and Texas. One can resurrect from the archives a mention of how Filipinos were dispatched by the French pirate Jean Laffite to join the forces of Andrew Jackson in the Battle of New Orleans in 1812. But it was our colonization by the U. S. military, a primal loss suffered through the Filipino-American War (1899–1902) and the protracted resistance ordeal of the revolutionary forces of the First Philippine Republic up to 1911, that opened the way for the large-scale transport of cheap Filipino labor to Hawaii and California, inaugurating this long weary, tortuous exodus from the periphery to the metropolis with no end in sight. We are here, but somehow it is still a secret.

Our invisibility has been less a function of numbers than an effect or symptom of that persisting colonial oppression by the United States to which no other Asian immigrant group, with their thousands of years of Buddhist/Confucian culture, has been subjected. We do not have to review Hegel's phenomenology of bondsman and master to understand why Filipinos are quick to identify themselves as "Americans" even before formal citizenship is bestowed. It seems that the loss of autonomy is compensated for by identification with U.S. ego ideals, from Lincoln to Elvis Presley. Filipinos find themselves "at home" in a world they have lived in before—not just in Hollywood fantasies but in the material culture of everyday life, from the American English of commercial music to consumer goods, from U.S. weaponry in military bases to sumptuary rituals at MacDonald's to Avon cosmetics to condoms to celluloid dreams of the good life. (Jessica Hagedorn's 1990 novel *Dogeaters* provides a neat catalogue of these symbols and artifacts syncopated with survivals from the palimpsest tablets of an archaic past.) When they encounter rejection or discrimination in the United States, they are at first puzzled, wounded, feel culpable for not having read the signs correctly, mutely outraged. The psychological reflex is familiar: They vow to prove themselves twice as good as their "tutors."

The Filipino has been produced by Others (Spaniards, Japanese, the *Amerikanos*), not mainly by his or her own will to be recognized: his or her utterances and deeds. Four hundred years of servitude to Spanish feudal suzerainty preceded our famous U.S. "tutelage," a racial experience that made us a fortuitous tabula rasa for the doctrine of market liberalism and meritocracy that at the turn of the century wrote its signature in our psyches in the form of U.S. "manifest destiny," the White Men's Burden of civilizing the barbarian natives into free, English-speaking, forever adolescent consumers. The traumatic fixations began in those forty years of "compadre colonialism" and patronage. When formal independence was granted in 1946, after the harrowing years of Japanese imperial occupation, U.S. "tutelage"—to use this academic euphemism—assumed the form of a perpetual high- and low-intensity warfare of "free world" democracy led by the United States over our souls and bodies threatened by the evil forces of communism. Recently, the U.S. government's gospel of salvation redeemed us from the evils of Ferdinand and Imelda Marcos. You can read this version of contemporary events in Stanley Karnow's (1989) *In Our Image*, now a Pulitzer prize winner, and his three-part TV documentary (San Juan 1989a; Tarr 1989). And you can read an oblique commentary of Karnow's narrative (which Peter Tarr calls the "Immaculate Conception" view of U.S. imperial history) in Hagedorn's *Dogeaters*, the first novel I have read that seeks to render in a unique postmodernist idiom a century of U.S.-Philippine encounters: The novel can be conceived as a swift montage of phantasmagoric images, flotsam of banalities, jetsam of clichés, fragments of quotes and confessions, shifting kaleidoscopic voices, trivia, libidinal tremors and orgasms, hallucinations flashed on film/TV screens—virtually a cinematext of a Third World scenario that might be the Philippines or any other contemporary neocolonial milieu processed in the transnational laboratories of Los Angeles or New York.

Long before Filipinos—as immigrants, tourists, or visitors—set foot on the U.S. continent, they—in body and sensibility—have been prepared by the thoroughly Americanized culture of the homeland. This is true in particular for the second and third waves of immigrants, from 1946 to the present. Here, I disagree with those who claim that the majority of Filipino immigrants after 1965 carried with them traces of the growing nationalist sentiment in the Philippines before and after the declaration of martial law in 1972 (Occeña 1985). The records show that it was the first wave of immigrants in the twenties and thirties who demonstrated an intransigent recalcitrance, a spirit of militant resistance born, it seems, from "the political unconscious" of the popular mass struggles against Spanish and U.S. aggressors in the last decade of the nineteenth century and the first decade of the twentieth. Popular memory counterpointed the path of migration. Thus, Filipino workers in Hawaii (about 20,000 strong) initiated the first major interethnic strike against the sugar planters on June 19, 1920, which lasted seven months. Again, in April 1924, about 31,000 Filipino workers staged an eight-month strike that closed down half of the plantations in Hawaii; this bloody confrontation—police killed sixteen workers, wounded four, imprisoned sixty and blacklisted hundreds—earned Filipinos the reputation of being dangerous and rebellious workers. With the birth of the United Farm Workers Union from the historic Delano grape strike of Filipino workers in September 1965, an era ended; this heroic archetype of the Filipino worker (McWilliams 1964; Kushner 1971) is now a nostalgic topic for aging veterans of that class war and their kin in retirement villages, an epoch memorialized in Carlos Bulosan's epic chronicle *America Is in the Heart* ([1946] 1973). This epic theme of immigration is now anachronistic, displaced by the genre of forced exile, CIA intrigues, and sensationalized court trials (Marcos, Duvalier, Noriega), as well as the "warm body export" of over a million Filipinos scattered all over the planet.

The 1898 conjuncture in Philippine history, the explosion of revolutionary nationalist passion among workers, peasants, middle strata, and intellectuals, has never been replicated so far, not even by the rise of the First Quarter Storm in 1971 or the February urban insurrection of 1986. So, despite the U.S. tutelage of the first three decades, which converted Carlos P. Romulo and his ilk (most of whom sang alleluia in the pages of the *Philippine News* when Bush sent airplanes to rescue the beleaguered Aquino) into Taft's "little brown brothers," at least two generations of Filipinos (some of whom immigrated to the United States like Bulosan and Buaken) experienced the vicissitudes of life as subalterns in revolt against white Western domination. When they came to the United States, however, they had to undergo another education, an apprenticeship in disillusionment. Manuel Buaken writes:

> Where is the heart of America? I am one of the many thousands of young men born under the American Flag, raised as loyal, idealistic Americans under your promises of equality for all, and enticed by glowing tales of educational opportunities. Once here we are met by exploiters, shunted into slums, greeted by gamblers, and prostitutes, taught only the worst in your civilization. America came to us with bright-winged promises of liberty, equality, and fraternity—what has become of them? (1940, 410)

Bulosan for his part witnessed the many faces of racist violence at the heart of liberal free enterprise society, registering in his sentimental and melodramatic style the fabled shock of recognition: "I came to know afterward that in many ways it was a crime to be a Filipino in California. I came to know that public streets were not free to my people. We were stopped each time those vigilant patrolmen saw us driving with a car. We were suspect each time we were with a white woman. . . . It was now the year of the great hatred; the lives of Filipinos were cheaper than those of dogs" (1983b, 145; 1995b, 173).

America Is in the Heart, as everyone knows, ends with a utopian hope. Such a vision is possible only because Bulosan's testimony of growing up, an ethnic *Bildungsroman*, is sedimented with the popular memory of folk resistance and numerous peasant uprisings in Pangasinan where he was born; his roots in the dissident folk tradition and communal life preserved a certain cunning in his years of exile that enabled him, by an autodidact's luck, to forge the "conscience of his race" at a time when Filipino guerillas were fighting the Japanese occupation forces, the very same guerillas (descendants of *Katipuneros* and *Colorum* insurgents)[8] who later joined the Huk uprising and were ruthlessly suppressed by the CIA-supported Magsaysay regime in the heyday of McCarthyism. Today, Bulosan, after being discovered in the early seventies, has fallen back into oblivion.

Why do I linger on this historical specificity of persisting U.S. domination of the Philippines? Because without fully understanding the process of subjectification of the Filipino psyche (the division of the subaltern into the "I," grammatical subject of the statement that defines the fictional ego positioned by class, gender, race, and so on, and the "I" as the speaking subject, matrix or locus of the free play of signifiers), it is impossible to understand the forms of contradictory or antinomic behavior the Filipino is capable of manifesting as ethnic/racial subject in the terrain of U.S. late capitalism. This analysis of the effect of ideology in defining the position (what others would call "identity") of Filipinos as class, gendered, ethnic agents in the U.S. racial formation who are capable of being mobilized or pacified, depending on varying conjunctures, has not yet been systematically carried out. Research on structural constraints to social mobility preoccupy graduate students. But, so far, studies on the historical development of the Filipino community in the United States have been sketchy, superficial, and flawed in their methodology and philosophical assumptions. What prevails up to now is a reliance on the expertise of white male sociologists whose strategy of "blaming the victim" is still repeated in numerous textbooks, the commonsense wisdom echoed by opportunistic Filipino leaders themselves when they exhort the community to engage in united political activity for the Democratic or Republican party.

I should like to cite here one example, the explanation offered by the well-known scholar H. Brett Melendy for Filipino marginality. Melendy's entry on Filipinos in the authoritative *Harvard Encyclopedia of American Ethnic Groups* (1980) begins with a description of indigenous Filipino society. He recites the surface details of history and economics, focusing on the family and kinship structure: "The [*compadrazgo*] system required an individual's strong sense of identity with and acceptance by the group, and served to promote beliefs that kin relationships tolerate no disagreement; that an individual should maintain his proper station in society, neither reaching above nor falling below it; and that a person's acts should contribute to his self-esteem but not cause embarrassment to others" (356). Melendy also reports on the prevalence of gambling as part of barrio celebrations to show that this predilection prevented Filipino immigrants from saving money despite their diligence.

It was the power of these "cultural backgrounds and values systems" that, from the structural-functionalist point of view, compelled Filipinos to marry Hawaiian, Portuguese, and Puerto Rican women, not the social taboo or legal prohibition against miscegenation. Although Melendy alludes to the peculiar status of Filipinos as "nationals," neither citizens nor aliens, a twilight zone of indeterminacy that excluded them from naturalization but also prevented their deportation, he does not give this the emphasis it deserves. What is worse is that for Melendy the Filipinos came to the United States burdened with values and attitudes that not only encouraged prejudice or caused their not being accepted by the dominant white majority but also explain their political nullity as citizens today:

> The Filipinos, confronted with prejudice both in Hawaii and on the West Coast, divided their world even more sharply than formerly into compadres and enemies. The alliance system that evolved in most California towns was based upon Filipino traditions of reciprocity, obligation, loyalty, and unity; those outside the group were suspect. As in Hawaii, compang groups developed in camps and cities. In the evenings and on weekends these provincial clans partied together and fought others in the local pool hall, bar, gambling house, or dance hall; most of the drunken battles were over women. In contrast to the plantation Filipinos, the West Coast single men moved around constantly seeking work; there was little semblance of permanent community. . . .
> Filipino loyalty to family and regional group has militated against their achieving success in American politics. They see no clear reason to form a Filipino political organization, and their tendency to group exclusiveness makes it difficult for any one Filipino to gain widespread support from the others. . . . Provincial allegiances and personality clashes lead Filipino organizations to multiply rather than coalesce. (360–62)

Like snapshots or painted tableaux, this authorizing and authoritarian text has frozen thousands of Filipinos in some kind of hermetically sealed ethnographic museum or time warp in the mythology of secular predestination. Unfortunately, it is still quoted as textbook wisdom, sophisticated common sense.

Given the advance of Third World demystifying scholarship signaled by Frantz Fanon's writings and Edward Said's *Orientalism* (1978), among others, we can now see that the problem of Melendy

and other experts on ethnicity stems from the failure of bourgeois social science in general to grasp the historical specificity of global capitalism in its imperialist phase. This is the source of its failure to comprehend the differential incorporation of racial groups into the social
formation of developing U.S. capitalism from the nineteenth—for example, Chinese labor in railroad construction, genocidal campaigns
against the American Indians, annexation of Puerto Rico and the
Philippines—to the twentieth century. In the seventies, the project of
constructing a theory of "internal colonialism" with specific reference
to the Chicanos, blacks, and American Indians called attention to this
historical specificity, only to be overwhelmed by the cult of paneth-
nicity and the mock-pluralist individualism of the Reagan dispensation (Steinberg 1996). What actually underlies this inability of liberal
intellectuals to overcome racist ideology inheres in the paradigm of
Cartesian knowledge and its allochronic discourse whereby the West
exercised its power of transforming the Other (colonized subjects) into
scientific knowledge. In *Time and the Other*, Johannes Fabian demonstrates how Western anthropology in particular, with succeeding theories of evolutionism, relativism, and structuralism, refused coevalness—"the problematic simultaneity of different, conflicting and
contradictory forms of consciousness"—to non-Western peoples
(1983, 146). Consequently, Western knowledge about other peoples
concealed the historic agenda of imperialist conquest through
schemes claiming to promote civilized progress, development, or enlightenment upholding the banner of "freedom," "diversity," "integrity," and so on; relativism, on the other hand, fetishized taxonomy
(classification as a mode of essentialism) and homogenized all differences, thereby ignoring time and history altogether.

Here, then, is the problem of reinventing Filipinos in the United
States, articulating their silence and invisibility, for creative artists:
The master narrative of the migrant workers' odyssey used by Bulosan
and the quasi-existentialist interior monologues of Bienvenido Santos's expatriates marooned in the megalopolis can no longer serve as
generic models. The plenitude of classic realist narrative, a mimesis of
the bourgeois success story, is bound to distort the heterogeneous initiatives of the past three decades.

In a useful introduction to Filipino American literature, Sam Solberg argues that the immigration epic can be renewed by younger
writers whereas for the older generation, "The Filipino dream of independence fades into the American dream of equality" ([1975] 1991,
lxii). Suspended in a metonymy of dreams, otherwise known as the
Lacanian realm of the Imaginary, the Filipino cannot possess any identity worth writing about. No loss is experienced; the castration crisis

of colonial disruption has been forgotten—nay, it has been repressed. He or she becomes simply a mimicry of the white American, a mock image born of misrecognition. At this point, a struggle for control of the signifying practice linked to the "I" of the speaking subject, site of the polysemy of representations, becomes imperative.

There is, I think, no alternative: A beginning must be made from the realities of immigrants in the eighties, and from the experience of Filipino Americans born in the United States in the sixties and seventies.[9] And this cannot be done without evoking the primal scene coeval with the present: the neocolonial situation of the Philippines and its antecedent stages, the conflicted terrain of ideological struggle that abolishes the distinction/distance between Filipinos in the Philippines and Filipinos in the United States. Continuities no less than ruptures have to be articulated for an oppositional practice to emerge. The terrain is less geographical than cultural—culture defined as the complex network of social practices signifying our dominant or subordinate position in a given social formation. Nor would the triumphalist rhetoric of *Line of March* claiming the Filipino community as part of the proletarian vanguard provide a viable starting point. I believe that we are still in the stage of recuperating and sublating the gains of the sixties in a time when the U.S. Establishment is celebrating the defeat of "actually existing socialism," the failure of Marxism, and the victory of the giant supermall and the religion of endless consumerism—shop until you drop! To allude to the revolutionary situation in the Philippines and the presence of left guerillas contesting the U.S.-backed regime would sound, for a middle-class audience in the United States, as anachronistic and weird as talking of the Watsonville Riots of January 1930 or the staged blowing-up of the *Maine* in Havana harbor in 1898. This, I think, is the achievement of Hagedorn's novel: The unfolding of the historical crisis of U.S. hegemony in the Philippine context (marked by the Aquino assassination, the hovering presence of the New People's Army, the scandalous decadence and corruption of the elite polluting the whole body politic, and the persistence of the same in the succeeding administrations of Corazon Aquino and Fidel Ramos) conveyed through a postmodernist, inescapably complicitous myth.

Of all the Asian American groups, the Filipino community is perhaps the only one obsessed with the impossible desire of returning to the homeland, whether in reality or fantasy. It is impossible because, given the break in our history (our initiation into the Imaginary or mirror stage of colonial existence), the authentic homeland does not exist except as a simulacrum of Hollywood or a nascent dream of *jouissance* still to be won by a national-democratic struggle. Its presence (invoked in Hagedorn's novel as the pre-Oedipal matriarch invested in various characters) is deferred, postponed, the climax of a trajectory of collective and personal transformative projects. One such project can be fulfilled through a reinterpretation of the past: What Ronald Takaki in his chronicle describes as the addiction to gambling, dancing, and pursuit of white women could be read as the eloquent realization of what George Bataille (1985) calls the principle of expenditure, the fulfillment of the need to lose and destroy, a drama that sublimates the agon of class struggle and subverts the rule of capitalist utility and its calculus of reification. Sacrifice of energy, money, time engenders the sacred. In such acts of gift exchange or symbolic reciprocity, the Filipino community reinvents itself in a conjuncture (*kairos*) in which structure and event coincide, charting boundaries and affirming its solidarity vis-à-vis the alienating world of commodity fetishism. Conviviality and carnival (in Bakhtin's sense) replace solitary nostalgia, dissolving guilt into shame. But this is of course not the route pursued by post–World War II Filipino American writers.

I quote a characteristic statement from three Filipino American writers who address the hybrid or schizoid sensibility of Filipinos presumably straddling Eastern and Western cultures:

> Being born or reared in America is like being put into a kettle with other ethnic groups, simmered by years of racism, identity crises, and subsequent ethnic rejection, and then coming out with a blend of many influences from that environment. Thus, we have Filipinos who are more versed in other ethnic cultures and who talk, act, and actually believe themselves to be white. . . . Although geographically and racially he is Oriental, the Filipino is so influenced by Western ways that many adopt and imitate anything American. The Filipino-American, aware of the contradictions in American society, is thus confused and dismayed when he visits the Philippines and finds brown faces with white minds. . . . The Filipino American writer is seeing and writing about the myth of the American dream, while the Filipino is drawn by the dream that is perpetuated by the heavy American influences in his country. (Chin et al 1975, 49, 54)

This was written in the early seventies. It reflects the vocabulary and temper of those days, especially the impulse to assert one's identity to surmount the putative identity crisis (Erik Erikson 1980) and the proverbial "melting pot." Self-assertion is conducted by drawing demarcation lines between the Filipino American (who can penetrate through the masks of myth) and the mystified Filipino. This taxonomy not only ignores precisely the problem of colonial subordination and racial victimage, but it also represses the truth that the revolutionary process in the Philippines has far outstripped the counterculture rhetoric of California and Greenwich Village. A spurious identity,

"Filipino American," is exhibited here as mere form, without real substance. The lesson of poststructuralism is that all these binary oppositions are inscribed in a field of textuality, of difference, where meaning is relational and processual. In other words, the Filipino American cannot be defined without elucidating what the problematic relation is between the two terms that dictates the conditions of possibility for each—the hyphen that spells a relation of domination and subordination. Let us not so peremptorily elide the differences subsisting at the core of a temporary synthesis. Lacking this totalizing and historical view, the critique of racism and imperialism implied by our writers rests on an unquestioned metaphysics of the subject, seemingly autonomous, universal, and free, which is precisely the philosophical and ideological foundation of imperial hegemony that undermines their collective project, their will to self-determination.

Now it is easy to resolve one's problematic situation of being situated on the borders, or on no man's land, deterritorialized by powers whose operations seem mysterious, by making a virtue of necessity, so to speak. It is easy to perform the unilateral trick of reversing the negative and valorizing that as positive: for example, "Black is beautiful," and so on. Or else, we can take pride in the fact that we are beneficiaries of both cultures, East and West, and that our multicultural awareness, our cosmopolitanism, enables us to partake of the feast of humanity's accomplishments—from Egyptian funerary art and Plato's Ideas to the latest IBM computer. This is in fact the fashionable axiom of postmodernist theorizing. The postmodernist technique of pastiche, aleatory juxtaposition, virtuoso bricolage carried to its logical culmination, is what presides in the first part of *Dogeaters*—a flattening of heterogeneous elements approximating Las Vegas simultaneity—until the introduction of Joey Sands, symbol of what is actually meant by "special Filipino American relations," forces the text to generate a semblance of a plot (cause-effect sequence, plausible motivation, and so on) whereby the scenario of sacrifice—Joey's slaughter of Taruk, iconic sign for the surrogate father who also functions as castrator/betrayer and for all the other patriarchs upholding the code of filial piety—is able to take place and the discourse to end in a prayer to the Virgin "mother of revenge." But that vestige of the traditional art of storytelling, in which irreconcilable victims of a neocolonial regime end up in a revolutionary guerilla camp plotting retribution, finds itself embedded and even neutralized by a rich multilayered discourse (exotic to a Western audience) empowered by what Henri Lefebvre (1971, 1976) calls the capitalist principle of repetition. This culture of repetition (pleonasm; tautology; recycled simulations; in effect, Baudrillard's [1984a, 1984b] world of pure mediations) of which the telltale index is the Hollywood star system (and its counterpart in the commercial mass culture of the Philippines: the regurgitated routine of clichés, stereotypes, debased sexual rituals) conditions most postmodernist art, reducing even parody, satire, and irony to aspects of a relativistic and redundant cosmos against which the "Kundiman" or prayer of exorcism concluding *Dogeaters* can only be a stylized gesture of protest.

For Asian American artists in general, not just for Filipino writers, the seduction of postmodernism as an answer to racism and ethnic marginality can be intoxicating and well-nigh irresistible. But we need to address these questions (see Mascia-Less et al. 1989; Fraser and Nicholson 1990): Does the antifoundational favoring of difference and identity politics abolish prevailing norms and hierarchies? Do polyvocality and positionality erase power differentials? Can the fragmentary, dialogic approach of EuroAmerican intellectuals (specific and local, as Foucault [1980] cautions us) claim to be more faithfully "representative" of people of color than the latter's *metarecits* of justice and liberation? Can pragmatism and new historicism empower the victimized subalterns at the mercy of the corporate elite of northern industrialized nation-states? Can Lyotard's paradigm of the "justice of multiplicities" and heterogeneity eliminate private appropriation of surplus value and the authority of capital? In the ultimate reckoning, is not this postmodern strategy of "otherness" a none-too-subtle mode of recuperating the totalizing mastery of liberal, pluralist discourse? For whom is modernist and postmodernist theory constructed? Not only Asian Americans but all artists of color have substantial stakes in how these questions are answered.

Since all art in a commodity-centered society is ultimately reduced to exchangeable value—and literature is no exception—we can see that the style of postmodernism and its philosophical justification in cultural pluralism (floating monads in Bloomingdale?) easily becomes instrumentalized to serve the very ends that it originally sought to counter. A certain form of postmodernist art functions to replicate the commodity as eternal recurrence of the same, the paradigm of repetition. The dialectic of art as a substitute for radically transforming praxis, of aesthetic fantasy as substitute for the body's protean transaction with the real world, may also be perceived in the exploitation of illusion embodied in commodities, a phenomenon analyzed by W. F. Haug in his *Critique of Commodity Aesthetics:*

> An innumerable series of images are forced upon the individual, like mirrors, seemingly empathetic and totally credible, which bring their secrets to the surface and display them there. In these images, people are contin-

ually shown the unfulfilled aspects of their existence. The illusion ingratiates itself, promising satisfaction: it reads desires in one's eyes, and brings them to the surface of the commodity. While the illusion with which commodities present themselves to the gaze, gives the people a sense of meaningfulness, it provides them with a language to interpret their existence and the world. Any other world, different from that provided by the commodities, is almost no longer accessible to them. How can people behave, or change themselves, when continually presented with a collection of dream-images that have been taken from them? How can people change when they continue to get what they want, but only in the form of illusion? (1986, 52)

To paraphrase those urgent questions: How can postmodernist writing, offspring of commodity aesthetics, break off from its narcissistic captivity? One effective way I would suggest is by a return to modernist reflexiveness and self-critique, in particular to the defamiliarizing practice of Bertolt Brecht or Roland Barthes. Expose the mechanisms producing illusions, reveal the anatomy of the production process, bare the devices of erotic sublimation. These guidelines may catalyze the imagination of the nomadic artist crisscrossing the borders toward a fundamental interrogation of itself and its social presuppositions. With the writer's complicity, they may help empower the reader/audience, even the ethnic community, to thwart the homogenizing and integrative force of hegemonic standards and norms and perhaps facilitate movements demanding the democratic control of the apparatus of intellectual/cultural production once envisaged by Walter Benjamin.[10] Creative writers are, to be sure, astute fabricators and purveyors of illusions, beleaguered or compromised as they compete with corporate mass media (in particular, movies and television). If Asian American writers are not to be merely unwitting agents for the reproduction of capital and its racializing virulence, is it exorbitant to expect them to study and understand the dynamics of U.S. cultural hegemony and in the process commit themselves to a minimum program of demystification? Everyone knows each writer must decide for whom his or her art is destined, whose complicity he or she seeks to instigate.

In conclusion, I want to emphasize the necessity for ethnic artists, Asian American writers in this case, to grasp that a liberal democratic society constituted by manifold antagonistic interests can function only when hegemony (consent of subjects to be ruled) obtains—that is, when a particular set of values, attitudes, or beliefs, together with its accompanying complex network of practices I alluded to earlier, is accepted as consensus; when people voluntarily act and think in accordance with a certain worldview or structure of feeling associated with a class or historic bloc of groups who dominate what Louis Althusser

(1971) calls "Ideological State Apparatuses." Hegemony in the symbolic order (in the public sphere, civic society) guarantees not only production for profit but also reproduction of the total structure of society, reproduction of itself—endless repetition, with just enough phenomenal diversity or variety to hide the boredom and produce the impression of orderly, peaceful change toward more improvement, more progress, and more illusory individual gratification.

In line with this concept of hegemony (borrowed from Gramsci and modified by Raymond Williams), the plurality of cultures or lifestyles in any given social formation is a mirage that, although palpable and temporarily satisfying, maintains the political hegemony of a particular group whose view of the world prevails precisely by virtue of this illusion (which Haug discussed previously). Culture is nothing else but the complex network of social practices that signify or determine positions of domination, equality, or subordination. U.S. normative pluralism denies this definition of culture by concealing the contradictions and conflicts of interests in society. Through postmodernist articulations of formal differences without substantive changes in the structure of power, it seeks to impose a unity of all groups (sexual, racial, economic); achieving a temporary harmony of all by marginalizing the dissidents and neutralizing the unfit or deviant, it maintains the hegemony of a particular constellation of groups or interests who benefit from the status quo. But because uneven and nonsynchronic development informs all levels of society (economic, ideological, political), a totalizing and permanent hegemony by definition is impossible. Gaps, fissures, cleavages may be discovered in numerous (but not infinite) spaces where negotiation of positions can be the agenda for struggle. Conjunctural opportunities can be seized by the popular forces even within the confines of rigid structural constraints. Within this framework, even postmodernist strategies of expression and representation can be inflected for alternative or oppositional ends; hence the ambiguous, equivocal effect of such works as *Dogeaters*.

Ideally, the critique of hegemony should precede any exploration of one's racial or ethnic identity—subject position, to be precise—because one's place can be discovered only in the field of multiple relationships. But I would argue that we should first disabuse ourselves of the notion that there is equality of cultures and genuine toleration of differences in a stratified society by bearing in mind this very cogent perspective that Hazel Carby proposes for our careful judgment:

> By insisting that "culture" denotes antagonistic relations of domination and subordination, this perspective undermines the pluralistic notion of compatibility inherent in multiculturalism, the idea of a homogeneous

national culture (innocent of class or gender differences) into which other equally generalized Caribbean or Asian cultures can be integrated. The paradigm of multiculturalism actually excludes the concept of dominant and subordinate cultures—either indigenous or migrant—and fails to recognize that the existence of racism relates to the possession and exercise of politico-economic control and authority and also to forms of resistance to the power of dominant social groups. (1980, 64–65)

The special predicament of Filipino writers in the United States whose historical roots I have tried to outline here may now be diagnosed as a symptom of the weakening of U.S. hegemony in the face of revolutionary challenges to its continued violent institutionalization in the Philippines. But because of the appeal of acquisitive/possessive liberalism and market-oriented individualist freedom in the context of access to certain goods and satisfactions in the metropolitan center, especially because of the power of commodity aesthetics that pervades all space in capitalist society, Filipino writers in the United States still cannot escape the pleasure-filled trap of hyphenation. Perhaps they consider themselves a special case whose destiny seems incommensurate with that of African Americans, Chicanos, American Indians, and so forth; or with that of their brothers and sisters in the neocolony. Perhaps their signifying practice, the whole repertoire of their métier, refuses to register the immense loss, the huge expenditure incurred in the thrall of colonial domination. Such a refusal perpetuates the compulsion to repeat. Their liberation from the postmodernist mirage cannot be attained without a historical retrospective settling of accounts with the ghosts of the past—all those workers of Bulosan's generation sacrificed to the potlatch of free enterprise democracy—and the present victims of U.S. low-intensity, counterinsurgency warfare in the Philippines and elsewhere. Of course, for Filipino writers in the United States, the struggle is within and outside the institutions of the racializing state whose imperial foreign policy is the chief source of oppression, misery, and death for millions of Filipinos in the homeland. Spatial distance yields to temporal coevalness: the recognition of the authentic Other as one's possibility. Writing in English, an alienating medium for the majority of 70 million Filipinos, Filipino writers based in the United States (whether sojourners, expatriates, or permanent residents/citizens) can communicate only to a limited audience in the neocolony. But here they can announce the news that the "dogeaters" will soon take their ultimate revenge when a sacrifice of the patriarchal totem of a dog-eat-dog world is enacted in the presence of all those who dared risk their lives, who dared to live and suffer through the expenditure and the loss to fashion a less destructive, more liberating ecosystem.

3

Arming the Spirit, Writing in Times of Emergency

The tradition of the oppressed teaches us that the "state of emergency" in which we live is not the exception but the rule. We must attain to a conception of history that is in keeping with this insight. Then we shall clearly realize that it is our task to bring about a real state of emergency.

Walter Benjamin

The starting point is of course our reality.

Renato Constantino

Ever since the United States annexed the Philippine Islands in 1898, the discourse of capital has always been reductive, monological, and utilitarian. Although luminaries such as Mark Twain, William James, and William Dean Howells denounced the slaughter of the natives during the Filipino-American War of 1899–1902, the Filipino presence was not registered in the public sphere until Filipinos' singular commodity, labor power, appeared in large numbers on Hawaii and on the West Coast between 1907 and 1935. Until 1946, when formal independence was granted, Filipinos in the metropolis (numbering around 150,000) occupied the limbo of alterity and transitionality: neither slaves, wards, nor citizens. Carey McWilliams believed that these "Others" belonged to "the freemasonry of the ostracized" (1964, 241). How should we address them, and in what language? Can they speak for themselves? If not, who will represent them?

Called "little brown brothers," barbaric "yellow bellies," "scarcely more than savages," and other derogatory epithets, Filipinos as subjects-in-revolt have refused to conform to the totalizing logic of white supremacy and the knowledge of "the Filipino" constructed by the Orientalizing methods of U.S. scholarship. Intractable and recalcitrant, Filipinos in the process of being subjugated have confounded U.S. disciplinary regimes of knowledge production and surveillance. They have challenged the asymmetrical cartography of metropolis and colony, core and periphery, in the official world system. Interpellated within the boundaries of empire, Filipinos continue to bear the stigmata of three centuries of anticolonial insurgency. Given this indigenous genealogy of resistance, which I have traced elsewhere (San Juan, 1992b), the Filipino writer has functioned not simply as *porte-parole* authorized by the imperium's center but more precisely as an organic intellectual (in Gramsci's sense) for a people whose repressed history and its "political unconscious" remain crucial to the task of judging the worth of the U.S. experiment in colonial "tutelage" and to the final settling of accounts with millions of its victims.

Up to now, however, despite the Philippines' formal independence, the texts of the Filipino interrogation of U.S. hegemony remain virtually unread and therefore unappreciated for their "fertilizing" critical force. Not demography, but a symptomatic reconnaissance of contested territory seems imperative. An inventory of the archive (by a partisan native, for a change) is needed as an initial step toward answering such questions as I raised earlier. Foremost among these is why the Filipino intervention in the U.S. literary scene has been long ignored, silenced, or marginalized. Although the Filipino component of the Asian–Pacific Islander ethnic category of the U. S. Census Bureau has now become the largest (O'Hare and Felt 1991, 2), and in the next decade will surpass the combined total of the Chinese and Japanese population, the import of this statistical figure so far has not been calculated in the existing Baedekers of U.S. high culture.

Literary surveys drawn up in this era of canon revision ignore the Filipino contribution. In the 1982 Modern Language Association (MLA) survey, *Three American Literatures*, edited by Houston Baker Jr., the Asian American section deals only with Chinese and Japanese authors. This omission is repeated in the 1990 MLA guide, *Redefining American Literary History;* no reference is made to Filipino writing except in a meager bibliographic list at the end under the rubric "Philippine American Literature" (Ruoff and Ward 1990, 361–62). In this quite erroneous citation of ten authors' "Primary Works," three authors would not claim at all to be Filipino American: Stevan Javellana, Celso Carunungan, and Egmidio Alvarez.[1] Nor would Jose Garcia Villa, the now "disappeared" inventor of modern Filipino expression in English, who is a permanent U.S. resident but not a citizen (Villa died in February 1997 after this chapter had been written), make this claim. The classification "Philippine American" may appear as a harmless conjunction of equal and separate terms, but in fact it conceals subsumption of the former into the latter. In everyday life, the combinatory relay of American pragmatic tolerance easily converts the "Philippine" half into a routinized ethnic phenomenon, normalized and taken for granted. How then do we account for the absence, exclusion, and potential recuperability of Filipino writing in this society—at least that portion conceded recognition by institutional fiat?

Historicizing Texts

In general, the production, circulation, and reception of texts are necessarily though not sufficiently determined by the dynamics of class and race. Everyone agrees that in this system numbers do not really count unless the community exercises a measure of economic and political power. Filipinos in the United States remain an exploited and disadvantaged group, not at all a "model" minority. A 1980 study of income distribution among Filipinos found that young men (80 to 86 percent of whom are employed in the secondary sector in California) received only about two-thirds of the income of white males whereas the older men get only half; women, on the other hand, receive one-half the income of white men. Such income disparities persist despite comparable investments in human capital (education, work experience, and so forth) that generate low returns, an incongruity "suggestive of race discrimination" (Cabezas and Kawaguchi 1989, 99). Filipinos rank third among Asian Americans in median household income, behind Japanese and Asian Indians. Another survey (Nee and Sanders 1985, 75–93) concludes that although Filipinos have a higher educational attainment than whites or recent Chinese immigrants, their average income is lower than Japanese Americans and Chinese Americans because they are confined to low-skilled, low-paying jobs.

Except in the past few years, Filipinos in the United States have not participated significantly in electoral politics (notwithstanding recent breakthroughs in California and Hawaii), a fact attributed by mainstream sociologists to the inertia of "provincial allegiances and personality clashes" (Melendy 1980, 362). Collective praxis, however, is not an a priori given but a sociohistorical construct. This implies that we have to reckon with the tenacious legacy of four centuries of Spanish and U.S. colonial domination to understand the Filipino habitus. What passes for indigenous music or architecture turns out to be a mimesis of Western styles, whereas the refined skills of reading and writing needed for the production and distribution of the knowledge monopolized by the elite (compradors, landlords, bureaucrat capitalists) serve business interests. In brief, cultural literacy is geared to soliciting the recognition of U.S. arbiters of taste and brokers of symbolic capital. We may have talented writers but certainly have had no sizable and responsive audience of readers and commentators up to now. And so this predicament of the community's powerlessness, together with its largely imitative and instrumentalized modality of cultural production/reception, may shed light on the invisibility of Filipino writing in the academy and in public consciousness. But its exclusion and/or marginalization cannot be grasped unless the irreducible historical specificity of the Philippines as a former colony, and at present as a virtual neocolony, of the United States, and Filipinos as subjugated and conflicted subjects are taken into full account.

This dialectical perspective explains the irrepressible centrality of Carlos Bulosan's oeuvre in the shaping of an emergent pan-Filipino literary tradition affiliating the U.S. scene of writing. What distinguishes Bulosan's role in this field of Filipino American intertextuality is his attempt to capture the inaugural experience of uprooting and bodily transport of Filipinos to Hawaii and the North American continent. In Bulosan's life history, the itinerary of the peasant/worker-becoming-intellectual unfolds in the womb of the occupying power (the United States) a narrative of collective self-discovery: The traumatic primal scene of deracination is reenacted in the acts of participating in the multiracial workers' fight against U.S. monopoly capital and valorized in interludes of critical reflection (San Juan 1972, 1984). And this solidarity, forged in the popular-democratic crucible of struggling with whites and people of color against a common oppression, stages the condition of possibility for the Filipino writer in exile. In effect, writing becomes for the Filipino diaspora the transitional agency of self-recovery. It facilitates a mediation between the negated past of colonial dependency and a fantasied, even utopian, "America" where people of color exercise their right of self-determination and socialist justice prevails. Bulosan's historicizing imagination configures the genealogy of two generations of Filipinos bridging the revolutionary past and the compromised present and maps a passage from the tributary formation of the periphery to the West Coast's "factories in the fields" and canneries in *America Is in the Heart* (1946, reprinted 1973; hereafter *America*) that cannot be found in the sentimental memoirs of his compatriots.

History for Bulosan is what is contemporary and prophetic. In "How My Stories Were Written," he evokes the childhood of Apo Lacay, the folk sage who inspired his vocation of allegorical remembering chosen during "the age of great distress and calamity in the land, when the fury of an invading race impaled their hearts in the tragic cross of slavery and ignorance" (1983b, 25). The allusion here is to the scorched-earth tactics of U.S. pacification forces during the Filipino-American

War and the ruthless suppression of a nascent Filipino national identity—a foreign policy "aberration" in most textbooks, but recently
vindicated by Stanley Karnow's apologia, *In Our Image* (1989). In stories like "Be American," in the quasi-autobiographical *America*, and
in his novel *The Power of the People* (original titled *The Cry and the
Dedication* [1995a]), Bulosan renders in symbolic forms of fabulation
how the U.S. conquest exacerbated feudal injustice in the Philippines
and accomplished on a global scale an iniquitous division of international labor that transformed the United States into a metropolis of industrial modernity and the Philippines into an underdeveloped dependency: a source of cheap raw materials and manual/mental labor with
minimal exchange value.

Since it is impossible to ignore Bulosan's works in dealing with Filipino "ethnicity"—recall how his essay "Freedom from Want" (1943),
commissioned by the *Saturday Evening Post* to illustrate President
Roosevelt's "Four Freedoms" declaration, was subsequently displayed
in the Federal Building in San Francisco—how does the Establishment
handle the threat posed by their radical attack on capitalism? In other
words, how is Bulosan sanitized and packaged to promote pluralist U.S.
nationalism? Instead of rehearsing all the possible ways, it will be sufficient here to give an example of a typical recuperative exercise from
The American Kaleidoscope (1991) by Lawrence Fuchs.[2] He writes:

> The life of Bulosan, a Filipino-American, illustrates the process by which
> the political struggle against injustice and on behalf of equal rights often
> turned immigrants and their children into Americans. ... Disillusioned,
> Bulosan considered becoming a Communist; at another time, he became
> a thief. But his principal passions were American politics and American
> literature, and these stimulated him to organize the Committee for the
> Protection of Filipino Rights, and to start a small school for migrant
> workers where "I traced the growth of democracy in the United States"
> ... recalling that his brother had told him "America is in the hearts of
> men." ... When, after months of illness and debility, he finished his au-
> tobiography, he called it *America Is in the Heart*, using words similar to
> those of President Roosevelt to Secretary of War Stimson, "Americanism
> is simply a matter of the mind and heart," and those of Justice Douglas,
> that "loyalty is a matter of the heart and mind."
> ... Bulosan, the Filipino migrant worker, much more than Dillingham,
> the scion of an old New England family, had proved to be a prescient in-
> terpreter of American nationalism. Those who had been excluded longest
> from membership in the American civic culture had rushed to embrace it
> once the barriers were lifted. (237–38)

Earlier, Fuchs paternalistically ascribes to Bulosan the fortune blacks
did not have of being befriended by a half dozen white women. Some-

how Bulosan was also endowed with the exceptional gift of having access to a secret knowledge denied to other minorities: "When he spoke of the American dream he wrote of his migrant-worker students that 'their eyes glowed with a new faith ... they nodded with deep reverence.' ... Bulosan identified with the experience of the Euro-Americans who had come to this country as immigrants" (147–48). Shades of Andrew Carnegie, Horatio Alger, the Godfather? As if that were not enough, Bulosan is lined up with "Carl Schurz, Mary Antin, and tens of thousands of other self-consciously Americanizing immigrants" (357).

Bulosan is thus appropriated by official discursive practice to hype a putative "civic culture" of "voluntary pluralism" by occluding the historical specificity of his anti-imperialist politics. Both his materialist outlook and his paramount commitment to genuine national sovereignty for the Philippines and to socialism are buried in the abstraction of a "political struggle against injustice." The strategy of containment here is one of tactical omission; calculated redeployment; selective emphasis; and, more precisely, decontextualization. Its mode of uprooting certain words and phrases from their historical habitat of political antagonisms recapitulates President McKinley's policy of "benevolent assimilation" and the duplicitous discourse of pacification from William Howard Taft to the latest scholarship on U.S.-Philippine relations. It can also be read as a textual analogue to the Hawaiian Sugar Planter's Association's (HSPA) raid of peasant male bodies from occupied territory between 1906 and 1946. By such ruses of displacement and complicity, Bulosan is recruited by his enemies, the imperial patriots, who celebrate his romantic naivete at the expense of his egalitarian principles and his repudiation of chauvinist-fascist apartheid founded on wars of conquest and the dehumanization of people of color.

The refunctionalization of Bulosan for the cause of white supremacy cannot simply be ascribed to missionaries like Fuchs. Multicultural evangelists from the Asian American camp have purveyed their share of factual errors and misleading judgments; one example is Elaine Kim's guide, *Asian American Literature* (1982). Kim might be chiefly responsible for the defusion of Bulosan's insurrectionary aesthetics by ignoring the vicious subjugation of the Filipino masses. This is because she subscribes to the immigrant paradigm of EuroAmerican success criticized long ago by Robert Blauner (1972) and others when she claims that Bulosan "shares with the Asian goodwill ambassador writers a sustaining desire to win American acceptance" (57). (Because the term "America" denotes a complex overdetermined but not indeterminate relation of peoples and nationalities, I urge that its use should always be qualified, or replaced by other terms.) In spite of her good intentions, Kim's pedestrian conformism disables her from perceiving the deviancy of Bulosan's text. Like Fuchs, she fosters the instrumentalist prejudice that *America* is unilaterally "dedicated to the task of promoting cultural goodwill and understanding"(47), an opinion induced by her completely uncritical endorsement of the patronizing banalities of reviewers and the damaged mentalities of her native informants. Indeed Kim's prophylactic handling of Asian American authors for systemic recuperation and fetishism proceeds from the assumption that ethnic texts are produced by the minds of lonely, disturbed, and suffering immigrants, helpless and lost, but somehow gifted with inner resources capable of transcending their racial oppression and sundry adversities by way of hard work, genius, and circumstantial luck. At best, in the spirit of a philanthropic liberalism shared by apologists of Anglo missionaries, Kim says that to become part of U.S. society one can always rely on "the urge for good, for the ideal" which is "lodged permanently in the human heart" (51).

Reading (as Fuchs and his ilk practice it) turns out to be an act of violence in more ways than one. What all these reappropriations of Bulosan signify is the power and limits of the hegemonic consensus and its apparatuses to sustain its assimilative but ultimately apartheid-like project to absorb the Asian "Other" into the fold of the unitary hierarchical racial order. In the case of Filipinos settling in the United States, it forgets the original deed of conquest and elides the question how did Filipinos come to find themselves in (as Jose Marti puts it) "the belly of the beast"? From a world system point of view, it is the continuing reproduction of unequal power relations between the Philippines and the United States that is the matrix of the disintegrated Filipino whose subjectivity (more exactly, potential agency) is dispersed in the personae of migrant worker, expatriate intellectual (the major actant in Bienvenido Santos's fiction), cannery or service worker, U.S. Navy steward, and solitary exile. We should remind ourselves that Filipinos first appeared in large numbers in the landscape of an expansive military power, not as fugitives (the "Manillamen" of the Louisiana bayous) from eighteenth-century Spanish galleons but as recruited laborers transported by the HSPA.[3] Reinscribed into this context of differential power relations, the Filipino imagination thus acquires its fated vocation of disrupting the economy of "humanist" incorporation by transgressing willy-nilly the boundaries of interdicted times and tabooed spaces.

Crisis of Representation

What is at stake is nothing less than the question of Filipino self-representation, of its articulation beyond commodity reification, postmodern narcissism, and paranoia. In lieu of the usual atomistic and hypostatizing view, I submit this principle of world system linkage (the colony integrally situated as the double of the imperial polity) as the fundamental premise for establishing the conditions of possibility for apprehending Filipino creative expression in the United States. Lacking this cognitive/reconstructive mapping, one succumbs to sectarian fallacies vulnerable to the divide-and-rule policy of laissez-faire liberalism.

An instructive case may be adduced here. In their foreword to the anthology *Aiiieeeee!* (1975), Oscar Peñaranda, Serafin Syquia, and Sam Tagatac fall prey to a separatist adventurism and thus inflict genocide on themselves: "No Filipino-American ("Flip" born and/or raised in America) has ever published anything about the Filipino-American experience. . . . Only a Filipino-American can write adequately about the Filipino-American experience" (37–54). Writing in the early seventies, a time when Filipinos in the United States born during or after the war were undergoing the proverbial "identity crisis" in the wake of Third World conscientization movements that swept the whole country, our Flip authors contend that Santos and Bulosan, because of birth, carry "Filipino-oriented minds" whereas "the Filipino born and reared in America writes from an American perspective" (50). What exactly is "an American perspective"? Flawed by a crudely chauvinist empiricism, this position of identifying with the hegemonic order and its transcendent claims that validates the "exclusively Filipino-American work" becomes supremacist when it dismisses Philippine literature produced in the former colony as inferior, lacking in "soul" (510).[4]

From the same milieu, Serafin Malay Syquia displays a more nuanced, sophisticated conceptualization of the linkages between metropole and periphery that goes beyond the reified, separatist dogmatism of the Flips. He is enabled here by his sensitivity to the "signs of the times," the massive anti-imperialist ferment of the sixties, and his mature sense of accountability. Consider his statement concerning the dialectical fusion of worlds and sensibilities:

> The commonality that bridges white and Third World poets is politics, politics defined as the outside forces and pressures that shape every human being in this planet. To face the reality of politics as the factor that governs our lives is a necessary step in the development of a consciousness that transcends an elitist concept of poetry. Poetry is the reflection of life and life is determined by politics. Yet, the word politics still produces anxiety because it often is synonymous with only newsprint, television faces and radio voices that seem so distant from our day to day lives.
>
> But politics is much more than that. To write a nature poem describing the tranquillity of the woods and the beauty of the birds and wind at the

same time the trees are being cut down, birds being poisoned and shot, and wind being polluted seems facetious, at the least. This isn't to say that nature poems per se are irrelevant. It may well be that the nature poet sees only beauty and tranquillity in his sheltered wood. However, the times render his vision of beauty and tranquillity harmful to both the poet and the reader if both agree that this is the way the world is. The nature of the times requires, no, demands realism, both in politics and poetry. A people starving cannot be fed on pictures of gourmet dishes. A people with nowhere to live cannot live inside 21-inch television sets. To feed people obscure thoughts perpetuates the obscurity of such thoughts. If poetry is to reflect life as it is, it must concentrate on the symptoms of the sickness that have necessitated the various escape mechanisms artists take in order to separate themselves from reality. Poetry should not nurture the symptom that created the sickness in the first place. It should help to cure the problems of the world by exposing the sickness and offering a sensitive response to the causes of the failures in society. . . .

It's important to remember that art in any society is shaped by that particular society's politics. If a country is in political chaos, it would be misleading to read of tranquillity and the magnificent silence emanating from a law and order dictatorship. . . . Poetry must communicate in order to survive because people must begin to listen and understand the politics that govern their lives in order for this world to survive. (Navarro 1974, 87–89)

I want to syncopate further two antithetical projects to buttress my point. In contrast to the aforementioned Flip manifesto, the singular virtue of the volume *Letters in Exile* (Quinsaat, 1976) (published a year later) lies in confirming the de-/reconstructive force of the premise of colonial subjugation I propose here. Its archival and countervailing function needs to be stressed. When the Philippine Islands became a U.S. colony at the turn of the century, its inhabitants succeeded the Africans, Mexicans, and American Indians as the "white man's burden," the object of "domestic racial imperialism" carried out through brutal pacification and co-optative patronage (Kolko 1976). The first selection in *Letters in Exile*, "The First Vietnam—The Philippine-American War of 1899–1902," provides the required orientation for understanding the Filipino experience of U.S. racism culminating in the vigilante pogroms of the thirties. Neither Chinese, Japanese, nor Korean history before World War II contains any comparable scene of such unrestrained unleashing of racial violence by the U.S. military (Vietnam later on exceeds all precedents). Without taking into account the dialogic contestation of U.S. power (mediated in American English) by the Filipino imagination judging its exorbitance and "weak links," the critique of U.S. cultural hegemony worldwide remains incomplete. Until 1934, when Filipinos legally became aliens as a result of the passage of the Tydings-McDuffie Act, their status was anomalously akin to that of a "floating signifier" with all its dangerous connotations. Wallace Stegner described the breathing of their fatigued bodies at night as "the loneliness breathing like a tired wind over the land" (1945, 20). This index of Otherness, difference incarnate in the sweat and pain of their labor, is the stigma Filipinos had to bear for a long time. Like it or not, we still signify "the stranger's" birthmark. Only in 1934 did the Filipino "immigrant" (at first limited to fifty) really come into existence; hence neither Bulosan nor Villa were immigrants. Nor were the laborers enraptured by dreams of success who were rigidly bound to contracts. In this context, the hyphenated hybrid called "Filipino-American" becomes quite problematic, concealing the priority of the second term (given the fact of colonial/racial subordination and its hallucinatory internalizations) in what appears as a binary opposition of equals. If the writings of Bulosan and Santos do not represent the authentic Filipino experience, as the Flips self-servingly charge, and such a privilege of "natural" representation belongs only to those born or raised in the U.S. mainland (which excludes territorial possessions), then this genetic legalism only confirms the Flips' delusions of exceptionality. It reinforces "the thoroughly racist and national chauvinist character of U.S. society" (Occeña 1985, 35) by eradicating the rich protean history of Filipino resistance to U.S. aggression and thereby expropriating what little remains for EuroAmerican legitimation purposes.

By contrasting the polarity of ideological positions in the two texts cited, I intended to demonstrate concretely the dangers of systemic recuperation and the illusion of paranoid separatism. Even before our admission to the canon is granted, as Fuchs shows, the terms of surrender or compromise have already been drawn up for us to sign. Who then has the authority to represent Filipinos and their experience? Answers to this question and to the problem of how to define Filipino cultural autonomy and its vernacular idiom cannot be explored unless historical parameters and the totalizing constraints of the world system are acknowledged—that is, unless the specificity of U.S. imperial domination of the Philippines is foregrounded in the account. From 1898 up to the present, the production of knowledge of, and ethicopolitical judgments about, Filipinos as a people different from others has been monopolized by EuroAmerican experts like W. Cameron Forbes, Dean Worcester, Joseph Hayden, and others. Consider, for example, H. Brett Melendy's discourse "Filipinos" in the *Harvard Encyclopedia of American Ethnic Groups* (1980), which offers the standard functional-empiricist explanation for Filipino workers' subservience to the Hawaii plantation system due to their indoctrination "to submission by the barrio political system known as caciquismo" (358). Melendy claims that their kinship and alliance system inhibited social adaptation and "militated against their achieving success in American politics" (362). Thus the Filipino becomes a "social problem." Not only does this expert blame the victims' culture, but he also acquits the U.S. state apparatus and its agents of responsibility for deepening class cleavages and instituting that peculiar dependency syndrome that has hitherto characterized U.S.-Philippine cultural exchange.[5]

From Transgression to Sublimation

The conventional wisdom of U.S. scholars studying Filipinos reflects the poverty of bourgeois social theory in general. Such poverty, however, has not contaminated the density, thickness, and multiplicity of Filipino utterance. In the hope of resolving the predicament of the intractable temper of Filipino subjectivity (I hesitate to use "subject position" here because it may suggest a shifting monad, a disposable lifestyle unanchored to specific times and places), one may be tempted to unduly totalize the heterogeneous trends of writing styles while at the same time preserving the fragmentation of writers into the categories of "old-timers," activists of "identity politics," and assorted expatriates. For analytic purposes, my present discourse seeks to articulate constellations of tropes, ethical postures, and idioms of habitus within a differentiated and provisional totality. I think it is facile if not falsifying to lump the multiplicity of incompatible cultural productions into a putative phenomenology of exile and displacement (see Campomanes 1992). Such an approach may be superficially provocative, inviting us, on one hand, to test the validity of Edward Said's conceptualization of exile as a reconstitution of national identity (1990, 359) and, on the other, to contextualize Julia Kristeva's psychoanalysis of every subject as estranged, the "improper" Other as our impossible "own and proper" (1991, 191–95). But how does it really protect us from the internal colonialism at work in high culture's idealizing of the worldwide division of mental/manual labor?

Although such a critical stance may foreground the fact of dependency and its libidinal investment in an archetypal pattern of exile and redemptive return, it indiscriminately lumps together migrant workers, sojourners, expatriates, pseudo-exiles, refugees, émigrés, and opportunists at the expense of nuanced and creative tensions among them.[6] The hypothesis of exile is heuristic and catalyzing, but it fails to discriminate the gap between Bulosan's radical project of solidarity of people of color against capital and the integrationist "melting pot" tendencies that vitiate the works of N.V.M. Gonzalez, Bienvenido Santos, and their epigones. Subjugation of one's nationality cannot be divorced from subordination by racial and class stigmatizing; only Bulosan and some Flip writers are able to grapple with and sublate this complex dialectic of Filipino subalternity and bureaucratic closure. In a typical story, "The Long Harvest," Gonzalez easily cures the incipient anomie of his protagonist by making him recollect the primal scene of his mother suturing his narcissism with artisanal commodity production at home (1990, 28). As long as those sublimating images of an archaic economy survive, the petit bourgeois expatriate can always resort to a conciliatory, accommodationist therapy of mythmaking and need never worry about class exploitation, racism, and national oppression.[7] Of course, it is the easy path to ethnic self-aggrandizement and a compensatory, ghettoized ressentiment.

This is the caveat I would interpose: Unless the paradigm of exile is articulated with the global division of labor under the diktat of U.S. finance capital (via IMF–World Bank, United Nations, private foundations), it simply becomes a mock surrogate of the "lost generation" avant-garde and a pretext for elite ethnocentrism. The intellectual of color can even wantonly indenture himself or herself to the cult of exile à la Joyce or Nabokov. Bulosan also faced this tempting dilemma: Stories like "Life and Death of a Filipino in the USA" and "Homecoming" (San Juan 1983) refuse commodity fetishism by fantasizing a return to a healing home, a seductive catharsis indeed. He writes: "Everywhere I roam [in the United States] I listen for my native language with a crying heart because it means my roots in this faraway soil; it means my only communication with the living and those who died without a gift of expression" (1979, 153–54). But he counters this nostalgic detour, this cheap Proustian fix, by reminding himself of his vocation and its commitment to the return of symbolic capital expropriated from his people: "What impelled me to write? The answer is— my grand dream of equality among men and freedom for all. To give a literate voice to the voiceless one hundred thousand Filipinos in the United States, Hawaii, and Alaska. Above all and ultimately, to translate the desires and aspirations of the whole Filipino people in the Philippines and abroad in terms relevant to contemporary history. Yes, I have taken unto myself this sole responsibility" (Kunitz 1955, 145).

Bulosan's transplantation from the empire's hinterland to the agribusiness enclaves of the West Coast coincides with his transvaluative mapping of the future—not the "America" of corporate business— as the space of everyone's desire and emancipated but still embodied psyche (San Juan 1992c, 1996b). When the patriarchal family disintegrates, the narrator of *America* (unlike Melendy's "Filipino") discovers connections with Chicano and Mexican workers, finds allies among white middle-class women, and taps the carnivalesque life energies of folklore in *The Laughter of My Father* (1944), Bulosan's satire of a money-obsessed society. He encounters the submerged genius loci of anti-imperialist solidarity in gambling houses, cabarets, labor barracks—sites of loss, excess, and expenditure that found a new social bond; points of escape that circumscribe the power of the American "dream" of affluence. Bulosan's strategy of displacement anticipates the insight that "a society or any collective arrangement is defined first by its points or flows of deterritorialization" (Deleuze and Guattari 1987, 220), by jump cuts, syncopations, and scrambling of positions.

Borders, of course, include by excluding. It might be surmised that when the conclusion of *America* reaffirms the narrator's faith in "our unfinished dream," an "America" diametrically opposed to the nightmares of history that make up the verisimilitude of quotidian existence, Bulosan suppresses history. One might suspect that he infiltrates into it a "jargon of authenticity" and forces art to fulfill a compensatory function of healing the divided subject. David Palumbo-Liu cogently puts the case against this kind of closure in ethnic textuality as capitulation to, and recapitalization of, the dominant ideology: "In ethnic narrative, the transcendence of the material via an identification with the fictional representation of lived life often suppresses the question of the political constitution of subjectivity, both within and without the literary text, opting instead for a kind of redemption that short-circuits such questions" (1993, 4). But, as Marilyn Alquizola has shown, a probing of *America*'s structure will disclose an ironic counterpointing of voices or masks, with numerous didactic passages and exempla critical of the system undercutting the naive professions of faith so as to compel the reader to judge that "The totality of the book's contents contradict the protagonist's affirmation of America in the conclusion" (1991, 216). Beyond this formalist gloss, an oppositional reading would frame the logic of the narrator's structuring scheme with two influences: First, the routine practice of authors submitting to the publisher's market analysis of audience reception (wartime propaganda enhances a book's saleability) and, second, the convention of the romance genre in Philippine popular culture that warrants such a formulaic closure. Further metacommentary on the subtext underlying *America*'s mix of naturalism and humanist rhetoric would elicit its Popular Front politics as well as its affinity with Bulosan's massive indictment of capital in "My Education," in his 1952 ILWU yearbook editorial and in numerous letters, all of which belie his imputed role of servicing the behemoth of U.S. nationalism. Ultimately, we are confronted once again with the masks of the bifurcated subject disseminated in the text, traces of his wandering through perilous contested terrain.

Forgotten after his transitory success in 1944 with *The Laughter of My Father*, Bulosan remained virtually unknown until 1973 when the University of Washington Press, convinced of Bulosan's marketability and impressed by the activism of Filipino American groups opposed to the "U.S.-Marcos dictatorship," reissued *America*. My current acquaintance with the Filipino community, however, confirms Bulosan's lapse into near oblivion and the unlikelihood of the Establishment initiating a retrieval to shore up the ruins of the "model minority" myth. This immunity to canonization, notwithstanding the possibility that the fractured discourse of *America* can lend itself to normalization by disciplinary regimes, is absent in the works of Bienvenido Santos, whose narratives cultivate a more commodifiable topos: the charm and hubris of victimage.

Santos's imagination is attuned to an easy purchase on the hurts, alienation, and defeatism of *pensionados*, expatriated *ilustrados*, petit bourgeois males marooned during World War II in the East Coast and Midwest, and other third wave derelicts. His pervasive theme is the reconciliation of the Filipino psyche with the status quo.[8] Since I have commented elsewhere on Santos's achievement (San Juan 1984, 1986), suffice it to note here his power of communicating the pathos of an obsolescent humanism such as that exemplified, for instance, by David Hsin-Fu Wand's celebration of the universal appeal of ethnic writing, its rendering of "the human condition of the outsider, the marginal man, the pariah" (1974, 9) in his introduction to *Asian American Heritage*. The patronage of the American New Critic Leonard Casper might be able to guarantee Santos's efficacy in recycling the ethnic myth of renewal, the born-again syndrome that is the foundational site of the hegemonic American identity. Casper's technique of assimilation differs from Fuch's in its reactionary essentialism. Bewailing Filipino society's alleged loss of "agrarian ideals that guaranteed cultural uniformity and stability," a loss that supposedly aggravates the traumatic impact of the "America of individualism" on poor tribal psyches, Casper superimposes his antebellum standard on his client: Santos is "offering an essentially timeless view of culture, which transcends history limited to the linear, the consecutive, and the one-dimensional" (1979, xiv–xv). But read against the grain, Santos's *Scent of Apples*, and possibly his two novels set in San Francisco and Chicago, derive their value from being rooted in a distinctive historical epoch of Filipino dispossession. As symptomatic testimonies of the deracinated neocolonized subject, they function as arenas for ideological neutralization and compromise, presenting serious obstacles to any salvaging operation and any effort to thwart recuperation because they afford what Brecht calls "culinary" pleasure, a redaction of the native's exotic susceptibilities for tourist consumption and patronage. So far we have seen how Fuch's extortive neoliberalism can hijack the transgressive speech of Bulosan into the camp of "American nationalism" (!) and how Casper's paternalistic chauvinism can shepherd Santos up to the threshold of the Western manor of polite letters. Appropriated thus, our authors do not really pose any threat to the elite proprietorship of administered learning. Does that apply to Villa, the avant-garde heretic now *desaparecido*, who once scandalized the colony's philistines?

Brown Orpheus

When Jose Garcia Villa arrived in the United States in 1930, he was already acclaimed as a modernist master by his contemporaries in the Philippines. His stature was further reinforced when his two books of experimental and highly mannered poems, *Have Come Am Here* (1942) and *Volume Two* (1949), came out and earned praise from the leading mandarins in the Anglo-American literary establishment, among them Edith Sitwell, Marianne Moore, e. e. cummings, Richard Eberhart, and Mark Van Doren. His poems were then anthologized by Selden Rodman, Conrad Aiken, and W. H. Auden (although, as far as I know, no textbook of American literature has included Villa). He has received numerous prizes, including the American Academy of Arts and Letters Award and the Shelley Memorial Award; he was nominated for the Pulitzer Prize in 1943. Villa claims that he was denied a Bollingen Prize because he was not a U.S. citizen. On June 12, 1973, the Marcos government bestowed on Villa its highest honor, "National Artist of the Philippines." After the publication of his *Selected Poems and New* in 1958, however, Villa immediately sank into obscurity—an enigmatic disappearance that I think can be plausibly explained (apart from rapid changes in taste and fashion) by the immense reifying and integrative power of mass consumer society to flatten out diverse or antithetical visions and philosophies.

Villa had no problems being hailed as an "American" poet by the celebrities mentioned earlier, including the editor of *Twentieth Century Authors*. For this reference guide, he confessed the reason why his poems were "abstract" and lacked feeling for detail and particularity:

> I am not at all interested in description or outward appearance, nor in the contemporary scene, but in essence. A single motive underlies all my work and defines my intention as a serious artist: The search for the metaphysical meaning of man's life in the Universe—the finding of man's

selfhood and identity in the mystery of Creation. I use the term meta-physical to denote the ethic-philosophic force behind all essential living. The development and unification of the human personality I consider the highest achievement a man can do. (Kunitz 1955, 1035–36)

Thirty years later, Werner Sollors tries to smuggle Villa back into the limelight by focusing on the poet's reactive idiosyncracy, not his metaphysical selfhood, that substantiates the myth of U. S. exceptionalism in which the languages of consent (to assimilation) and descent collaborate to Americanize almost any immigrant. Villa's indeterminate status in the United States motivated his fabrication of a new poetic language of "reversed consonance" (Sollors 1986, 253–54). Positing the imperative of syncretic belonging, Sollor's pastiche of ethnic genealogy thoroughly cancels out Villa's descent. Meanwhile S. E. Solberg "naturalizes" Villa and so annuls Filipino collective self-determination, labeling the poet's spiritual quest a "personal and idiosyncratic fable, a protean version of the 'making of Americans' " (1991, 54).

Elsewhere I have argued that Villa's poems can be properly appraised as "the subjective expression of a social antagonism" that constitutes the originality of the lyric genre (Adorno 1974, 376; San Juan 1992b). What preoccupies Villa is the phenomenology of dispossession or lack in general, a malaise that translates into the double loss of the poet's traditional social function and audience when exile overtakes the Filipino artist. What is staged in Villa's texts are scenarios for overcoming the loss by the discovery and ratification of the imagination as a demiurgic logos expressing the poet's godhood, a process that also reciprocally evokes the forces of alienation and reification the poet is wrestling with; in short, both the reality effect and the domination effect (Balibar and Macherey 1981) are fused in the grammar of poetic enunciation. Such contradictions, pivoting around the themes of revolt against patriarchal power, psychomachia, negativity, and bodily uprooting, elude the neocolonizing maneuvers of Villa's critics and the parodic mimicry of his epigones.

It is not too much, I think, to suggest that Villa has refused the "ethnic" trap by challenging imperial authority to recognize his authentic artist self and so validate his equal standing with his white peers. But this also spelled his premature redundancy, since reconciliation via aestheticism is nothing but the hegemonic alternative of healing the split subject in a transcendental restoration of plenitude of meaning. We can observe this in the way the crisis of exile, rendered as metonymic displacement in "Wings and Blue Flame: A Trilogy" and "Young Writer in a New Country" (in *Footnote to Youth* [1933]), is dissolved by metaphoric sublimation: In his visionary re-presentation of

the primal loss (exile as castration; expulsion by the father), the antinomic discourses of place, body, inheritance, and need converge in the
self-exiled native being reborn in the desert of New Mexico where the
Oedipal trauma (the loss of the mother's/*patria*'s body) is exorcised by
a transcendent trope of the imagination. Art then functions as the resolution of the conflict between solitary ego and community, unconscious drives and the fixated body, symbolic exchange and the imaginary fetish; between subjugated people and despotic conqueror.

In his sympathetic introduction to Villa's stories, Edward J. O'Brien
intuits a "Filipino sense of race" or "race consciousness" embedded in
the text, but this consciousness swiftly evaporates in the "severe and
stark landscape of New Mexico" (1933, 3). Such a gesture of alluding
to difference acquires a portentous modality when Babette Deutsch,
again with the best of intentions, apprehends something anomalous in
Villa's situation only to normalize it as strange: "The fact that he is a
native of the Philippines who comes to the English language as a
stranger may have helped him to his unusual syntax" (1962, 56). But
the stigmata of the alien is no hindrance to Villa's creation of "lumi-
nous and vibrant" poems "concerned with ultimate things," a sacrifi-
cial rite whose antiutilitarian telos may not be so easily instrumentalized as Bulosan's idealism for the sake of vindicating the ethos of the
pluralist market. Even if difference as plurality is granted, it is only at
the expense of its subsumption in the sameness/identity of the artist
whose self-contained artifices, predicated on the organic reconciliation of ego and alter, transcend the exigencies of race, nationality,
class, gender, and all other segmentations integral to profit accumulation in the planetary domain of the late bourgeoisie.

At this juncture, the quest for Filipino self-representation reaches
an impasse. Villa's "abject" response to the world of commodities and
the cash nexus combines both acquiescence and nausea, given our hypothesis that the lyric form harbors social antagonisms and yields
both reality and domination effects. His work might be read as a
highly mediated reflection of the vicissitudes of conscienticized Filipinos who are driven from the homeland by economic crisis, alternatively nostalgic and repelled, unable to accommodate themselves to
their new environment. Villa's "disappearance" is but one episode in
the allegory of the Filipinos' pre-postcolonial ethnogenesis.[9] The
group's persistently reproduced subordination arises from its belief
that it owes gratitude for being given an entry visa, and that by imitating the successful models of Asians and other immigrants who made
their fortune, it will gradually be accepted as an equal; at the same
time, it cherishes the belief that it originated from a distinct sovereign
nation enjoying parity with the United States. To salvage Villa, we

have to read his work symptomatically for those absent causes that constitute its condition of possibility, even as those very same ruptures and silences betray the manifold contradictions that define the imperial "American civic" consensus. Villa's agenda is integration of the personality, ours the reinscription of our subject-ion in the revolutionary struggle to forge an independent, self-reliant Philippines and in the resistance of people of color everywhere to the violence of multiculturalizing white supremacy.

Counterhegemonic Resistance

In this emancipatory project to build the scaffolding of our cultural tradition, we can learn how to safeguard ourselves from the danger of reclamation by a strategy of retrospective mapping (performed previously) and anticipatory critique. To advance the latter, I comment on two modes of narrating Filipino self-identification: Jessica Hagedorn's *Dogeaters* (1990) and Fred Cordova's *Filipinos: Forgotten Asian Americans* (1983).

Conflating heresy and orthodoxy, Hagedorn's novel possesses the qualities of a canonical text in the making—for the multiculturati. It unfolds the crisis of U.S. hegemony in the Philippines through a collage of character types embodying the corruption of the Americanizing oligarchic elite (see San Juan 1991b). In trying to extract some intelligible meaning out of the fragmentation of the comprador-patriarchal order that sacrifices everything to acquisitive lust, she resorts to pastiche, aleatory montage of diverse styles, clichés, ersatz rituals, hyperreal hallucinations—a parodic bricolage of Western high postmodernism—whose cumulative force blunts whatever satire or criticism is embedded in her character portrayals and authorial intrusions. This narrative machine converts the concluding prayer of exorcism and ressentiment into a gesture of stylized protest. Addressed mainly to a cosmopolitan audience, Hagedorn's trendy work is undermined by postmodern irony: It lends itself easily to consumer liberalism's drive to sublimate everything (dreams, eros, the New People's Army, feminism, anarchist dissent) into an ensemble of self-gratifying spectacles. At best, *Dogeaters* measures the distance between the partisanship of Bulosan's peasants-become-organic-intellectuals and the pseudo-yuppie lifestyles of recent arrivals. As a safe substitute for Bulosan and as one of the few practitioners of Third World/feminine "magic realism," Hagedorn may easily be the next season's pick for the Establishment celebration of its multicultural canon.[10]

From another perspective, that of an Italian feminist, Hagedorn's fiction cannot be co-opted by an omnivorous U.S. multiculturalism because it is a cyborg's manifesto. Giovanna Covi argues that the main protagonist's movie-novel is not just stereotypical representation; its rhetoric aims for "a semiotics capable of producing a discourse on the neo-colonial condition of the Philippines in the context of the Americanization of world culture" (1996, 74). So far, it is Covi who, to my knowledge, is the only critic who enunciates most cogently the internationalist horizon of *Dogeaters* for a cosmopolitan audience:

> Hagedorn expresses the Gramscian version of nationalism as the national-popular: she articulates the sense of her own country as the sense of her own place, of herself as occupying a given position whose social meaning derives from belonging to a historically-defined tradition. She rejects the nationalism of the nation-state, which is supported by the identification with a specific ideology. . . . Precisely because the Philippines [is] an American colony—and this is not an invention—*Dogeaters* is not only a realistic portrayal of the cultural, social, and moral fragmentation derived from centuries of dependence on first the Spanish and later the Americans, but also—in Gramscian terms—the expression of a sociality which is historical and ethico-political and which is the condition for the artistic rendering of a genuine and fundamental humanity. (1996, 65–66)

My previous remarks on *Dogeaters* should now be contextualized in terms of the metacommentary of Chapter 6 on Hagedorn's *The Gangster of Love* (1996). In contrast to the quasi-surrealistic montage of her first novel, Hagedorn's second novel centers on the adventures of a young Filipina in the United States growing up against the background of the obsolescence of the rock/hippie/youth counterculture of the sixties, the decline of civil rights struggles and "Third World" revolutions, and the resurgence of reactionary ideology and practices. Can nostalgia replace the shock of living through alienation and commodity fetishism, racial bigotry and sexism, in the imperial metropolis? What is the fate of the post-1965 Filipino immigrant generation? Rocky Rivera's search for a viable community (the rock band functions as temporary surrogate and compensatory device) dramatizes the predicament of the adolescent Filipina stranded in the milieu of the neoconservative United States. Rocky decides to be a mother and replace patriarchal culture (signified by her aging mother still fixated on the absent philandering father) with the shifting positionality of a nomadic subject—Covi's cyborg—who somehow survives the predatory disasters of her "flower-power" companions. She deploys tactics of mimicry, satire and burlesque, comic ruses, and happenstance stratagems. Her situation can be read as an allegorical rendering of the post-1965 cohort of Filipino immigrants whose neocolonial roots can only prompt a clinging to fragments of indigenous, damaged culture while aping the suburban lifestyle of conspicuous consumerism. The narrative stages Rocky's return after her mother's death to face the dying father in the Philippines and what he comes to symbolize: the decadent world of the Marcoses (a return of the past sacrificed in *Dogeaters*) and the moribund oligarchy. A politics of memory emerges, the libidinal figuration of which captures the uneven, unsynchronized social formation of the neocolony.

In the final analysis, Hagedorn's production of a "postcolonial" minoritarian discourse depends for its condition of possibility on what it denies or represses: the culture of resistance symbolized by the Manongs and by extension the revolt of the Filipino masses erased by Jimi Hendrix and Hollywood. On the other hand, one can argue that impulses of resistance are not completely extinguished but manifest themselves here in the form of grotesque characters, melodramatic juxtapositions, breaks and discontinuities in style and idiom, above all in the absurd and fantastic incidents whose bizarre texture reflects precisely the profound crisis of late global capitalism registered in the bodies and performances of Hagedorn's "gangsters of love," temporarily disbanded and/or routed, in quest of laws and authorities they need to defy.

Meanwhile, the Filipino remains subalternized by putative rehabilitation. Examining Fred Cordova's (1983) photographic montage, we encounter again our Otherness as "fertilizer" for the Hawaiian farmer and "little brown brother" for the bureaucrats. We discern here a symptom of the conflicted neocolonized subject compensating for his or her lack by impressing the public with an overwhelming multiplicity of images of family/communal togetherness, simulacra of smiles and gestures that animate the rituals of the life cycle and the repetition of which seems enough to generate illusions of successful adjustment and progress. Filipinos turn out to be "first" on many occasions. Despite the negative witness of parts of the commentary, the surface texture of those images serves to neutralize the stark evidence of a single photo (on page 42) that captured stooping, faceless workers caught in the grid of a bleak, imprisoning landscape. Nothing is mentioned of why or how these alien bodies were transported and smuggled in. What is suppressed here can be gleaned from a comparable though abbreviated photographic discourse made by another outfit, *Pearls* (Bock et al. 1979). Its section titled "Pinoy" offers an apologetic history and the usual documentary exhibits of Filipinos adapting to their new habitat, but the inclusion of newspaper cutouts headlining anti-Filipino riots serves to demystify the ideology of adjustment and compromise that informs such officially funded enterprises as Cordova's.[11] *Pearls* records a vestigial trace, a lingering effect, of what *Letters in Exile* strove to accomplish: a reconstruction of the historical conditions of possibility of the Filipino presence in the metropolis and Filipinos' struggle to affirm their humanity by acts of refusal, solidarity, and remembering.

The Marcos dictatorship interlude (1972–1986) in Philippine history, which brought a flood of exiles and pseudo-refugees to the United States at the same time that Washington amplified its military and economic aid to the national security state, has foregrounded again the reality of U.S. domination of the homeland that distinguishes the Filipino nationality from other minorities. Our neocolonial stigmata renew the signifiers of difference.[12] I reiterate my thesis that the creation of the vernacular resume, of Filipinos' experience of limits and possibilities in the United States, can only be theorized within the process of comprehending the concrete historical particularity of their incorporation in the U.S. empire and the ecology of this unequal exchange.[13]

In the context of recent demography, Bulosan seems to be a "rural" misfit. The transplantation of recent Filipino immigrants to the urban wilderness of Los Angeles, San Francisco, Seattle, Chicago, and New York City has impelled young writers to conjecture the emergence of an "urbane" sensibility, adoptive and adaptive at the same time, born from the clash of cultures and memories. The trajectory of the proletarian imagination from Hawaii's plantations to California's Imperial Valley to Washington's Yakima Valley no longer crosses the paths of "dogeaters" and "Flips." Recent subaltern anxiety, however, seeks legitimacy from the universal archetypes found in archaic folklore and myth—an ironic aporia, indeed. How can this recover from the "backwaters" the writings of Serafin Malay Syquia, for example? And how can it valorize the paradigm of the *sakada's* redemptive agon in *Istorya ni Bonipasyo: Kasla Gloria Ti Hawaii* for its lessons of inventing "history from below"?[14]

Only disconnect and recontextualize—that is our motto. What makes such disparate events as Fermin Tobera's killing in 1930 and the murder of Silme Domingo and Gene Viernes in 1981 the condensed turning points of the Filipino odyssey in the United States?[15] You have to conceive of both occurring in the space of the heterogeneous Other occupied by U.S. "civilizing" power. Although the texts of the nationality's autochthonous tradition are interred in the imperial archive that cries for inventory and critique—I am thinking of the oral histories of the "Manongs"; interviews with veterans of union organizing; testimonies in letters and journals of immigrant passage; reportage and videofilms of various struggles, such as that over the International Hotel in San Francisco; and other nonverbal signifying practices—unfortunately there are few discerning and astute commentaries or informed reflections on these circumstantial texts. We need to disconnect them from the hegemonic episteme of Fuchs and Melendy, contextualize them in the resistance narrative of peasants and workers, and then re-configure them in the punctual lived experiences of Filipinos today. Therefore, I consider the production of transformative critical discourse a priority in the task of identifying, generating, and selecting the anticanon[16] of Filipino agency and praxis that in varying degrees have resisted co-optation and incorporation. Toward realizing this agenda of searching for our "representative" speech, I propose Bulosan's corpus of writings as central touchstone and researches like *Philip Vera Cruz: A Personal History of Filipino Immigration and the Farmworkers Movement* (Vera Cruz 1992; see Chapter 5) as crucial linkages between popular memory and individualist dissidence. In this syllabus, we include Santos's and Gonzalez's fiction on the diaspora as loci for renegotiation, together with Villa's entire production as salvageable for counter-hegemonic rearticulation in spite of his status as a legendary classic. Meanwhile, the prodigious creativity of a conspicuously avant-gardist generation—among them Jessica Hagedorn, Nick Carbo, Marianne Villanueva, R. Zamora Linmark, M. Evelina Galang, and many more who participated in the annual exodus from the Philippines in the last decade—remains a reservoir of practices for future hermeneutic appraisal and reader/writer empowerment.

Among the most recent exhibits that blend the residual and the nascent is Fatima Lim-Wilson's award-winning collection of poems, *Crossing the Snow Bridge* (1995). As expected, the conventional reviewers praise her for a new brand of the exotic: apocalyptic and "sumptuous evocations of stolen islands and multiple fires." That, of course, is highly misleading. From her meditations on the ironic resonance of her craft in "Alphabet Soup" and "Sestina Written in a Cold Land" to more geopolitical commentaries on habitat/location in "Luzviminda," "Market Day," and "Positively No Filipinos Allowed," Fatima Lim-Wilson demonstrates her unusual gift: She is that rare artist who never sacrifices ethical commitments for the easy seductions of performing as a fashionable "postcolonial" aesthete. This is because the dominant symbolic and thematic action linking the poems in her volume stages the drama of confronting the ambiguities and paradoxes of identity, hence the cartographic motifs and the recurrent tropes of mapping scenarios, borders, territories. The speaking subject of her poems draws from indigenous reservoirs of memory, folklore, and national history as well as from cross-cultural encounters of a personal nature the raw materials that she then reconstitutes in precisely contoured narrative lives. These "happenings" almost always succeed in avoiding the lure of verbal legerdemain so common to exiles or émigrés obsessed with cutting off ties and/or claiming ambidextrous virtues (like dual citizenship). Lim-Wilson's poems evince a nuanced and graceful control of experience that can only be expected from a "Third World" woman artist who has conscientiously wrestled with the dangers and blandishments of metropolitan culture. Her performance thus yields both instruction and pleasure—an accomplishment transcending the parochial ethnic measure imposed by academic opportunism.

To accomplish this project of discovery, rescue, and affirmation of Filipino agency against recolonizing strategies from above, we need a radical transformation of grassroots consciousness and practice, a goal addressed by Marina Feleo-Gonzalez's playbook, *A Song for Manong* (1988). What is at stake here is a recovery of the inaugural scene of Filipino subjectification and insurgency as a dialectical process. We find this event dramatized here when the script unfolds the figure of Pedro Calosa, a leader of the Tayug uprising in Pangasinan, from which milieu of sedition and dissidence Bulosan emerged, as one who learned the craft of resistance from the Hawaii interethnic strikes of the twenties. Feleo-Gonzalez chooses to circumvent any easy return to a pristine homeland by concluding the performance with the solidarity-in-action of EuroAmericans and Third World peoples in the campaign to preserve the site of the International Hotel from corporate modernization.[17] Feleo-Gonzalez's intervention reawakens the community's conscience and redeems its "collective assemblage of enunciation" (to use Deleuze and Guattari's [1986] phrase) from the fate of recoding by the celebrated "melting pot" religion.

One such assemblage is Manuel Buaken's neglected book *I Have Lived with the American People* (1948). Indeed, Buaken returns to haunt us with the lesson that no fable of dredging up a coherent and synchronized identity through memory alone, no privileging of the therapeutic power of art, no sacred ceremony of reminiscence by itself can cement together the fragments of our uprooting from the ravished homeland and repair the tragic disintegration of the nation's spirit. In the breakdown of Buaken's "goodwill autobiography" as a teleological fable, we find a counterpointing discourse: Our quest for linkage and autonomy encounters the testimonies of such early migrants as Francisco Abra (117–20) and Felipe Cabellon (121–24), soliciting empathy and justice, interrupting our pursuit of wholeness. With the Filipino nationality in the United States still mind-manacled and the islands convulsed in the fire of the people's war for liberation, the practice of writing by, of, and for Filipinos in the United States remains nomadic, transitional, hybrid, metamorphic, discordant, beleaguered, embattled, "always already" in abeyance. Such a genre of "minor" writing, which I define as a praxis of becoming-what-is-other-for-itself, is (to quote Deleuze and Guattari [1986, 19]) "the revolutionary force for all literature."

4

Bulosan's Metamorphosis: The Return of the Alter/Native

... by abandoning your hungry fingers / to the mercy of suspect pages ...

Alvaro Cardona-Hine, "Bulosan Now"

So it remained for Marpo to bring the word of God to Yoneko. ... Marpo, who was twenty-seven years old, was a Filipino and his last name was lovely, something like Humming Wing, but no one ever ascertained the spelling of it.

Hisaye Yamamoto, "Yoneko's Earthquake"

Works and Days

I am sure of myself and what I can do in the world. ... I know deep down in my heart that I am an exile in America. ... Yes, I feel like a criminal running away from a crime I did not commit. And the crime is that I am a Filipino in America.[1]

More than fifty years after the publication of *America Is in the Heart* ([1946] 1973; hereafter cited as *America*), Carlos Bulosan (1911–1956) is now beginning to be recognized as one of the first "Third World" revolutionary writers who memorialized the struggles of people of color in the United States and in all quarters of the empire against the global system of capital. With militant candor, Bulosan expressed the principal contradiction within the core of the migrant community's existence in the United States. In December 1937, he wrote to a

95

friend: "Western peoples are brought up to regard Orientals or colored peoples as inferior, but the mockery of it all is that Filipinos are taught to regard Americans as our equals. . . . The terrible truth in America shatters the Filipinos' dream of fraternity" (1995b, 173). This shattering of the "dream of fraternity" induced the birth pangs of national/class consciousness in the colonial subject.

Although Bulosan, just like thousands of his compatriots, discovered the explosive truth that "It was a crime to be a Filipino" in the metropolitan center of power, he could also indulge in wish fulfillment: "America is in the hearts of men that die for freedom; it is also in the eyes of men that are building a new world" (1995b, 212). To convert the rubric "America" into a utopian metaphor and thus arrest the vertigo of its historical reference without qualification is, I think, misleading. Bulosan, the subaltern tribune of the colonized, inflected "America" as a popular Imaginary constituted by the lived experiences of millions who suffered, fought, and died for the freedom and justice of all.

Was Bulosan assuming the mask of an ecumenical prophet in the twilight days of the empire? This is in hindsight quite anachronistic: Bulosan's maturation occurred years after the Bolshevik Revolution of 1917 and six years before one-fourth of humanity would conclude its "long march" in the victory of the Chinese People's Liberation Army in October 1949. Perhaps, by invoking the Latin American shibboleth "our America" (formulated in the Second Declaration of Havana) and identifying it with the anti-imperialist tradition of oppressed peoples, we could explain more credibly the shifting contours of Bulosan's imagination as stages in the evolution of a "Third World" socialist consciousness. This is confirmed, as we shall see, by the way the paradigmatic struggle for recognition and equality in Bulosan's writings transvalues all social relations. In the process, the agent of historical change emerges in the solidarity of groups in action.

> Do you know what a Filipino feels in America? He is the loneliest thing on earth [surrounded by] beauty, wealth, power, grandeur. But is he a part of these luxuries? . . . He is enchained damnably to his race, his heritage. He is betrayed, my friend.

After centuries of oppression by Spanish colonialism, the natives of this southeast Asian archipelago revolted in 1896 and established the first Philippine republic in June 1898. But the invading U.S. forces, under the slogans of "manifest destiny" and "benevolent assimilation," suppressed the aspirations of the newly emancipated millions and aborted the birth of a sovereign nation. The Spanish-American War of 1898 marked the emergence of the United States as an imperialist power. It offered the pretext for the brutal conquest of a remote group of islands several thousand miles from the North American continent. Workers, peasants, and the intelligentsia mounted a formidable resistance throughout the Filipino-American War from 1899 to 1902, with sporadic guerilla attacks lasting until the eve of World War I. Although defeated in open warfare, the revolutionaries switched to other tactics of dissent and refusal that continue up to this day, when overt political, economic, and military dependency belies any claim of the client regime to independence.

While the United States spent over $600 million, deployed 126,468 troops, and suffered over 80,000 casualties, the revolutionaries endured tremendous sacrifices, with about a million killed in counterinsurgency atrocities (Francisco 1987). The first My Lais occurred in this period, when the U.S. ruling class implemented a policy of indiscriminate slaughter to "pacify" the recalcitrant natives. In the famous campaigns in Samar and Batangas provinces, for example, the U.S. military used scorched-earth terrorist tactics, burning villages and annihilating all inhabitants in contested areas—men, women, children—suspected of being guerillas or their allies. In this first episode of people's war in Asia, over a million Filipinos were slain in pursuit of the U.S. government's desire to—in President McKinley's words—"civilize" and "Christianize" the natives.

For four decades, this resistance of a "peripheral" formation, as Lenin emphasized in *Imperialism: The Last Stage of Capitalism* (1939), delivered fierce blows to the U.S. ruling class. This resistance is alive and well today.

At the time when the U.S. war machine was occupied in a genocidal campaign against the Muslim population of southern Philippines, Bulosan was born in the province of Pangasinan, northern Luzon, on November 2, 1911. He was too young to grasp the horror of what happened at the battle around Mt. Bagsak near Jolo City, Sulu, where more than a thousand men, women, and children were ruthlessly slaughtered (Davis 1989). Before he died, Bulosan took up the gun where the Moros dropped it and led a counterattack. He lambasted the McCarthy reaction of the fifties in his editorial for the 1952 yearbook of the International Longshoremen's and Warehousemen's Union (ILWU), Local 37:

> Continued U.S. exploitation of the Philippines and continued violent attacks on the workers and peasants have produced the colonial pattern of riches for the few and poverty for millions. Despite the arrest of their leaders (like Amado V. Hernandez, president of the Congress of Labor Organizations), Filipino trade unionists are fighting energetically to end U.S. intervention in the Philippines, . . . to secure the withdrawal of

American military and economic advisers, to regain their democratic rights and their national independence. Filipino workers are demanding friendship with People's China and strongly protesting the rearming of Japan and the U.S. aggression in Korea. (1952, 27)

Why did Bulosan, like thousands of Filipino young men in the first three decades of U.S. occupation, leave the colony? What was the outcome of the much-publicized intention of "civilizing" the benighted inhabitants? In his autobiographical testimony written in the mid-thirties, Bulosan articulates a response. He captures in microcosm the social background of thousands of Filipino workers in Hawaii and on the West Coast:

> My father was a small farmer, but when I was five or six years old his small plot of land was taken by usury. [Usury, Bulosan comments elsewhere, used to be the "racket" of the Filipino oligarchs, but later the Americans employed it to extract surplus value from serflike tenants.] My father became a sharecropper, which is no different from the sharecroppers in the Southern States. Years after, because of this sharecropping existence, my father fell into debt with his landlord, who was always absent, who had never seen his tenants—and this was absentee landlordism even more oppressive than feudalism. Then my father really became a slave—and they tell me there is no more slavery in the Philippine Islands! (1995b, 215)

Because of such privations thanks to Anglo-Saxon tutelage, Bulosan's dream of securing a formal education evaporated, leaving in its wake the line of escape to the metropolis.

We see then, on one hand, the heightening of semifeudal exploitation of the peasant majority and its systematic dispossession, a plight traceable to the intensified underdevelopment of a narrowly based agrarian economy (devoted to a few export crops like sugar, tobacco, hemp) under the control of U.S. finance capitalism. On the other hand, we face the increasing demand of West Coast and Hawaii planters for cheap labor when the passage of the Exclusion Act of 1924 finally cut off their supply of Chinese and Japanese workers. In collusion with steamship companies, U.S. agribusiness engaged in deception and fraud to recruit Filipino peasants with promises of education, high wages, decent working conditions—in short, a phantasmal prospect of affluence. It must be recalled that from 1900 the educational apparatus in the Philippines functioned to instill in the old and young generation the values of competitive and self-centered individualism coupled with Eurocentric chauvinist ideas and attitudes, all of which were then valorized by the slogans of "democracy" and "liberty."

Bulosan's life may be conceived of as an epitome of the migrant's *agon* in a protracted sojourn in the "New World." It exhibits the process of his coming to understand that the history of all society is characterized by class struggle in various forms, a continuum punctuated by racist violence, anomie, and impulses of solidarity. Initiated into the exposed life of peasants victimized by landlords and usurers and by debt peonage, Bulosan quickly perceived how state power was used by the property-owning classes to enforce their authority and thus insure their privileges. Folk superstitions, tributary mores, and the retrograde sanctions of the church reinforced the state's coercive apparatuses. Bulosan grasped the structural causes of the widespread poverty, malnutrition, illiteracy, and savage wrath of the masses—the still unawakened gravediggers of the occupying Leviathan.

In the middle of imperialism's breakdown, the Depression of the thirties, Bulosan found himself confronted with problems from which, he thought, he had successfully fled: hunger, poverty, racial apartheid, class violence. These experiences radicalized the young Bulosan. They tempered his naivete, his penchant for sentimental moralizing. They aroused anger and compassion; they provoked a defiant resolve to help the disenfranchised, the pariahs and outcasts. His ordeals gave him a penetrating knowledge of social crisis and its overdetermined nature, intuitively apprehending its causal dynamics. He became what Marx calls a "social individual," who thought and felt deeply about the predicament of the nameless "Others" in the farms, factories, prisons; in the war zones of his unforgotten birthplace. Exile, for Bulosan, became the crucible of character and the matrix of destiny.

After landing in Seattle in 1931, Bulosan reminisced, he was sold for five dollars to a labor contractor. Exploited in the salmon canneries, he soon began to live the truth of the predatory system. One contemporary observer depicted the milieu of Bulosan's initiation, the life of the "Alaskero":

> The men toil like slaves from morning till night and are often called upon to work overtime. Some are paid by the piece—three cents for handling a cooler of 168 cans, and others are paid fifteen cents an hour. The work might not be so bad if the workers were well housed and fed, but the opposite is usually the case, as regards the "Asiatic" workers at least. They are miserably housed in crowded quarters and the feed is of the poorest— salted fish or meat and rice, supplied by the labor contractor. Only when the contractor's supplies run low is salmon ever eaten. (Cruz 1933, 46)[2]

In these circumstances, Bulosan's maturation could not be anything else but a process of conscientization and praxis. His education was mediated by situations of recurrent crisis in which he absorbed the lessons (more precisely, knowledge of rationally intelligible laws of social development) gained by his compatriots in the realm of perceptual and sensory experience. In the artifices of his imagination, all these disparate elements coalesced. He produced a multilayered conception of life propelled by antagonistic class interests. This is the reason why, in spite of the ironic texture and iterative architectonic of *America*—ironic in the sense that the massive dossier of victimization contradicts the fictive narrator's assertion of his faith in the United States as the incarnation of freedom, equality, justice (Alquizola 1991)—we are not confused. A complex historicizing vision enabling a grasp of the social totality, critical distance, and nuanced ethical discrimination invests Bulosan's major texts with a powerful transformative charge.

In one autobiographical testimony, Bulosan provides us an insight into the synthesizing principle of his art:

> I was very young when I landed, and the savage impact of a machine country only splintered the frail vestiges of the civilization into which I was born. . . . There were suicides everywhere among the "important" and "rich" men who were "touched" by the economic concentration. But I am wondering to this day why there were no suicides among the very poor, the very miserable and homeless. . . . And I found out that the bond between the poor is tighter than that between the rich and important. Of course this is not to be found in books or in any history, because the poor man does not write books; he is too busy looking for something to fill his stomach. . . . Thus the history is not yet written. (1995b, 215)

That history, though unwritten, was then being lived through in diverse ways, constituting the virtual force field of his imagination. As Bulosan attested to in a letter written on the eve of World War II: "And I was a part of it all: starving in foul toilets . . . crying at night and in the morning, . . . shouting for something that was not in America, demanding for tenderness of love." This confessional, even mawkish, register of discourse must be assayed in the context of such episodes in the life of a dark-skinned colonial ward bereft of the rights enjoyed by ordinary citizens, a life distorted by ostracism, insults, lynchings. Returning to this inaugural scene, Bulosan retrieves occluded meanings and deciphers the palimpsest of experience. Instead of adopting the cliché of assimilation, he posits a rhizomatic figure of "gravitation" that counterpoints the eccentric itinerary of *America* with the ritualized performative speech acts in *The Cry and the Dedication*:

> When I landed in Seattle, I was met by a swaggering countryman, a dapper Filipino, who sold me to an agricultural labor contractor for $7.50. There were seventy-five of us, all under twenty-five years old, who were cheated this way. I worked for a month under this unforgettable deal. At

the end of the month the contractor vanished one night with all our money. I starved on that farm; then I escaped to become a dishwasher: $7.00 a week. I ran away from this second job at the end of three weeks and starved again. I drifted to Santa Barbara where I worked for almost three months in a bakery. Then I came down to Los Angeles. I was out of work again. I found the members of the outer fringes of society: hoboes, tramps, gamblers, prostitutes, etc. I was absorbed by them. In spite of all that had happened I was still innocent. You should have seen how they protected me from sin and debaucheries. Because in Filipino society there is a by-path on which these "unfortunates" walk and often meet the "educated" ones, I soon discovered the college students, graduates, newspaper workers. Because one thing leads to another, I was soon thrown into one lap of radicals, progressives, social workers. I became one of them, not by adaptation but by gravitation—the general process from an ignorant farm worker, city worker, student, to a class-conscious individual. [letter to Dorothy Babb, October 9, 1937]

Because one thing leads to another "not by adaptation but by gravitation": this perspicacious rendering of change, this tactful configuring of motion and stasis, distills the Filipino artist's metamorphosis in the space of the heterogeneous, the contingent and "always already" interrupted. We confront here not social mobility but the fluctuations of the international capitalist division of labor. Subjects are reified into objects—but not without protest. All of what happened personally to him and to millions of people of color taught Bulosan the urgent need to be critical not only of his environment but also of himself as a product of historical circumstance and alternatively as its creative agent. He acquired from what Gorki called "the university of life" a visionary but also realistic mode of interpreting the world.

A year before he died, Bulosan renounced any politics of identity and the "genealogical anxiety" it entailed. He declared that he judged writers according to whether they are "for or against war, for or against life"—a broad criterion whose utopian thrust amid the menace of nuclear holocaust animates the rhetoric of one eloquent letter:

I will try to tell you a short story: Once when I was a little boy in that village where I was born, I dreamed that we could remake this world into a paradise. In such a world there would be no darkness, no ignorance, no brutality to man by another man. In such a world there would be no inhumanity, no indignity, no poverty. In such a world there would be no deception, no ugliness, no terror. In such a world there would be mutual assistance, mutual cooperation, mutual love. This is the dream which has sustained me down the terrible years, and it is with me still; only it is more lucid now, more terrifying in its vastness. I would like to give you a glimpse of this dream some day. [January 7, 1974]

Glimpses of this dream can be found in the story "As Long as the Grass Shall Grow" (Bulosan, 1983a), which pits the terrorism of the dominant society against the solidarity of Filipino workers with a white woman.[3] In *America*, what vividly stands out amid the antagonisms of race and class is the ineradicable reality of the victims, whites and colored people alike, sharing the pain and joy of work as a form of resistance that lacks any preemptive and sublimating closure. In "Be American" (see next section), the narrative dramatizes how the trusting otherworldliness of the migrant, experiencing the mutation of bodies to commodities, yields to the recognition of labor as the principal creator of value. This is conveyed by the "unwritten law of the nomad": friendship and kinship mediated through fruits, fish, and so on, appreciated not for their exchange value but for their use value. Circulation via the market is disrupted. This "Americanization" of the native is the translation of the dream the youthful Bulosan cherished, a conversion that aims to abolish the commodification of life and so naturalize the alien/stranger in a humanized environment. Thus, the itinerant ward from the empire's margin returns to "himself" as it were on a higher level, voids his alienation, and attains a new dimension of existence immanent in the world of his artifice.

The Example of "Be American"

*And we were all thousands of miles from our islands, alone (without even our women) in a strange, and often hostile, country.
. . . Most of us will die here because we can work here, and when we can work we will make a life for ourselves. Man always makes a life for himself from whatever he has.*

To illustrate the distinctive mode of production subtending Bulosan's craft, I offer these abbreviated comments on what I consider his most representative work, "Be American." This composition displays Bulosan's stylistic habit of organizing details of time and space within the pattern of a didactic or pedagogical fable, a teaching-learning organon (to use Brecht's [1964] terms). This anticanonical genre has been downgraded to an inferior status by the New Criticism, whose standard, tied to the practice of a limited number of selected writers in the Western canon, dogmatically privileges the mimetic-expressive convention. One distinction of this genre lies in its capacity to fuse the virtue of a quasi-documentary transcript of the protagonist's actions with the narrator's sublimated judgment, thus evoking both critical questioning and sympathy.

In "Be American," Bulosan attempts a ludic mapping of a commodity-oriented space in search of a locus of identity, a subject position that migrant workers can hope to achieve through work. One can argue that Consorcio's stance proposes a model for the praxis of resistance writing trapped momentarily in the center, in "the belly of the beast." This genealogy of entitlement can also be transcoded as an attempt to undermine the hegemony of commodity fetishism in the milieu of "factories in the field" where the bodies of people of color suffer reification, bought and sold for less than the price of their harvest. All the stations of passage for the Filipino contingent of stoop laborers are defined by certain vegetables or fruits converted as tokens that signify both presence and absence of the giver: Rhetorically viewed, metonymic linkage is displaced here by metaphoric equivalence. The workers utilize the fruit of their bodies' expenditure of energy/time to chart their journey as well as map their vanishing horizons, the orbits of their quests for personal dignity via solidarity. Their harvests communicate the message of survival and the ethics of desire (ethics in Spinoza's sense as the ratio of motion and rest, activity and passivity). On this arbitrary but not intractable constellation of signs pivots the proverbial search for identity of the deracinated Other who is neither citizen nor alien, in short, the Filipino suspended between necessity and chance.

In effect, I believe what we are pursuing here is the negotiated route of the migrant worker that etches his visage on the sociocultural map of the North American continent. It is an act of domiciling, a historical duration, diametrically opposed to the notion of private ownership of land, goods, and so on. It contradicts the law of permanent settlement as a qualification for appropriating things. It repudiates the fetishism of commodities and the alienation of the monadic ego in the marketplace. It connotes a shift from the network of ritual sacrifice to that of representation (Attali 1985). For the narrator, the law of the nomad is "finders keepers"—an anonymous random sharing of the products of human labor that dissolves the reification of market exchange and generates altruistic pleasures.

Given this problematic of vernacular self-definition, Bulosan's mode of mixing utopian and grotesque motifs might be construed as an attempt to elude the responsibility of class struggle through its sublimation into erotic fantasy. Hence, the narrator tends to refuse the temptation of history and accept instead the gratification offered by the myth of eternal recurrence. But the plot's trajectory inscribes its opposite between the lines. Indeed, the facts of quotidian life reassert themselves: the violence of war, racist exclusion, death. What is instructive for us is the narrator's belief that Consorcio fulfilled his ambition of realizing "his most cherished dream: American citizenship." At this point, the logic of entitlement degenerates to legalistic formalism while the pathos of the narrator's celebration of Consorcio becomes an easy compensatory resolution. It is obvious that the mystique of the land as female body overshadowing the greed of male rapists fails to salvage the dream. Notwithstanding this, I would contend that the conclusion foregrounds the irreconcilable conflict between the "wonderful dream" and the painful reality, between the narrator's "enduring love for the American earth" and that earth's retribution visited on those whose sacrifices have for so long sustained its beauty and abundance. The closure leaves us with the open-endedness of an order predicated on the ceaseless reproduction of class antagonisms—what enables individuals to exercise the right to own property, to buy and sell—without which surplus value, ressentiment, and hierarchy status cannot be realized.

What is at stake here is not the canny Hegelian "ruse of Reason" but more simply the cunning of Bulosan's imagination and its delayed redemptive effects. In "Be American," Bulosan projects a conjunction of opposites discernible on one level: Consorcio's naivete versus the narrator's seeming worldliness. This nexus of opposites then graduates to a stage of tension and polarity signified by Consorcio's disillusionment, his rejection of the narrator's docile acceptance of things qualified with, or heightened by, his wish fulfillment. This leads in turn to Consorcio's phase of "gravitation"—his association with other people of color through work that educates him until he acquires class consciousness. Juxtaposed with Consorcio's application of an intuitive dialectics, the narrator for his part moves to a phase of mysticism, his gesture of togetherness and (if one might pun here) his consorting with others serving as a pretext for the mock apotheosis of the dream of integration, what every immigrant supposedly brings with him or her to "the land of opportunity."

Scrutinizing further, we perceive how, within these manifold layers of ideologemes, a fundamental insight crystallizes: Consorcio unwittingly has become "an American" (read: conscious actor or participant in the class-and-race struggles determining his fate) "when he began to think and write lovingly" about the predicament of his fellow workers. He seized the means of representation to engender the "conscience of his race" in the possibilities opened up by historical circumstance. Nowhere was this "loving" attitude more clearly manifested than in Consorcio's solidarity with the workers of all nationalities and races in their fight for the right of self-determination. Uncannily, this change in Consorcio marks a qualitative leap that disrupts the notion of the Filipino as a passive lump, "beasts of burden" or "sex-crazed monkeys" devoid of any historicity. Thus Bulosan's humanism is not essentialist but intransigently materialist to the core.

"Be American" may then be said to posit a microcosm of the Filipino experience in the United States before World War II. It exemplifies Bulosan's sensibility as a bundle of contradictions, with the anarchist individualism of the petit bourgeois intellectual colliding with the discipline of the collective.

Petronilo Daroy, among others, has censured Bulosan for sentimentality and propensity to stress old-fashioned "human values" (1968, 202). There is indeed a backward tendency in Bulosan to succumb to metaphysics when he ignores class divisions and exalts the values of nativist communalism. This harbors a dangerous potential: the risk of endorsing a fascist mystique of the *Volk* that could be activated by the forces of reaction unless popular-democratic leadership can harness it to emancipatory ends.

Given Bulosan's background, this tendency may be inescapable. Because the content of that idea derives from the goal of national liberation, it enabled him on one hand to formulate a critique of the depersonalizing effects of bourgeois hegemony, the ultimate source of which was the exploitative market, the system of profit accumulation in general. On the other hand, it precipitated moments of despair even while he recognized that "It is dangerous for any man to live alone and to dwell in the delicate world of his mind." It drove him to conjure in certain passages of his chronicle (which might have been editorially inserted by his publisher with Bulosan's consent),[4] an imaginary space of unlimited freedoms, a cornucopia of abundance called "America" that concealed the basic antagonisms of class, gender, and race. Such utopian thinking is a token of the counterhegemonic impulses ascribable to the genre of the romance fable and its repertoire of utopian tropes. On the whole, however, this typical vacillation of the intellectual should be deemed a reflection of the living condition of the middle strata rooted in petty commodity production. It illustrates an artisanal mentality that informs the writer's craft honed in the turmoil of capitalist crisis. Bulosan lived through that interregnum described by Gramsci (1971) as a boundary zone between the dead past and the unborn future, a site where morbid symptoms of all kinds stage their macabre, pornographic dance.

In an autobiographical sketch entitled "My Education" (circa 1948), Bulosan recounts how he himself grappled with "American reality" (1995b, 124–30). A polarizing movement—one dividing into two or more trends—structures his quest, yielding a rhythmical and echoing counterpoint to Consorcio's plight in "Be American." This quest can be subsumed in the pattern of tragedy, with a vector of reversal (*peripeteia*) followed by a scene of recognition (*anagnorisis*). In Bulosan's art, however, the tragic denouement is often canceled by a comedic resolution in which the victims are empowered by their newly discovered gift of inscribing their signatures on the map of history. This is a catharsis for mobilizing, not defusing, creative energies. It accomplishes a Brechtian, not an Aristotelian, objective. It is within this framework that we can discern how Bulosan's life history discloses in its reflexive ambiance the overall significance of thousands of Consorcios, replications of the allegorical protagonist as avatar of change. Despite the excruciating nightmare of unemployment, hunger, and desperate loneliness, Bulosan preserved his faith in the 16 million unemployed and disinherited citizens. He despised the artists of the "lost generation" who fled to Paris, expelling themselves from the fecund terrain of socialist reconstruction—"America" as the reality effect of actual class wars.

I submit that a "Third World" writer like Bulosan is different from his EuroAmerican counterpart because his success in wresting control of the means of representation, the power of textualizing reality, is not a private affair; it cannot be divorced from his people's struggle to enfranchise and represent themselves as a dominated nationality. Bulosan the writer stakes the authorizing voice of the subaltern communities he speaks of, with, and for. In the final analysis, he was in quest of not a private identity but a vocation as fabulist of a transnational allegory: "I only want to expose what terror and ugliness I have seen, what shame and horror I have experienced, so that in my work, however limited in scope and penetration, others will find a reason for a deeper grievance against social injustice and a higher dream of human perfection."

There are protean aspects to his own re-presentation of himself: the persona at one moment functioning as a detached inwardness, at other moments a compatriot drawing strength and resources from the community. One cannot be fully disentangled from the other. This is why the ironical turns and repetitions crisscrossing the text of *America* render not only the circumscribed, fragmented world of the migrant worker but also the extemporizing of the imagination as it positions itself to contrive patterns and invent figures so as to shift the circulation of seemingly fated events and fixated characters onto the plane of historical contingency: "My hunger for the truth had inevitably led me to take an historical attitude. I was to understand and interpret this chaos from a collective point of view, because it was pervasive and universal" ([1946] 1973, 142). Reality, the dream betrayed, struck Bulosan full in the face. He once confessed that he could not "compromise" the picture of the United States he gleaned from the colonial textbooks with the "filthy bunkhouses" in which he and his compatriots lived, but he admitted the lesson of betrayal and sought to transcode that dream into the project of international emancipation inspired by reading noncanonical writers like Maxim Gorki, Pablo Neruda, Nicolas Guillen, Nazim Hikmet, Agnes Smedley, Theodore Dreiser, Richard Wright, Lu Hsun, Lillian Hellman, and assorted Marxist critics.

Bulosan acknowledged the catalyzing influence of progressive thinkers, anarchists, mavericks of all kinds. Of the highly eulogized modernists like Faulkner and Hemingway, he believed that "They were merely describing the disease" of U.S. society, "bestowing form on decay, not eliminating it." Bulosan asserted that "It was the duty of the artist to trace the origin of the disease that was festering American life," to diagnose the malaise that blighted the profligate imagination of Melville and Poe and locate its source in "the powerful chains and combines that strangled human life and made the world a horrible place to live in." He confessed that those books he read while he thought he was dying of tuberculosis "opened all my world of intellectual possibilities—and a grand dream of bettering society for the working man." From Gorki whom Bulosan calls "the founder of proletarian literature," he treasured a key seminal idea: Gorki showed that "We poor people in all lands are the real rulers of the world because we work and make things" whereas "Those rich bastards who kick the poor peasants around: they contribute nothing to life because they do not work. . . . Everything we see and use came from the hands of workers. . . . That is what this great Russian writer means when he said: 'Workers of the world you have nothing to lose but your chains!'" Not books in general but the ideal of liberation from class bondage was what enabled Bulosan to transvalue the repetition of victimage as well as the return to pastoral innocence that was for a time his formula for survival.

Even while Bulosan appreciated Whitman's cosmic empathy, his concern focused on the plight of people of color whose victimization became the pretext for the scenes of reversal and recognition I have noted earlier. With the closing of the western frontier, Whitman's republic evolved into an empire built on the corpses of American Indians, Mexicans, Cubans, Puerto Ricans, and Filipinos. Although the narrator-persona of *America* had picked hops with Indians near Mt. Rainier, pruned apples with poor whites in the rich deltas of the Columbia River, cut asparagus and peas with the Japanese in California and Arizona, and picked tomatoes with Negroes in Utah, this serialized cartography climaxed in his feeling that "I did not belong to America." Work to produce surplus value or profit did not coincide with the promise of the United States gathered from the colonial texts of missionaries. This experience of discordance forced Bulosan to withdraw to recuperate the submerged past, in particular the knowledge about the genesis of class/race antagonisms: "The nebulous qualities of the dream took hold of me immensely. . . . I was driven back to history." From the nightmare of the real to the awakening into history—this encapsulates the trajectory of *America*. Dream bred nostalgia; nostalgia precipitated Bulosan's fall into time. Ambiguity and paradox were resolved when the sleepwalking prophet embraced the earthbound combatant: "All these terrible humiliations gave me that courage to fight through it all, until the months passed into years of hope and the will to proceed became obdurate and illumined with a sincere affinity for America."

In the Middle of the Journey

I am grieved because [my brother] is going away; but history has determined our lives, and we must both work hard for what we believe to be the right thing for the Filipino people. . . . Our task is to live and explore the very roots of life, dig deep into the hidden fountainhead of happiness; and when we die, at last, we must die accepting death as a natural phenomenon and believing also that life is something we borrow and must give back richer when the time comes.

At the outset, Bulosan joined his brothers Dionisio and Aurelio in California in search of a life free from the poverty and oppression of rural life in Binalonan, Pangasinan, where he was born. Although Bulosan became involved in the union-organizing drives in 1933 and 1936 spearheaded by the Congress of Industrial Organizations (CIO), his radicalization began long before this, with his childhood exposure to landlord abuses in the Philippines evinced in his recollection of the Tayug uprising (memorably described in chapter 8 of *America*).[5] For a time, he collaborated with Filipino labor organizers and wrote articles for the *Philippine Journal, Commonwealth Times*, and other periodicals on behalf of striking workers. But I argue that it was his self-education in the Los Angeles Public Library and his friendship with the brilliant left-wing writer Sanora Babb and her sister Dorothy (who became intimate with Bulosan) while he was confined in the Los Angeles County Hospital (1936–1938) that largely accounts for his conversion to a socialist worldview. From 1932 to 1940, when he was alternating between public libraries and hospitals, Bulosan wrote poems and stories published in such journals as *Poetry, Lyric, Frontier* and *Midland, Tramp*, and *Voices* and later on in the *New Yorker*, where the stories in his best-selling collection *The Laughter of My Fa-*

ther (1944; hereafter *The Laughter*) first appeared. In 1952, he moved to Seattle to edit the ILWU Local 37 yearbook. During this time, he composed the novel *The Cry and the Dedication* (1995a; initially published as *The Power of the People* in 1986), probably in gestation since 1949, the outbreak of the Huk uprising in the Philippines.[6]

Unemployment, exploitation by labor contractors in the fields of Hawaii and the West Coast and in the salmon canneries of Alaska, attacks by white vigilantes, homelessness, and poverty—all these and more hounded over 100,000 Filipino migrants during the Depression. In 1934, the passage of the Tydings-McDuffie Act promising independence to the Philippines drastically curtailed Filipino emigration (to fifty a year) and the Repatriation Act of 1935 threatened Filipinos with summary deportation.

"Between 1931 and Pearl Harbor Day," Bulosan tells us that he immersed himself in the rapidly expanding labor union movement of fruit pickers and farmhands, learning and teaching (by writing) at the same time. Although Filipinos had participated in militant multiethnic strikes in Hawaii in the first two decades of the twentieth century, it was only in 1933 that they began forming the first unions and staging massive strikes in the West Coast. Carey McWilliams (1964) characterized the Filipino as "a real fighter" and his strikes "dangerous." One historian recalls the origin of the process that culminated in the formation of the United Farm Workers of America in a historic episode: "In August 1934, about 3,000 Filipinos went out on strike in the valuable lettuce fields near Salinas, California. On September 3, a union of white workers (Vegetable Packers Association Local No. 18211) employed in the packing sheds returned to work under an agreement to arbitrate. In fact they were told to return to work by Joseph Casey, an AFL official. But the Filipino workers refused to call off the strike" (McWilliams 1964, 265; see also Dewitt 1978). Because of his involvement, Bulosan became a target of physical threats; but none deterred him from his course. Up to his last days, he heeded the imperative for an organized and broad united front of all the oppressed—EuroAmerican workers and people of color—rallying behind the platform of fighting for the fundamental right of self-determination, for a just and fair distribution of social wealth, and ultimately for the overthrow of an iniquitous system of property relations.

In the crucible of uncompromising struggles with farmhands, stevedores, cannery workers, and elements of the progressive middle strata, Bulosan forged and sharpened his dialectical materialist conception of life. His fiction, poems, and essays demonstrate a practical comprehension of the contradiction between the productive forces impelling social motion and the constraining property relations. This knowledge was obscured by reactionary propaganda about abstract freedoms in the marketplace. Freedom for Bulosan was not just a formal concept or a chimera hatched by Locke, Mill, and other theoreticians of bourgeois jurisprudence. It meant something as down to earth as access to food, clothing, shelter, and other basic necessities. It is synonymous with how people actually live as concrete social beings with developing needs and aspirations.

Bulosan staunchly upheld his conviction that "We are not really free unless we use what we produce. So long as the fruit of our labor is denied us, so long will want manifest itself in a world of slaves." This eloquent statement comes from his essay "Freedom from Want" commissioned by the *Saturday Evening Post* (and published in 1943 with an illustration by Norman Rockwell) to publicize President Franklin Roosevelt's January 1941 speech on the "four freedoms." Although a half century has elapsed since then, we find Bulosan's words still valid today and even more urgently applicable to the situation of 70 million Filipinos suffering from poverty, bureaucratic corruption, and military brutality in a neocolonial formation. Wealth and privilege in the Philippines remain concentrated in the hands of a minority comprising oligarchic families—less than one percent of the population—who collaborate with transnational corporations and foreign governments to maintain their power.

In general, Bulosan contraposed his dialectical view to the mechanical and one-sided interpretation of received doxa. For him, the substance of individuality equals the totality of social relations at any given time and place. It springs from a sociohistorical process in which the needs and abilities of each person receive reciprocal esteem and validation only within the framework of mutually interacting productive forces. Thus, the free development of each individual in society depends integrally on the free development of all. Although influenced and affected by the mutable conditions in which they live, people also shape these inherited conditions and, in so doing, alter their own natures: The educators educate themselves, to echo Marx's "Theses on Feuerbach" (Marx and Engels 1968). There is then a dialectical relation between an individual's action and the objective necessities of one's lived situation. As Engels said, freedom is the recognition or appreciation of such necessities. For the radical thinker Spinoza, freedom and necessity, social potential and nature, are indivisible. Consequently, individuals make history but only within the delimited circumstances of their time, within the parameters of possibilities and constraints of a given social formation.

In the face of the Establishment dismissal of Bulosan's ideas as mere tokens of "economic determinism," we must point out that Bulosan predicates the full flowering of democratic culture and the all-round development of each person on the satisfaction of basic wants and immediate needs. This is the chief desideratum: the survival of humans as practicosensuous beings. This prerequisite is fulfilled in accomplishing the decisive tasks of a thoroughgoing social transformation of economic, political, and cultural structures leading to the actualization of a participatory socialist democracy. When Bulosan fails to make a lucid analysis of the system's internal contradictions and ignores the conflict between the exploiter and the exploited, then he regresses to the level of vacuous wish fulfillment. He calls his utopia "America," as though that label could arbitrarily be claimed by its victims without jeopardizing the critical rationality of discourse. When Bulosan confronts state troopers protecting armed thugs, scabs, and strikebreakers paid by agribusiness and banks or indicts corrupt labor contractors who preyed on their countrymen, then he elevates our consciousness to a perception of the totality and the antinomies of social motion. Thus, it is necessary to guard against the untenable opinion that Bulosan, like misguided Filipinos clamoring for statehood for the Philippines, sought the final reconciliation of colonizer and colonized in the capitalist United States. Nothing can be further from the truth.

Bulosan summed up the ordeal of his quest in "My Education." Initially, he believed that the roots he had been searching for were "not physical things but the quality of faith deeply felt and clearly understood and integrated in one's life" (1995b, 129), a "common faith" of which he could be a part. The organicist language of "roots" and "growth," combined with the image of Icarus escaping from prison, implies an orthodox reaction to what was considered at first as the horror of "technology," "crass materialism," and so forth.

After six years of encountering the same predicament and its traumatic repercussions, when his "awareness of not belonging" made him "desperate and terribly lonely" toward the end of 1935, Bulosan enacted a reorientation of principles: His support for the republican forces during the Spanish Civil War "gave coherence to the turmoil and confusion of [his] life." Such events precipitated a reaffirmation of his faith in the discipline of a revolutionary process: "The ruthless bombings of churches and hospitals by German and Italian planes clarified" and confirmed his "democratic beliefs." More important, the initiatives of the CIO reinvigorated his creative impulses. Denouncing "the false values of capitalism and the insidiousness of bourgeois prejudices," Bulosan then realized the singular lesson of his sojourn in the United States from 1930 to 1941. He finally faced his enemy, capitalism gone berserk: "Suddenly I began to see the dark forces that had uprooted me from my native land and had driven me to a narrow corner of life in America. At last the full significance of my search for roots came to me, because the war with Japan and against fascism revealed the whole meaning of the fear that had driven me as a young writer into hunger and disease and despair." In this fidelity to personal truth and its social conditions of possibility resides the emancipatory virtue of Bulosan's writings.

From the Cry to the Dedication

To listen to Scarlatti's violin solo, remembering a lost mountain village, is a beautiful and tear-provoking experience. To watch hundreds of workers building the towering scaffolding of a new bridge—well, that is breathtaking and tear-provoking too. But it would be tears of joy, seeing the magnificence of man's collective labor.

With the release of *The Laughter of My Father* in 1944, reprinted in several languages and even broadcast to the U.S. armed forces during the war, Bulosan finally enjoyed worldwide fame. Three previous books of poems, *Chorus for America* (1942), *Letter from America* (1942), and *The Voice of Bataan* (1944), went unnoticed. But his piece "Freedom from Want" made him a celebrity when it was published in the widely circulated *Saturday Evening Post* and displayed in a room of the Federal Building in San Francisco. In 1946, the publication of *America*, Bulosan's attempt to grasp the dialectic of dream and reality, climaxed this itinerary marked by the advent of the Cold War (San Juan 1979). This "social classic" deliberately blends fact and fiction to engender a unique *testimonio* of Filipino migrant lives from the twenties to the forties.

By 1947, with his face gracing the covers of national magazines, Bulosan had become the hero of a stereotyped immigrant success story that his own protagonists had tried to imagine but could not really comprehend. Now the next eight years of his life, according to some commentators, degenerated into one long train of alcoholism, illness, neurosis, and obscurity that ruined his writing career all because of a plagiarism charge brought in late 1946 and satisfactorily settled out of court. If he wrote at least two novels, numerous stories, poems, and letters after 1946, then the verdict of ruin seems premature. His relocation to Seattle testified to his active participation as union publicist and defender of the democratic rights of the whole Filipino community. And although he drank to deaden the chronic pain of his lung lesions, mitigate the loneliness resulting from his separation from the generous Babb sisters, and blunt his sensitivity to the malice of Filipino critics, I think Bulosan cannot be said to have succumbed to disaster in those fateful years, which saw the short-lived triumph of McCarthyism and the transitory eclipse of the Huk rebellion. On the contrary, he was as fertile, disarmingly unpretentious, and combative as ever.

At the height of the Cold War hysteria in the fifties, Bulosan renewed his unwavering commitment to radical change by participating in union resistance to Congressional witch-hunts and FBI surveillance. There was even a concerted attempt by the state to deport veteran activists, among them Ernie Mangaong and Chris Mensalvas, which was defeated by militant popular protest. In his editorial for the 1952 yearbook of ILWU Local 37, Bulosan asserted his thesis of a mobilized proletariat as the chief defense of democratic rights: "I believe that the unconditional unity of all workers is our only weapon against the evil designs of imperialist butchers and other profiteers of death and suffering to plunge humanity into a new world war" (1952, 4). U.S. armed aggression against the Korean people under the banner of the United Nations (prefiguring the 1991 war against Iraq!) and by proxy against Filipino workers and peasants was then in full blast.

Bulosan was intensely aware of the international configuration of forces. He affirmed once more the ethics of solidarity of all exploited groups enunciated in the poem "If You Want to Know What We Are" and in the satiric sequence of Uncle Sator didactic fables (Bulosan 1978). But, in Seattle, at this juncture, his dilemma assumed unprecedented urgency: He was no longer confronting Japanese fascism, which had brutalized his brothers and sisters at home by the time he was busy modernizing the raw material of folklore for *The Laughter*. He was now confronting the violence of finance capital ruthlessly destroying the bodies and spirits of Filipinos under the aegis of a CIA-sponsored populist hero, Ramon Magsaysay. In the ILWU yearbook, Bulosan rallied to the cause of the Huks and of Amado Hernandez, the great insurrectionary poet and union leader, who was imprisoned for alleged subversive activities such as his unwavering fight for social justice, popular democracy, and genuine national independence.

Although operating thousands of miles away from the islands, Bulosan never left the Philippines in mind and heart—he never became a U.S. citizen. In 1947, he wrote to a friend:

> The making of a great cultural heritage is so closely associated with the lives of those who make it: then, surely, we should write about them in a warm and loving way so that other generations would think of the magnitude of, say, a great epic poem with the life and times of the author.
>
> We should work like common people, absorbing, learning, remembering. It is only when we know the depth of the human soul, its tranquillity and violence, its magnificence and fragility, that we are really capable of writing something of significance and importance in men's life. The mag-

nitude of a creation of art (and other human endeavors) is measured by the suffering endured by the creator in the hour of its composition. The Philippines is undergoing a great tragedy: why are the writers not challenged by it? (Feria 1960, 233–34)

It was because Bulosan consciously wedded the Filipino people's struggle for complete and genuine independence with the migrants' efforts to oppose racist violence and persecution that in the process he discovered the resources of a critical and transformative imagination. This occurred when he was fabricating those tales in *The Laughter* that some misguided readers today consider "wacky" humor to be consumed for the benefit of the mentally fatigued. Such a discovery is essentially the central motivation, the controlling vision, of the magnificent novel, *The Cry and the Dedication* (1995a; hereafter *The Cry*)—so far the first and only sophisticated in-depth rendering of the 1949 Huk insurgency and its transcultural ramifications.

Indeed, Bulosan never left the Philippines in spirit: He joined the peasant revolt against tyrannical landlords, avaricious compradors, and corrupt bureaucrat-capitalists—the local clients/agents of the U.S. elite. One might say that he was engaged in the same struggle on two fronts. It was in this dialectic between the concrete practice of Bulosan the artist and the historical pressures of his identity-in-process as a Filipino migrant (unable to return home but also at the same time unable to make his peace with the enemy) that this novel germinated. The manuscript remained in hibernation for more than twenty years until the rise of the anti–Vietnam war movement in the seventies produced an audience for it. I hold that it is no exaggeration to claim that this novel is a substantial achievement by a Filipino artist of world stature, a countercanonical text expressing the predicament of an embattled formation such as the Philippines, a cultural performance equaled only by Rizal's novels and the poetry of Amado Hernandez.

The background of *The Cry* embraces the turbulent milieu of the early forties when the Philippines still functioned as the only direct Asian colony of the United States. It then supplied cheap raw materials and served as a market for expensive industrial goods. It was a time when intense union agitation in Manila and elsewhere signaled the rekindling of the indigenous revolutionary spirit. The onset of the Cold War not only brought forth a reactionary tide of repression but also intimated the decline of pax Americana marked by the victory of the People's Liberation Army in China in 1949 and the U.S. debacle in Korea. Meanwhile, the CIA was transplanting to Vietnam its counterinsurgency schemes tested in the Philippines. The postwar popularity of the Huks and the phenomenal growth of their peasant army may be attributed to the failure of the imperial system to stabilize a precarious order in which a privileged few battened on the misery of millions. The conjuncture of the Cold War in the late forties and early fifties for the first time afforded Bulosan that extraordinary shock of recognition in which he grasped the linkage between the national-democratic agenda of the Huks and the strikes of multiracial workers in the United States, a moment of recognition in which he seized the present as history (Libretti 1995).

In retrospect, *America* wrestled with the disjunction of past and present, of dream and reality, aspiring to project a vision of all peoples united in the crusade for freedom, justice, and equality. For Bulosan, the problem for the artist in the Cold War era is how to translate the forging of solidarity into dramatic terms, into cogent symbolic action. What we find Bulosan striving for is a transcultural allegory of actors or typical individuals establishing channels of communication, strategies of alliances. In crafting a narrative that tries to capture the mutations of ideas, wills, and desires, Bulosan borrows from the discursive archive of Marxism a precision instrument for cognitive mapping. Since the proletariat as a universal class, defined as the producer of all society's wealth and the only class that can liberate humanity from class bondage and alienation, has no country in the ultimate reckoning, Bulosan's account of peasant-worker revolts in the neocolony transcends its geographical provenance. By suturing these revolts occurring 10,000 miles from the U.S. mainland with the resistance of class-conscious, organized workers in the West Coast exploited by the racist state, Bulosan's writing praxis is able to reflect the emergent totality of the struggle against imperial capital. Specifically, this multiracial spearhead of the struggle in the U.S. during the forties derives from the antifascist popular front around the world that informs the narrator's search for a plausible coherent pattern, for some overarching purpose that would give meaning to the nomadic, deracinated existence of Filipinos in the United States.

In *The Cry*, Bulosan traces the development of the popular-democratic movement against caciquism into an anti-imperialist united front. When he writes about guerillas seeking to emancipate the masses from semifeudal bondage and marginality, he is also confronting the main source of racist violence, the incarnation of fascist barbarism: the rule of U.S. finance capital. And so it turns out that the Huk insurgency is a pretext that transcodes the struggle of oppressed people of color in "the belly of the beast." It prefigures the more difficult task of purging the beast from the colonized psyche. In the last analysis, one cannot divorce the national liberation struggle of the Filipino masses from the fight of Third World nationalities in the United States for the exercise of full democratic rights, including the right to autonomy and secession.[7]

At the peak of the Cold War, Bulosan expressed the controlling vision of his art: to realize the "grand dream of equality among men and freedom for all." What compelled him to write? His answer: "Above all and ultimately, to translate the desires and aspirations of the whole Filipino people in the Philippines and abroad in terms relevant to contemporary history" (1995b, 216). What is striking in this testament is the urge to conceive of the evolving Filipino diaspora as a unitary phenomenon, a reality effect of the dependent and distorted political economy of the Philippines in the wake of 300 years of Spanish mercantile colonialism and a half century of U.S. domination. To illustrate the depth and cogency of Bulosan's partisanship, I would like to quote at length from one of his letters, dated January 17, 1955:

> Why should I write about labor unions and their struggle? Because a writer is also a worker. He writes stories, for example, and sells them or tries to sell them. They are products of his brain. They are commodities. Then again, a writer is also a citizen; and as citizen he must safeguard his civil rights and liberties. Life is a collective work and also a social reality. Therefore the writer must participate with his fellow men in the struggle to protect, to brighten, to fulfill life. Otherwise he has no meaning—a nothing.
>
> Now culture being a social product, I firmly believe that any work of art should have a social function—to beautify, to glorify, to dignify man. This assertion has always been true, and it applies to all social systems. But always art is in the hands of the dominant class—which wields its power to perpetuate its supremacy and existence. Since any social system is forced to change to another by concrete economic forces, its art changes also to be recharged, reshaped and revitalized by the new conditions. Thus, if the writer has any significance, he should write about the world in which he lives: interpret his time and envision the future through his knowledge of historical reality. (1995b, 143)

The "sole responsibility" of interpellating a Filipino subjectivity-in-the-making coeval with the emergence of a truly sovereign nation is one that Bulosan assumed as he straddled the boundaries between two terrains, the neocolony and the imperial power. He helped move the periphery to the center in transcribing the political and ethical dilemmas of the characters in this novel. One can also propose that Bulosan's writings discharged the responsibility of unleashing the emancipatory energies locked in folklore, ethnic or indigenous tales, newspaper accounts, oral testimonies, photos, letters, journals, propaganda, and the rich bewildering texts of quotidian life—the site of warring hegemonic and oppositional inscriptions and voices, energies that can be harnessed for popular-democratic transformation. We can share in fulfilling the mandate of this responsibility. Shall we then allow imperialist diktat to silence those voices?

At the threshold of world-transforming upheavals in the fifties as pax Americana entered its epoch of decline, Bulosan summed up in this novel his ordeals and his passage through them as a conjuncture that bridged the Filipino war of resistance against U.S. imperialism at the turn of the century, the struggle of people of color in the thirties, and the communist-led Huk rebellion in the late forties and fifties. His project of social transformation was first inscribed in a suppressed revolutionary tradition that is only now being resuscitated. In his provocative idiom, which emulated if not paralleled the polemic exuberance of the 1896 *ilustrado* propagandists, Bulosan blasted "the vicious lies of the capitalist press and yellow journalism, the warmongering of big business, the race-hating hysteria of reactionary organizations" at the height of the McCarthy period. He attacked the "maniacal machinations" and "malignant designs" of the capitalist state. Such fiery words were penned by Bulosan when he was the beleaguered editor of the 1952 ILWU yearbook, a position emblematic of his quest to make the work of writing coincide with the labor of migrant workers in the North American continent and with the history of resistance of people of color everywhere.

When "Life Was Swift and Terrible in This Country"

Once I wrote a brief but beautiful piece about that world of fantasy called "To a Time Far Away" and it made me cry because what prompted me to write it was a vivid remembrance of my father's voice calling me one morning, that echoed with a soothing urgency down the valley of home. I always write about that life beautifully, but when I take another background like the U.S., I become bitter and angry and cruel. . . . If you have ever lived in one of the slums of the U.S., I know you would also be influenced by it. I lived in the slums of Los Angeles, and I never escaped its terrors, its soul-sickening atmosphere. . . . And do you know what happened to my companions? . . . What happened to me? I do not know myself.

In 1937, Bulosan felt he was dying in the city hospital in Los Angeles, California. Later on, he would have several more operations for leg cancer and lung lesions, until he was left slightly crippled, one kneecap and one kidney removed, his body frail and vulnerable. But he lived on until September 11, 1956 when, after a night of drinking with a labor lawyer who was a close friend, he wandered around the streets of Seattle; at dawn he was found comatose on the steps of the City Hall.

Was Bulosan ever haunted by the thought of his death? Like any normal person, he did reflect on the fragility of the body and its extinction, but always in the context of his vocation: "But as my body decays and slowly crumbles to uselessness, my mind becomes solid and crystallized. The most important thing for a young writer to have is health." It was not death but life that obsessed him, the struggle to preserve one's self and realize one's potential, to enjoy that freedom that comes from the wedding of intellect and nature: "It did not make me conceited that out of the slums and kitchens of California, out of the fear and hatred, the terror and hunger, the utter loneliness and death, I came out alive spiritually and intellectually! Instead it has made me humble and serious in my relations with my fellowmen."

A telling indication of the kind of civic or "social individual" Bulosan became may be discerned in this passage from a letter of April 15, 1947: "We are the only expatriates who really lived and worked with the people, and I'm very sentimental because of this fact. Sometimes I lose my historical perspective because of this sentimentality. . . . While we are all alive we must try to understand each other, give each other confidence, help, happiness and goodness." The theme of concern for the Other is further elaborated in a letter to his nephew in which he mentions his mother's approaching death: "It is good to cry. But don't let sorrow kill your life. We will all die: it is only in the affection that we give to each other when we are still alive that keeps the world moving" (March 8, 1948). In another letter, Bulosan counsels that "we all die, rich or poor, brown or white; that any time is as good as any other to you. But while I say all this to you, Fred, try always to seek the goodness in your fellow man. That is the greatest wealth of all: goodness. And beauty, too. The beauty that you find in all good things" (April 1, 1948).[8]

In spite of Bulosan's reiterated faith in life as "a continuum of desire, with shifting limits that are always displaced" (to borrow phrases from Deleuze and Guattari), the rumor is still around that Bulosan languished in "poverty, alcohol, loneliness, and obscurity," a canard no longer worth dignifying. Not negativity or a "sense of foreboding and despair" after the atomic bombs annihilated thousands in Hiroshima and Nagasaki but a trusting, bold, rapturous warmth suffuses the following excerpt from a letter of December 31, 1947: "Our task is to live and explore the very roots of life, dig deep into the hidden fountainhead of happiness; and when we die, at last, we must die accepting death as a natural phenomenon and believing also that life is something we borrow and must give back richer when the time comes." Amid the holocaust of the Korean War and the counterinsurgency carnage in the Philippines, Bulosan's thinking pursued the task of proposing alternatives that were not utopian but realizable because they inhered in the dream of a society of creative, enlightened participants:

Human life could truly be a paradise, in many respects, if the money spent for destruction were used for the elimination of disease, schools propagating tolerance, factories for necessary consumer goods, and research centers, clinics, hospitals, maternity wards, etc. In fact, we would have a Department of Peace in the cabinet, instead of a Department of War. Hate, greed, selfishness—these are not human nature. These are weapons of destruction, evolved by generations of experimenters in the service of ruling groups, be it a tribe, a clan, a prince, a king, a democracy. These destructive elements have finally become so subtle, so intricate, so deeply rooted in men's minds in our time, the era of international finance, that many people sincerely, though ignorantly, believe them to be the guiding forces of nature. Love, kindness, pity, tolerance, happiness, beauty, truth—these are the real human nature from which a galaxy of other relevant virtues spring, take root and flourish in manifold form in what we call brotherhood or common humanity, as the ideal of honest men in the world. (March 21, 1953)

Earlier, in 1948 and 1949, he wrote to his close friends:

Genius is not the sole property of one race or one class of men; and the possession of a soul which indicates the ability to appreciate the truth and beauty in all things belongs to everyone and to no one. . . .
   Writing is a pleasure and a passion to me—I seem to be babbling with multitudinous ideas, but the body is tired and weak. . . .
   What drives me is the force of the idea, the historical fact. (1995b, 180)

It was not death, neurosis, or obscurity that menaced Bulosan's texts—the militant activism of the late sixties and seventies resurrected these texts and unleashed their vernacular force—but the persistent exclusionary law of the EuroAmerican canon and its hegemonic reach. In 1953, he wrote:

What is this struggle? To live a little longer with the minimum of pain, close to each other in peace, and to contribute what we can toward the elevation of the human spirit. So short, so brief, so little is the infinite flame of life in all its forms—this is our life on this planet. Why do we hate and kill each other when we are going to die sooner or later? Where are the conquerors of yesteryears?
   Now when I write anything I am always propelled by the main forces of life and society . . . and now realize the heroism of men to make the world a better, happier place. (1995b, 182)

After Bulosan's death, his works were relegated to the museum precinct of Filipiniana. Judged from the sophistry of New Critical formalism that synchronized with the U.S.-led Cold War strategy of containing Third World revolutions, Bulosan's writings may appear trite and pedestrian compared to the sophistication of Jose Garcia Villa or Nick Joaquin. With their characteristic imperialist hauteur, U.S. critics of this persuasion usually dismiss *The Laughter*, for instance, as merely a potboiler dispensing "local color," a tourist brochure featuring a montage of quaint native customs and exotic costumes. One example would be the accusation by Leonard Casper (1966) that Bulosan is foisting on a gullible public "the oversimplified image of the Filipino as Peter Pan or as the lovable village idiot." With such superficial and glib observations, the high priests of bourgeois high culture flaunt their contempt of Bulosan's satire and wit, a craft designed for the conscienticization of the oppressed. This has been the fate of Bulosan in the hands of the reigning arbiters of literary taste, both local and foreign— until his rediscovery by the "third wave" of immigrants and the youthful generation of Filipino Americans growing up in the sixties and early seventies, radicalized by the praxis of the massive civil rights and antiwar movements in solidarity with people of color in Indochina, Cuba, Grenada, Iran, Angola, Mozambique, Chile, and elsewhere.[9]

Overturning the Patriarchal Law

I am not old enough to look back with nostalgia, but because I am away from home I have a longing for everything that was lovely and happy. It may be that I shall never again see my country, but I feel strong and powerful and immortal in the thought that I can still remember fragments of my childhood. I know that the years have somehow made me love my country more.

The stories in *The Laughter* and *The Philippines Is in the Heart* (1978) exhibit a wide range of themes and rhetorical inventiveness testifying to Bulosan's versatile craft. In an erudite essay, L. M. Grow (1995) calls attention to the trickster motif in *The Laughter* and the erotic charge of its folkloric themes. When his reviewers dismissed him as a mere purveyor of local color and exotic humor (proof of an unconscionable philistinism recently revived by P. C. Morantte and other "old-timers" who are pathetically trying to cash in on Bulosan's prestige), Bulosan responded (in a letter to a friend dated April 8, 1955) in terms that these carping readers might call pedantic or highbrow:

My politico-economic ideas are embodied in all my writings, but more concretely in my poetry. Here let me remind you that *The Laughter* is not humor; it is satire; it is indictment against an economic system that stifled the growth of the primitive, making him decadent overnight without passing through the various stages of growth and decay. The hidden bitterness in this book is so pronounced in another series of short stories, that the publishers refrained from publishing it for the time being.

In numerous essays, particularly "My Education," "I Am Not A Laughing Man," "The Growth of Philippine Culture," and others, Bulosan unequivocally asserted his fundamental Marxist orientation. Anyone trying to interpret and assess the texts for their emancipatory value can dismiss this at the risk of superimposing their own parochial prejudices and know-nothing anti-intellectualism. In a letter of January 8, 1950, for instance, he stated, "I have tried to explain our cultural growth from a materialist point of view. . . . What I am trying to do, especially in my writings since I left Stockton, is to utilize our common folklore, tradition, and history in line with my socialist thinking." Bulosan's intention is further elaborated in a letter of January 17, 1955:

> Filipino writers in the Philippines have a great task ahead of them, but also a great future. The field is wide and open. They should rewrite everything written about the Philippines and the Filipino people from the materialist, dialectical point of view—this being the only [way] to understand and interpret everything Philippines. They should write lovingly about its rivers, towns, plains; mountains, wildernesses—its flora and fauna—the different tribes and provinces. They should write about the great men and their times and works, from Lapulapu to Mariano Balgos. They should compile the unwritten tales, legends, folklore, riddles, humor, songs, sayings. They should illustrate that there was a culture before the Spaniards uprooted it. When these are written, they should extenuate and amplify. The material is inexhaustible. But always they should be written for the people, because the people are the creators and appreciators of culture.

Such words are not to be taken lightly or disposed of as "egghead radicalism," a fatuous quip that is the trademark of a certain bankrupt cynicism.[10]

In his ventriloquial article "I Am Not A Laughing Man," Bulosan registers his refusal to be stereotyped as a procurer of cartoon humor for a commercial audience. He traces the genealogy of his stories in the workplace, in their genesis from his anger at the conditions of his compatriots, especially from his anger at people who laughed when they read *The Laughter*. Incidentally, his "anger" reveals itself also as an expression of rivalry, a desire to outdo the fame of William Saroyan and Thomas Wolfe. The fable of authorship traced here via metonymy and spatial relays epitomizes what Deleuze (1993) would call the "rhizomatic" mode of deterritorialization, a rupture of the social field that "minor" literature invariably adopts to thwart the totalizing power of hegemonic discourse.

In another essay, "How My Stories Were Written," Bulosan revealed "the compelling force that propelled me from an obscure occupation to the rewarding writing of short stories. That force was anger born of a rebellious dissatisfaction with everything around me" (1995b, 109). Again here Bulosan invents a scenario of legitimation, an originary myth: He evokes the image of Apo Lacay, the fountainhead of all the stories he has recounted, so that the author is conceived of primarily as a transmitter or conveyor of the collective wisdom and history of a people. In invoking the old man's presence, Bulosan summons an image of the community maturing through struggle and sacrifice. The wisdom and pleasure of resistance find a voice in how Apo Lacay lived all the tales he had told generations of listeners "about a vanished race, listening to the gorgeous laughter of men in the midst of abject poverty and tyranny. For that was the time of his childhood, in the age of great distress and calamity in the land, when the fury of an invading race impaled their hearts in the tragic cross of slavery and ignorance" (1995b, 113—14). But he puzzled outsiders, for he was "now living in the first murmurs of a twilight and the dawn of reason and progress, was the sole surviving witness of the cruelty and dehumanization of man by another man, but whose tales were taken for laughter and the foolish words of a lonely old man who had lived far beyond his time" (1995b, 114). What Bulosan is striving to communicate here recalls to mind what George Bernard Shaw once said to a philistine audience: His jokes were all deadly serious.

Although I am not denying the humor of Bulosan's tales that stem mainly from our perception of incongruities, exaggerations, and witty deflations of pretense, I think it is ill-informed reductionism to narrow their appeal to mere visceral reflex. It is also a mistake to conflate humor with the function of satire and, more important, with the psychological catharsis and political aim of comedy as a cultural genre and social institution. Satiric exposure of vice and folly cannot be reduced to comic book humor, nor can the reconciling rituals of comedy and its pedagogical thrust be trivialized as formulaic routine acts stimulating hilarity or good clean fun.

Like Chaucer or Boccaccio, though under much more adverse conditions, Bulosan translated into practice a serious and even programmatic commitment: the trenchant exposure of excesses of all kinds, injustice, hypocrisy, perverse customs, and other social ills. Through such oblique modes of hyperbole, understatement, techniques of ironic juxtaposition, ribald dialogue, burlesque characterization, bawdy situations, and so on, the writer of "My Father Goes to Court" or "The Capitalism of My Father" (Bulosan, 1944) denounced feudal exploitation and colonial abuses normalized in the micropolitics of peasant life. The narrative style of Bulosan's fables had the burden of delivering a criticism of class-determined norms and practices through the portrayal of concrete types (to be distinguished from stereotypes) that reflected the vicissitudes of diverse historical contradictions in the Philippines during four decades of U.S. rule. Whether through the genre of fantasy (as in "The Angel of Santo Domingo" or "The Lonesome Mermaid") or its variants, the uncanny and marvelous forms (as in the stories "The Amorous Ghost Came to Town" and "The Rooster's Egg"), Bulosan (1978) explored the vagaries of folk/plebeian experience. He did not set out to contrive mechanical recordings of local mores or fake photographs of village idiots, rogues, and clowns. Rather, he fashioned highly stylized or gestural (in Brecht's sense) analogues of action possessing morally determinate qualities with the intention of provoking not just laughter but also critical judgments and corrective actions. Pursuing the logic of this method, he subordinated realistic plausibility to the demands of critique and of mobilizing his readers' intelligence even though the camouflage of comic wit might distract them from the larger and deeper purposes he had in mind.

Unlike the fabrications of *The Laughter,* the stories in *The Philippines Is in the Heart* convey the more acerbic resonance of Swiftian satire, of the "hidden bitterness" that Bulosan referred to in a letter I quoted earlier. In "The Betrayal of Uncle Soyoc" or "The Homecoming of Uncle Manuel," the figure of Uncle Sator displaces the heroic patriarch of *The Laughter.* He assumes the role of tribal trickster whose duplicity and callous greed victimize the other uncles, disintegrate the clan, and corrupt the whole village. Whereas the father is partly the redemptive agent of the victims and partly the neutralizer of jokes, a resilient incarnation of the life principle, here Uncle Sator condenses impulses of greed, sadistic opportunism, cruel indifference, egotism, and deception that to a large extent characterize the machinations of the native oligarchy and their flunkies. Folklore revitalized here thus vindicates the father (castrated by Western aggression) by transferring the patriarchal role to the unscrupulous *padrino,* the rich unmarried uncle, who knows neither obligation nor duty but only the gratification of his needs.

Viewed from the framework of Mikhail Bakhtin's (1968) theory of the carnivalesque exemplified by Rabelais's oeuvre, however, Uncle Sator personifies a ludic principle shattering the boundaries of social conventions, laws, traditional morality, and contracts. This comic figure mocks all officially sanctioned rules that stifle the instincts and inhibit the flow of polymorphous drives. The uncle-hero as trickster with a liminal status can also be conceived as a sublimation of the outcasts and subalterns driven underground by a repressive system. He functions as a symbol of the generative force of the earth and of nature in general. Although the play of the erotic drive ruffles the narrative surface of *The*

Laughter but does not threaten the safety of the readers, the narrator of the Uncle Sator cycle takes great risks to offend and even shock. What this uncle embodies is nothing less than the urge to consume and the appetite to occupy others' territories and to pillage them—a parodic mirror image of imperial conquest. The drive to accumulate and transform wealth into a fetish predominates as a subversive current destroying orthodox pieties. It is an obsession countered only by the power of music freely offered by the nephew, whose aesthetic gift in turn reduces money to nullity. Indeed, this Orphic motif of art as a weapon against despotism and reification decenters the coherence of the stories by its arbitrary, non sequitur appearance. On the whole, the Uncle Sator cycle targets the monolith of a political economy centered on money, the cash nexus, the circulation of exchange value (versus use value) that underpins the ideology of individual freedom and comprador fascism sustained by U.S. military and economic aid.

In one sequence of stories, we encounter angels serving as androgynous agents of change (as in "The Lovely Angel" or "The Angel in Santo Domingo). One can discern here the contraposition of the pleasure principle (sexuality) and the death drive (fetishized money). In combining the supernatural with the erotic (as in "Amorous Ghost"), Bulosan tries to envisage the refusal of what exists, namely the status quo of a dehumanizing society in which feelings are deformed by reduction to cash and everything of value (psyches as well as bodies) converted to commodities. Although it is possible to gloss this as a way of instrumentalizing the conservative reflex of the folk to block secularizing pressures, one can also consider it a device of ideological critique. Like the intrusion of the trickster, the artist's preferred persona, into a milieu of scarcity and injustice, stories that stage the irruption of the irrational (the humanity negated by exchange) in the degraded routine of everyday life may serve to foreground the crisis of existing social relations. They intuitively gesture to the breaks and gaps where radical transformations can push through. These thematic ambiguities sutured together by the generic laws of comic satire then become the source of discordant messages enunciated by various critics who are themselves determined by the critical frameworks they operate. Such frameworks also act as the conditions of possibility enabling alternative discriminations.

Pursuing this track of investigation, one can apply the neo-Aristotelian concept of the *apologue* or Kenneth Burke's (1964) notion of "perspectives by incongruity" to elucidate the precise nature of Bulosan's project and the resources it deploys. Another instructive critical apparatus can be drawn from structuralism, for example, Tzvetan Todorov's (1981) schema for delineating the genre of the fantastic that hinges on "that hesitation experienced by a person who knows only the laws of nature, confronting an apparently supernatural event," and its corollaries, the species of the uncanny and of the marvelous. But since form is only a moment of content embedded in the total artistic configuration, I think it is necessary to ground the hermeneutic enterprise—if we do not repudiate it altogether—in a materialist conception of society to insure an all-sided, balanced estimate of any writer's achievement. At any rate, the poststructuralist approach espoused by Barthes, Kristeva, and others seems more open-ended but ultimately less historically plausible than Deleuze and Guattari's (1986) theory of "minor" writing extrapolated from Kafka's textual practice.

What does it mean to say that Bulosan's writing is "minor"? It means that his "machine" of expression is one that privileges the immanence of desire in history. It opposes teleology, the transcendence of an impersonal law, subjectivity, and naturalistic representation. It is designed to subvert the Oedipalizing code of the archetypal father (colonial bureaucracy, feudal hierarchy, and imperial capital, which have dethroned the native father) by inventing a montagelike concatenation of incidents that defies organic continuity. The destruction of the social order, the erosion of its authority, occurs when the narrator as subject of enunciation traces a line of escape, a becoming-trickster or becoming-exile, that negates the signified subject position (the dutiful son, the serflike tenant); this nomadic schizoid line in turn disrupts the sedentary Oedipalizing line and inaugurates the space for a range of multiple actions—an ensemble of possibilities, opportunities for schisms, reversals, interventions. Against centralizing interiority, idols and icons, mimetic representation, the metaphysics of state and private property, Bulosan's signifying machine assembles molecular indices and intensities so as to dismantle the apparatuses of hegemonic power (bourgeois textuality, negativity, aestheticism). It endeavors to plot the trajectory of immanent desire from the prisons to the frontiers of an interminable, liberating continuum of joy. In this light, we begin to appreciate why Bulosan, in his challenging poem "If You Want to Know What We Are," called revolution "the desires of anonymous men everywhere" (1995b, 167).

Beyond "Manifest Destiny"

I only want to expose what terror and ugliness I have seen, what shame and horror I have experienced, so that in my work, however limited in scope and penetration, others will find a reason for a deeper grievance against social injustice and a higher dream of human perfection.

On the eve of World War II, Bulosan reviewed the past and took his bearings before entering the bountiful period of *The Laughter* and *America*:

> It is almost impossible for a Filipino to write like himself, to be a part of the great American arena of writing, because he is always a Filipino, he is always a slave to his country's traditions and history. . . . Living in America, I can't escape from its doom. That is why sometimes in my writing, in my poetry and stories, the pangs and anxieties of a doomed society are visible. I can't escape from society, but I can't also escape from my country's history. These two forces make me hysterical as a living person and as a writer trying to explain my life in a doomed society. (March 1, 1941)

This was also a poignant anticipation of the divided self of the protagonists in *The Cry* and the dilemma of the traitor-paramour that always haunted him up to the end of his life: "the agonies of a Filipino lover loving a white woman in America" (Feria 1960, 235).

Looking back ten years after the anti-Filipino riots, Bulosan summed it all up in a letter of March 8, 1948: "In those days, life was swift and terrible in this country. . . . It was the beginning of my life of terror, my defiance against a system that treated human beings like rotten animals. . . . We have lived in a changing time, when confusion reigned supreme. And that was our gain from it all: we were able to see through the darkness of our time into another period where happiness could reign supreme." Observing the amnesia that afflicted Filipinos in the United States and how elitist professionals among them took pride in their subservience, Bulosan tried to remind the community of the sources of their passion, creativity, and hope. They spring from the common resistance to capital both in the United States and at home, in the life of the insurgent masses, in the national heritage of centuries of revolt against tyranny that those who claim to be Filipino cannot renounce, a legacy irresistibly affirmed or betrayed in one's thoughts and deeds. This task of shaping a historical imagination for the community impelled Bulosan to articulate his commitment to the cause of the multiethnic proletariat conceived as a universal class whose world mission is to destroy the basis of class oppression.

> But we must be born again, I guess, to find a place in [the post–World War II world]. We must reconstruct our thinking and living in order to be of use in its realization. . . . Like most serious artists I believe that content and form are inseparable elements of good artistic creation: one generates the other, but both are generated by a noble theme of universal significance. I do not believe that art is alien to life: it is a crystallized reflection of life, deepened or heightened by our individual perceptions and sensibilities. (Feria 1960, 228)

Bulosan's writings indisputably belong to the corpus of world proletarian writing that functions today as a cultural weapon in the hands of the insurgent masses in their fight against a moribund neocolonial (not postcolonial) system, for the goals of instituting participatory democracy and a caring, cooperative society. In this context, intertextuality annuls neutrality. What informs the technique, style, organizing premises, and philosophical assumptions of Bulosan's finest works is the cardinal principle underscored by Mao Tse-tung in his classic manifesto, *Talks at the Yenan Forum on Literature and Art*: "In the world today all culture, all literature and art belong to definite classes and are geared to definite political lines" (1960, 86). All art is inherently political, though highly mediated. Every discourse promotes the interests of one class or group against another, though the mode of expression or representation varies from the mimetic and illusionistic to the reflexive and didactic depending on the imperatives of the sociohistorical moment. As Bulosan counseled the radical poet Amado Hernandez, imprisoned by the comprador government for sympathizing with the Huk rebellion: "Every word is a weapon for freedom" (1983a, 17).

All of Bulosan's writings strive to explore the specific historical contradictions of his age, elaborating the major themes of class struggle in the era of late capitalism. They seek to elucidate the forms of alienation and subjugation in a dependent society, the forces that atomize individuals and block the emergence of class and national solidarity. Particularly in *America* as well as the Uncle Sator cycle, Bulosan seizes on the nodes or conjunctures of diverse social forces at the moment when residual and dominant institutions, habits, and values collapse, battered by new dissident ideas, by oppositional emergent "structures of feeling." Probing "the idea behind the historical fact," Bulosan seeks to exhibit the dynamic tendencies that constitute what Georg Lukács (1973) calls "the intellectual physiognomy of character" and its subversive resonance. His stories project an image of the Filipino as a self-critical, resourceful actor. They foreground the migrant ensemble as a collective agency resisting the dehumanizing onslaught of the fascist United States, its mystifications and violence, by being able to distance himself from his situation so as to interrogate and negate it. Bifurcated by his transplantation to an inimical environment, the Filipino in Bulosan's texts preserves his integrity via a metathesis of local knowledge, kinship interaction, and personal experience. Dialogic subterfuge and affiliation supersede discrepant translocality.

One central obsession pervading Bulosan's oeuvre is the will to vindicate the principle of the historical determination of art. This is accomplished through the strategic conjunction of opposites, in particular between metaphysical thinking and the violence of a class-torn society from which such thinking cannot be extricated. In the process, his art subverts the widely diffused bourgeois notion that supranatural forces dictate what's going on in the world. On the contrary, Bulosan would argue, the actual dynamics of class conflict imbricated in the national liberation struggle afford the only valid measure for ascertaining the value of any theory or idea. It is social practice, not correspondence to transcendental forms or an abstract standard, that substantiates or refutes the validity of any conception of life. And at the core of social practice is partisan commitment:

> And these are times that demand of the writer to declare his positive stand—his supreme sacrifice—on the question of war or peace, life or death. The writer who sides with and gives his voice to democracy and progress is a real writer, because he writes to protect man and restore his dignity. He writes so that this will be a world of mutual cooperation, mutual protection, mutual love; so that darkness, ignorance, brutality, exploitation of man by another, and deceit will be purged from the face of the earth. A writer should be political also. Governments or states are always in the hands of the ruling classes, and so long as there are states, there are also tyrannies. In a bourgeois state, under capitalism or imperialism, the tyranny is against the working class, against the majority. (1995b, 143)

Bulosan's art thus aims to uphold the view that humans inhabit concrete historical formations that are ultimately conditioned by overlapping modes of production—how people produce and reproduce their own existence, uneven formations that harbor manifold contradictions. And it is this collective effort of humans to transform their natural-social worlds to satisfy needs and desires that determines the constellation of norms, values, epistemes, and paradigms that operate in a constantly changing milieu.

> We must destroy that which is dying, because it does not die of itself. We must interpret the resistance against the enemy by linking it with the stirring political awakening of the people and those liberating progressive forces that call for a complete social consciousness. (1995b, 211)

Today, Bulosan's writings serve as militant witness to the protracted endeavor of Filipino peasants, women, workers, ethnic groups, and middle strata to free themselves from neocolonial barbarism, from the unrelenting exploitation of transnational capital. Bulosan was not only a courageous witness, the conscience of his community; he was also a battle-tested protagonist in the confrontation between warring classes on several fronts: between the multinational proletariat and the privileged minority of U.S. finance capital, between Third World subjects and the racial elite of the industrialized nation-states of Europe and North America. To the end of his life, Bulosan tried to fuse both the political imperative of art serving the masses through the popularization of egalitarian principles and the artistic demand for coherence, plausibility, and evocativeness. The synthesis he achieved was an uncompromising and lucid critique of the ironies, discrepancies, and paradoxes of social life. His purpose was to convince, persuade, instigate people to action. Although he died about a decade before his compatriots initiated the epoch-making Delano grape strike in 1965, Bulosan may be said to have already prefigured that event in his creation of oppositional actors in his fiction, in the invention of socially typical characters, incidents, and destinies that registered both the constructive and destructive tendencies of his epoch.

From the vantage point of this turn-of-the-century appraisal of his career, I consider Bulosan a revolutionary artist whose significant contribution to constructing the narrative of popular-democratic liberation inheres in his project of rearticulating the Filipino cultural heritage in a new direction. One goal of this project is to purge the colonial poison from the mentality of his migrant compatriots, a poison that then disguised itself with the labels "identity crisis," "culture shock," "marginality," transmigrant doubleness, and so forth. Colonial ideology in general functions as an obscurantist miasma shrouding the objectively existing condition of exploitation of people of color; in the process it reproduces and legitimizes the contradiction between the labor that produces social wealth and the private control of that wealth by a privileged minority. This miasma of surveillance and control can only be dissipated by grounding one's life on native soil, in the body of a nation materializing from the convergence of individual acts of revolt. And so he counseled his nephew: "If some day you discover that you are a genius, do not misuse your gift; apply it toward the safeguarding of our great heritage, the grandeur of our history, the realization of our great men's dream for a free and good Philippines. That is real genius; it is not selfish; it sacrifices itself for the good of the whole community. We Filipinos must be proud that we had the greatest genius in Jose Rizal, who sacrificed his life and happiness for the people" (April 1, 1948). Contra the amnesia of the colonized ego and the seductiveness of monadic consumption, Bulosan reminded his nephew to "never forget your town, your people, your country, wherever you go. Your greatness lies in them."

For a decolonizing expatriate like Bulosan whose vocation is complicit with the fate of his people, the responsibility of the writer is "to find in our national struggle that which has a future" since "literature is a growing and living thing." Writing then acts as the midwife to a cultural renaissance. The old world is dying, a new world is being born from the ruins of the old—such is Bulosan's crucial insight into the birth of the Filipino nation, a birth in which the spirit of national solidarity can be mobilized to sustain and energize the sharpening class consciousness of workers and peasants.

It might have been difficult then for the U.S. public and even for a Filipino audience now to grasp the import of this message, especially given the suspicion of plagiarism and innuendoes of Bulosan's alcoholism and despondency spread by well-meaning admirers as well as sycophants of the manipulated media. What is exceptional is that Bulosan did not waste his energies repudiating those malicious rumors; moreover, he never compromised his commitment to an agenda of socialist reconstruction that he reaffirmed a few years before his death even as he envisaged in his novel the exile's fidelity to the homeland of the imagination: "I felt that I would be ineffectual if I did not return to my own people. I believed that my work would be more vital and useful if I dedicated it to the cause of my own people" (1995b, 180).

Bulosan's life recapitulates the complex, often tragicomic unfolding of Filipino life in the United States in the crucial decades between World War I and the Cold War. He is by consensus the first Filipino writer from the colonial working class (with roots in the peasantry) who succeeded in capturing in language the savage truth of national, racial, and class oppression of Asians and other people of color, in recording the twists and turns of their struggle. But unfortunately what we call "the Filipino experience" has been mystified by countless scholars and opportunist "leaders" of the community; it has been reduced to a pathetic willingness to be assimilated. This tendency ignores and even denigrates the other aspect of this experience, namely, the persistent struggle of the community to affirm its national identity, which has up to now been either suppressed or displaced to a struggle for reforms to improve individuals' position in the racially stratified system.[11]

In his art Bulosan envisioned the contours of a socialist society that would spring from the political awakening of the U.S. multinational working class, an event that could be precipitated by the defeat of imperialism by the armed organized masses in the Third World.

Bulosan died before the popular-democratic victories in Cuba, Vietnam, Nicaragua, and several countries in Africa. In his 1952 ILWU yearbook editorial, he asserted that "The fundamental principles of our union are the mainsprings of a society" centered on "the collective interest and welfare of the whole people." In an earlier testament of his convictions, he declared: "Writing was not sufficient. Labor demanded the active collaboration of writing. . . . I drew inspiration from my active participation in the worker's movement. The most decisive move that the writer could make was to take his stand with the workers." In his allegorical and mimetic dramatizations of how Filipino workers united with progressive sections of U.S. society in their fight against predatory capital, in his affirmation that workers and people of color in metropolis and periphery constitute the principal motive force in the making of world history, Bulosan rendered a powerful articulation of the vast potential of "the wretched of the earth" to transform exploitative structures and uncover the wellspring of freedom, beauty, and goodness in the self-renewing creativity of labor.

For all these reasons, Bulosan's name today has come to symbolize the implacable revolutionary spirit of Third World people everywhere combating racist oppression and exploitation by transnational capital, fighting for the right to self-determination, for justice and authentic human dignity. Empowering the oppressed and celebrating the sanctity of life, Bulosan's works will endure to give pleasure and knowledge and above all to disturb the peace of tyrants and nourish the spirit of revolt. I consider it permanently timely to summon the specter of Filipino resistance (via Bulosan's voice) to haunt the pacified regions in the North American continent where the cries of victims now laid to rest still reverberate.

I was completely disillusioned when I came to know this American attitude [of race hatred]. . . . I shall never forget what I have suffered in this country because of racial prejudice.

In spite of everything that has happened to me in America I am not sorry that I was born a Filipino. When I say "Filipino" the sound cuts deep into my being—it hurts. . . .

I will never forget you: never. I will never forget what you have given me. I hope you are happy. As for myself, I don't care if I am happy or not.

I am proud that I am a Filipino. I used to be angry, to question myself. But now I am proud. . . . Everywhere I roam I listen for my native language with a crying heart because it means my roots in this faraway soil; it means my only communication with the living and those who died without a gift of expression. My dear brother, I remember the song of the birds in the morning, the boundless hills of home, the sound of the language. (San Juan 1995b, 209; Feria 1960, 269)

5

Resistance, Intervention, Deliverance

Lessons from Philip Vera Cruz

It is now time for the light of truth to shine; it is now time for us to show that we have feelings, honor, shame and mutual coopera- tion. . . . Therefore, O my countrymen! let us open the eyes of our minds and voluntarily consecrate our strength to what is good in the true and full faith that the prosperity of the land of our birth, which is aimed at, will come to pass.

Andres Bonifacio

Before Spain ceded its southeast Asian colony to the United States in December 1898, the revolutionary government headed by Emilio Aguinaldo sent Felipe Agoncillo, a nationalist intellectual, to rally progressive forces in the United States to support the Filipino national liberation struggle. Unless one considers Agoncillo the pioneer, the first radical Filipinos in U.S. territory were the preunion militants in the sugar plantations of Hawaii. One of them was Pedro Calosa, who helped his brother organize (circa early 1920s) an association called Be-ginning of Progress that planned a general strike of workers (Sturte-vant 1976, 273). After a prison term, he was deported in 1927 back to the Philippines where he led the 1931 anti-imperialist and antifeudal peasant insurrection in Tayug, Pangasinan.

Recruited mainly by the Hawaiian Sugar Planters Association, the early Filipinos were sojourners with peasant or proletarian roots. The main historic figure among them was Pablo Manlapit, who spear-headed the organization of the Filipino Federation of Labor in 1911 and the Filipino Unemployed Association in 1913. In 1919, their members formed the Higher Wages Association to demand better pay and working conditions, including eight weeks of paid maternity leave for women. On January 19, 1920, 2,600 Filipinos struck ahead of their Japanese counterparts; they were later joined by Spaniards and Puerto Ricans, their combined strength reaching 8,000. To counter charges of anti-Americanism, 3,000 Japanese and Filipino strikers marched in Honolulu carrying U.S. flags; pictures of Lincoln; and signs such as "We Are Not Reds, God Forbid, But Are Brown Workers Who Produce White Sugar," "We Want to Live Like Americans," and so forth (Chan 1991, 85–86). When open union agitation was prohibited, Filipinos resorted to establishing secret, nationalist-oriented societies (with rituals and secret initiation ceremonies modeled after freemasonry) for mutual aid, among them the Legionarios del Trabajo, Gran Oriente Filipino, and the Caballeros de Dimasalang.

With the decrease of Japanese labor in Hawaii and California, the Filipinos became the chief Asian group that engaged in labor agitation in politically repressive environments. When Manlapit was arrested in September 1924, Filipinos staged massive actions in Hanapepe plantation, Kauai, which the police fired upon, killing sixteen, with many others wounded. Manlapit was tried, convicted, and later freed in 1927 on condition that he never return to Hawaii. In 1932, he returned to Hawaii from California and revived the Filipino Federation of Labor with the help of Manuel Fagel and Epifanio Taok. (Manlapit was subsequently arrested and deported to the Philippines.) With the help of two organizers from the American Communist Party (Chan 1991, 87), Fagel mounted the last "ethnic" strike at Puunene in 1937. He was beaten up by the police, who defied the protest of the Congress of Industrial Organizations (CIO). Before the CIO appeared, only the Industrial Workers of the World extended solidarity to Filipinos.

The Japanese American activist Karl Yoneda (1988) names Danny Roxas as one of the eight Communist Party members who, in 1930, tried to organize 10,000 Mexican, Japanese, and Filipino field-workers in the Imperial Valley, California. All of them were arrested, convicted, and imprisoned under the criminal syndicalism law.

In 1933, 4,000 Filipino lettuce pickers in Salinas and Stockton, California, formed the Filipino Labor Union (FLU) when the American Federation of Labor (AFL) refused their plea for help. In 1934, the Filipinos merged with the Vegetable Packers Association and struck in Monterey County; later, the association rejected the FLU because it was branded as a Communist-front group by the farm owners (Dewitt 1978, 11). Severe repression—from arrests to violent burning of the workers' camps—forced the Filipinos to end their strike.

In his quasi-documentary ethnobiography, *America Is in the Heart* ([1946] 1973), Carlos Bulosan recounted the CIO-led activities of Filipinos during the Depression (San Juan 1986). He cited the participation of Filipino members of the Communist Party, assisted by individuals like Alice and Eileen Odell; Dora Travers (a member of the Young Communist League); and Anna Dozier, who collaborated with the "first Filipino Communist" in Los Angeles (1973 [1946], 267). Bulosan cooperated with the legendary Chris Mensalvas, who was instrumental in forming the United Cannery, Agricultural, Packing and Allied Workers of America (UCAPAWA). Bulosan contributed to *New Masses* and edited a left newspaper, *The New Tide,* and later the yearbook of the International Longshoremen's and Warehousemen's Union (ILWU), Local 37, in Seattle, Washington (San Juan 1995a, 38). Filipinos also figured prominently in the ILWU 1946 strike in Hawaii (Takaki 1989, 407–11).

In 1940, the AFL chartered the Federated Agricultural Laborers Association of Filipino farm-workers after it led a series of strikes. In the Alaskan salmon-canning industry, Filipinos were exceptionally active in 1933 and 1936. Ernie Mangaong was elected to head the Seattle-based Cannery Workers and Farm Laborers Union. In 1938, the union got rid of the corrupt system of labor contractors. In the sixties, Larry Itliong and Philip Vera Cruz, who headed the Filipino Agricultural Workers Organizing Committee, launched the historic 1965 grape strike in Delano, California, that led to the founding of the United Farm Workers of America.

At the height of the McCarthy era, seven Filipino leftists with the ILWU Local 7 (among them, the veteran leaders Ernie Mangaong and Chris Mensalvas) faced deportation on charges of Communist Party membership. This included Simeon Bagasol, an ILWU member in Hawaii. Only with the massive support of liberals and communities of people of color were their cases won finally in 1955 (Vera 1994).

In the twenties, Vicente Lava, a distinguished intellectual who later became general secretary of the Communist Party of the Philippines, studied at the University of California and Columbia University (Taruc 1953, 86). Several Filipinos who later became Marxists inside or outside the party also studied in the United States in the twenties and thirties. James Allen, a party activist, was sent to the Philippines by the Communist Party in 1936–1938 to render "fraternal assistance"; his memoir does not mention any of the Filipino labor militancy I have summarized here, but he refers to two Filipino communists whom he knew earlier: Pedro Penino, a veteran of the Lincoln Brigade, and Jorge Frianeza, who was killed as a combatant in the Communist-led Huk uprising of 1949–1954 (Allen 1993, 98).

It was not until the late sixties that a sizable segment of the Filipino intelligentsia became involved in various left formations through organizations (now all defunct) like the Union of Democratic Filipinos (KDP; Katipunan ng mga Demokratikong Pilipino) and other anti–martial law coalitions resisting the Marcos dictatorship (1972–1986). As the 1981 slaying of Gene Viernes and Silme Domingo by agents of the Marcos dictatorship illustrates (see Churchill 1995), many lessons from the days of Manlapit to Mensalvas have not been absorbed by sectarian and dogmatic elements who have now flipped over to glorification of hedonistic, consumerist lifestyles of the rich (evinced by the chic glossy magazine *Pilipinas*). Individuals from the Filipino community in the United States (now the largest of the Asian cohort) may at present be affiliated with groups like the old Communist Party, Workers World Party, Democratic Socialists of America, Committees of Correspondence, Solidarity, and others; but they tend to be more concerned with arousing support for the national-democratic struggle in the Philippines than in propagating Marxist or broadly socialist ideas to their fellow immigrants or expatriates in the United States.

Easily the most distinguished of the first generation of Filipino immigrants who weathered the savage racism of the twenties and thirties and emerged as an exemplar of a rare species of multiracial internationalism is Philip Vera Cruz.

Why should we, relatively privileged culturati of the postmodern world, read his autobiography (mediated to us via Craig Scharlin and Lilia V. Villanueva) published by the UCLA Labor Center and the UCLA Asian American Studies Center (1992)? [1]

One reason is given by the epigraph to the book, a quote from Carey McWilliams, a friend of Carlos Bulosan's and other people of color: "Personal history is one means by which the politics of the recent past can be made relevant to present history." Such relevance, limited by the existing modalities of representation, can promote either an assimilative politics of "model minority success," which is the liberal alibi for "doing business as usual"—the punctual system of the work ethic as inflected by contemporary neo–Social Darwinism—or it can serve a project of resistance, enabling individuals in a collective to express their power and freedom in an immanent process of becoming. Vera Cruz's life, in short, can be used to fashion an emancipatory constituent subject with "a memory of the future" (Deleuze 1993, 246). It can restore to primacy the value-creating practice of associative labor, the power of the multitude (first theorized by Spinoza), including the network of productive cooperation that generates society and mediates the state. It can help recover the rights of racialized collectivities marginalized or excluded by the bourgeois system of contracts and the apparatus of commodification so as to renew the revolutionary practice of the masses—the autonomy, the productivity, and the constitutive drive (conatus) of popular democracy.

Easily, we can say that this life history, like the genre of immigrant autobiographies, operates on various levels. It can be read as a "national allegory," a literary type in which (as Fredric Jameson argues) "the story of the private individual destiny" can be interpreted as "an allegory of the embattled situation of the public third-world culture and society" (1986, 69). In the past, I have glossed Carlos Bulosan's texts in this way (San Juan 1992b, 109–12). But can we not, at least for this occasion, suspend this allegorizing hermeneutic and examine this multiply authored text (literally and figuratively) as an attempt to produce a determinate pattern of events defining a new, emergent "Filipino" subjectivity? Can we not read this text as a narrative the "efficient causality" of which, its proportion of passion and action, enables the emergence of a new protagonist articulating ethnicity, race, nation, and class in a way that undermines postcolonial/postmodern verities?

In this experiment, I think we can appreciate more genuinely the creative power of the Filipino imagination instanced in Vera Cruz's (1992) reconstruction of his life. For what is imagined or dramatized here is the ethos of a singular existence conceived as a syncopated rhythm of motion and rest, activity and passivity. This is an idea captured in his statement: "When it comes to political ideologies I have always thought practical was a better word than radical" (20). "Practical" here, I take it, is equivalent not to business pragmatism reinforced by a theory of "rational choice" and the mythology of an underclass. I consider it a term for a realistic inventory of what is possible, given the human inability to apprehend the multiplicity of affects surrounding our body in relation to others. Vera Cruz's rendering of his life unfolds a productive dynamic that transforms passive into active affections, contingent passions to necessary actions. His refusal to repress a Filipino national identification within the Chavez-dominated United Farm Workers of America (UFW) extinguishes the pathos of his self-effacement and the years of victimage behind it. His revolt against the personality cult—a mirror image of elitist individualism—ushers the joy of affirming his critical power, a self-valorizing practice that disentangles the knotted strands of his past and locates his individuality in the multiplicity of rich, complex relations with others. This persistence of the desire to surpass instrumental and commodified social relations leads to the incorporation of moral passions and sensuous activities of militants into the freedom of the multitude.

Within this logic of transformation, I envisage three practical effects or consequences of Vera Cruz's intervention in present-day ethnic or multicultural studies. It is not without significance that other Asian

American voices (Kent Wong and Glenn Omatsu, in particular), as well as the miscegenated "authors" Scharlin and Villanueva, have situated Vera Cruz's vernacular within the constraints of a determinate historical conjuncture. First, this testimony with its decolonizing itinerary undercuts the dominant paradigm of Filipino American immigrant history institutionalized in the textbooks (Omatsu 1994, iv–v), sanctioned by the disciplinary archive of Ethnic Studies and replicated in the folklore of quotidian common sense. This signals the demise of the hegemonic sociological paradigm and its constitution of the acculturable subaltern. Second, Vera Cruz's ethical stance critiques the authoritarian style of leadership personified by Cesar Chavez and attacks the labor-aristocratic opportunism mimicked by the UFW hierarchy. This marks the bankruptcy of ethnic chauvinism, its corollary identity politics (including the worship of the charismatic hero), and the sectarian mentality it entails. Third, the last use signifies the obsolescence of vanguardist and/or workerist politics framed by U.S. "exceptionalism" and its moralizing neoliberal globalism. Unless U.S. radicals can undertake a thoroughgoing critique of the "racist culture" (Goldberg 1994) that pervades Western civilization, including the U.S. variant, all claims to internationalist solidarity for the sake of "world revolution" will only be self-serving. Dialectically, all chauvinisms and reverse or reactive nativisms (Afrocentrism, *la raza*, and so on) also need to be examined for their exclusivist and sectarian implications.

Vera Cruz's discovery of the futility of a return to the homeland opens up a space for another exodus, this time not to the archaic utopia of an "America" idealized in Bulosan's now canonical mosaic of lives, *America Is in the Heart* ([1946] 1973), but to a terrain of immanence where diverse social assemblages coalesce in the global struggle against transnational capital.

Such effects are of course contingent on the adequacy of our ideas to the play of power, the lines of forces and intensities structuring the narrative. In the epilogue written in 1991, Vera Cruz recounts the illness that spoiled his brief sojourn in the Philippines, a visit the import of which he could not fully discern until much later. His bodily pain was a symptom of this inadequacy. It was intensified by his greater chagrin at witnessing his relatives' seeming lack of comprehension of "who I am and the things I stand for" (145). The Aquino charisma compounded by traditional piety intervened to foil any intention he had of binding his singular finitude with sympathetic bodies. He did not get the chance to rehearse the circumstances that enabled him to sacrifice his ambition so that his brother and sister could be saved from poverty and ignorance—"I made it possible for them." Indeed, throughout his account, Vera Cruz never tires of reiterating that decision to subordinate his desire to what he considered a prior obligation, which is also his claim to surrogate fatherhood. The spatial mobility of his labor power in the metropolis made possible a relative improvement of the life chances of his kin in the colony. And this possibility of changing the life trajectories of others, with its habitus of dependency produced by U.S. colonial tutelage—a figure taken by most commentators as the telos or motivation for Filipino immigration—functions as a leitmotif that conceals what really underlies it: the rebellion against the status quo of inequality and injustice. We cannot legitimately postulate a telos to this narrative; there is none except what coincides with the persistence of the desire to vindicate the passion to overthrow alienated, racist and exploitative social relations. Familial *pietas* serves as the initial grounding for Vera Cruz's principle of commitment to the welfare of the dispossessed and disinherited. Everything else is overdetermined. At any rate, what is dangerous is for readers to recognize that Vera Cruz is a figure for everyone who, by overcoming fear and the superstitions constituting the ideology of the neocolonized subaltern, releases the power of the multitude to realize liberatory transformations in society (on this Spinozist perspective, see Balibar 1989; Hardt 1995).

In most textbooks anatomizing the predicament of the Filipino diaspora in the United States, we are offered the usual paradigm of a narrative that is compartmentalized into three sections. In this synoptic background, the inaugural scene of the U.S. imperialist conquest of the Philippines in 1898, especially the genocidal violence inflicted on the millions of peasants and workers (not excluding thousands of Moro women and children) who supported the revolutionary Philippine Republic during the Filipino-American War (1989–1902), is erased from public memory.

In their textbook *Asian Americans* (1988), Harry Kitano and Roger Daniels recount the three waves of Filipino migration: the first wave of *pensionados* (government-funded students, not really immigrants but sojourners) from 1903 to 1910; the second (from 1910 to 1934), of recruited workers for the Hawaiian sugar plantations; and the third, after a hiatus when entry was limited to fifty bodies per year during the Philippine Commonwealth (1935–1946), from 1946 up to the present when professionals or "brain drain" immigrants mixed with World War II veterans, tourists, students, and recruits in the U.S. Navy. After the 1965 immigration act abolished the national-origin system and gave priority to the reunification of families, Filipino "new wave" immigration more than doubled each decade from 181,614 in 1960 to 336,731 in 1970; 774,652 in 1980; and 1,419,711 in 1990 (Kitano and Daniels 1988, 87). A mechanical causality predicated on numbers governs this neat division of the passage of bodies from colonial territory to the metropolis: The colonial state unilaterally determines such passage through legislation, administrative regulations, state incentives to agribusiness, needs for cheap labor, and the ideological imperatives of World War II and the Cold War. No doubt, this is the master narrative of an imperial state machinery obeying the exigencies of capital accumulation and the world market.

Following this standard classification, scholars like Melendy, Bogardus, Pido, and others seek to establish the diversity of Filipinos in terms of rural/urban background, occupation, language, customs and rituals, education, and other ascribed characteristics the totality of which equal Filipino ethnicity. Functionalist analysis helps maintain the neocolonial disintegration of the Filipino nation-people (see San Juan 1994b). Various official reports have acknowledged that racist exclusion, discrimination, and violence have prevented the "Americanization" of Filipinos from the beginning up to World War II. In the case of the new "fourth wave" immigrants, however, Pido asserts that "Pilipinos are now discarding the hyphenated 'Filipino-American' and are instead asserting themselves as American who are Pilipinos" (1986, 99). By fiat, nationality or race is presumably displaced by the sovereign U.S. citizen who can manipulate the signifiers of ethnic alterity—a postmodern game performed in the Imaginary register of the psychic economy. To underwrite the demarcation between the second wave (to which Vera Cruz is assigned) and the professionals of the post-1965 influx, the historian Peter Stanley considers the latter successors not to the "Manongs" but to the *pensionados;* an irrecoverable divide separates the generations who all "found it difficult to conceive of each other as sharing a national identity" (1985, 45). What is accomplished by the experts' divide-and-rule methodology is clear: The spectacle of Filipinos is purveyed as the paragon of postmodern difference, postcolonial hybrids or syncretized role models celebrated by multicultural arbiters of taste in New York or Australia but otherwise rendered indifferent in the heterogeneous milieu of the global marketplace.

Vera Cruz's mode of witnessing, his quest for a hypothetical communal virtue, renders inutile such historiographic anatomy. Linear or chronological time—the segmentary line of binary oppositions—yields to a nomadic and wayward mode of narrative recall marked by interruptions, refrains, and sidetracking maneuvers. What recurs throughout—the breakthrough or messianic Now-time (following Walter Benjamin's [1969] terminology) that counterpoints punctual time—is the 1965 Delano strike and the subsequent "crisis" of Vera Cruz's life in the UFW. Compartmentalization is anathema here.

Vera Cruz's account begins with the announcement of his resignation in 1977 from the UFW. After a brief overview, the text doubles back in chapter 2 to his recollection of his parents and his brother Martin, then to the pivotal Delano strike of 1965 in chapter 3 and the circumstances that led up to it. In chapter 4, he returns to the time of his arrival in Vancouver in 1929 and eventually his sojourn in Chicago up to the outbreak of the war. Chapters 5, 6, 7, and 8 focus on his contribution to the formation of the UFW via earlier union organizing and the crucial break with Chavez over the latter's support for the Marcos dictatorship in 1977. He protests the lack of internal, participatory democracy in the union. Chapter 9 attempts to conclude this genealogy of his intellectual formation as a radical internationalist freed from the corporatist exclusivism and ethnic dogmatism exemplified by the Chavez clique. The concluding chapter turns out to be premature since the "Epilog" (written fourteen years after chapter 9)—a distance partly explained by the temporary censorship of a university press to which the manuscript was first submitted—seeks to vindicate his stand against Marcos's martial-law despotism by identifying with the populist image of President Corazon Aquino. Is there a suggestion here of the "return of the repressed" mother/sexuality/homeland? Reversals, flashbacks and foreshadowings, non sequiturs, repeats and quotations of earlier scenes, molecular flux, and so on characterize what Deleuze calls the "molar line of rigid segmentarity" (1993, 228–29) threading the earlier episodes. When chapter 5 foregrounds the struggle of Filipino farm-workers, cracks and ruptures in the molar line begin to predominate, culminating in a line of gravity or velocity, the line of flight, when Vera Cruz accumulates the insurrectionary energies of the Filipino workers, and compels him to repudiate class treachery.

Vera Cruz's departure from the UFW coincides with the profound mutation in the class composition of the Filipino community by the seventies. The time of the Manongs is over; more precisely, its thematic residue has blended with the ongoing dispersal of Filipinos across occupational, status, and class boundaries. Nonetheless, what Vera Cruz's montage effects in the early sections of his memoir exceeds the notion of postmodern decentering and the postcolonial sublime of Homi Bhabha, Trinh Minh-ha, Gayatri Spivak, and other traveling theorists. For it is not just the shattering of the three/four-waves schema, together with the doctrine of push/pull factors, in the mainstream sociological paradigm that Vera Cruz achieves. Vera Cruz also discombobulates the orthodox left fixation on ethnic workerism as the vanguard force supposed to catalyze a wholesale proletarian mobilization in North America. We are reading a narrative of substitutions, not of contiguity. We ask not what will happen next but what greater degree of understanding we gain as we grasp the syncopated rhythm of passive and active affections, the order of efficient causality, immanent in this life history. From Washington and Alaska (1924–1934) to

Chicago (1934–1942), then to the shanty towns of the San Joaquin Valley in 1943, Vera Cruz's trajectory deviates from the route of Filipino workers who land in Hawaii or California. His stay in Chicago for eight years unsettles the conventional pattern of "second wave" spatial mobility. It was only in 1943 that the binary overcoding of his life by the immigration apparatus halted as he was discharged from the Second Filipino Regiment and began working in the Delano-Richgrove vineyards. The chronology here is blurred as a disruptive line of differentiation begins with Vera Cruz's leadership of the Delano local of the National Farm Labor Union in 1949–1950, followed by an enigmatic hiatus in 1950–1960. In 1960, he continues the line of flight with his joining the Agricultural Workers Organizing Committee (AWOC), an affiliate of the American Federation of Labor/Congress of Industrial Unions (AFL-CIO), which leads to the founding of the UFW after 1965.

Conflicting lines of movement intersect in the section beginning with chapter 4. Vera Cruz returns to what I call the "primal scene" of deracination" (San Juan 1992c, 23–29): he reenacts the passage of the native via steerage in Bulosan's *America Is in the Heart* up to the arrival in Seattle six years before Bulosan. In April 1927, he entered Lewis and Clark high school in Spokane and in 1931 Gonzaga University, an aborted imitation of the *pensionado* experience (since he was also working at odd jobs in restaurants, homes, and so on) somehow prefiguring the phenomenon of exported Filipino domestic labor in the last three decades of this century. He associated with Filipinos of petty bourgeois orientation and befriended politicized Americans like Maurice Landisman and Bill Berg. Vera Cruz's education speeded up on contact with Larry Itliong, Chris Mensalvas, and Ernesto Mangaoang, authentic organic intellectuals of the Filipino migrant workers, who mediated the experience of the peasant/proletarian generation of the twenties and early thirties with that of the post–1965 professionals. These exemplary activists (to which Vera Cruz now belongs) then embodied an emergent notion of popular sovereignty, perhaps an exercise in grassroots self-management, in contradiction with the racist violence and regimentation of the larger society.

By the time Vera Cruz argued for a low-rental retirement home (the Agbayani Village) for the Manongs in chapter 5, he had already traversed several thresholds of microbecomings and dissolved the quarantining borders between the second and third waves. By a series of displacements and realignments, Vera Cruz can refer to people of his age as "old-timers" and underscore their peculiar predicament in contrast to the Mexicans:

Unlike the Mexicans, who had plenty of their own people around, and could even go back to Mexico if need be, the Filipino would have had to go 8,000 miles across the Pacific to find a Filipina to marry. Some of them had just stopped working in the fields for the first time when they came to live in Agbayani, and they were 70, 80, and even 90 years old. These were the old Filipino workers who were used by Cesar and Dolores Huerta to establish funds for a retirement home from the first table grape contract signed with Lionel Steinberg. (Scharlin and Villanueva 1992, 83).

Later on, when Vera Cruz confronts the Marcos-appointed Secretary of Labor Ople in one UFW convention and was prevented from speaking up by Chavez, he joins the children of second and third wave Filipinos who have been radicalized by the antiwar and civil rights movement of the sixties and early seventies, thus bridging the segmentary trenches inscribed in the history of Filipino deracination and resettlement.

In retrospect, the process of correlating molar and molecular lines, segmentary and irruptive flows, in Vera Cruz's life yields the insight that power inheres in the coalition of individual forces. In chapter 9, Vera Cruz addresses young Filipino students and exhorts them to learn from the example of the unlettered farm-workers. The lesson he selects is an internationalist concern for the fundamental human rights of everyone, including illegal aliens now converted into pariahs by Proposition 187. In this, he opposes UFW orthodoxy: "It is the job of the labor movement to unite all workers regardless of their color, nationality, language, or whatever" (Scharlin and Villanueva 1992, 128). Although change is slow, it is permanent. So far, it is evident that the process of change in Vera Cruz's life does not privilege certain social subjects with a monopoly of transformative agency. Events as a rule overtake intellect and intuition. The production of the constituent subject proceeds through the cognitive mapping of the field of immanent forces, of mutations and multiplicities. This constituent subject subtends Vera Cruz's worldview that "the situation was changing all the time" and what is fundamental is the sense of "responsibility" so that when Filipinos are in a position of power, "they will be able to represent people fairly" without discrimination, privileging one group against another.

On this matter of representation, we come to the second use of Vera Cruz's narrative. This involves the unrelenting critique of an authoritarian style of leadership. Vera Cruz challenges the mystique of representation based on charismatic personalities like Chavez that ultimately serves bureaucratic top-down business rationality. The cult of the heroic personality is decomposed by Vera Cruz's refusal to sublimate Filipino grievances. He rejects the transcendental aura or fetishism ascribed to leadership: "You see, when an individual is built up too much and made to seem like God, then you start defending him when you shouldn't. And you start confusing that person with the union. One person is not a union" (Scharlin and Villanueva 1992, 111). In one encounter, Vera Cruz deploys his own astute knowledge of human character in demystifying charismatic power: "You know, Cesar is sometimes kind of intimidating. But he cannot scare me. I know how much he can do and I know what he can't do. He does not own me" (Scharlin and Villanueva 1992, 112). Before this, Vera Cruz described the debate over Agbayani Village, and earlier the incompatibility between Filipino union organizers like Larry Itliong (who actually catalyzed the formation of the UFW when he helped merge AWOC and NFWA in 1966 into UFWOC, AFL-CIO) and Chavez. Years of independent struggle and cooperative work have given Vera Cruz the ethical courage, skeptical patience, and stamina to resist conformity to the opportunism and undemocratic style of the Chavez clique, notwithstanding the humanistic pronouncements of its liberal and religious sponsors.

At this juncture, Vera Cruz is afflicted with sad passion precipitated by the decomposition of his relationship with a union to which he had given so much of his life. He suffers because he has not yet formed an adequate idea of the rationality, the synchrony, between particular circumstances and specific human conduct. His diagnosis enables him to elucidate why reciprocity does not exist among singularities in a mass process of union struggle. His critique seeks to discern the rationality in the conjuncture of contingent events and malleable personalities: "When [Larry Itliong] came back to Delano he passed away shortly thereafter. I have felt so terrible about this. The first time we could have really talked and it was too late. The Filipino leaders in the farmworkers movement should have tried to be closer, to be friends and talk more about our mutual problems. Our unity in the union was always very weak because we never got together to discuss things. We always went our own ways, had our own pride. This wasn't good for our unity" (Scharlin and Villanueva 1992, 77).

Analyzing the colonial distortion of the Filipino psyche and its contagion in the lack of principles displayed by some Filipino community "leaders" (originating from the corrupt contractual labor system), Vera Cruz strives to grasp the internal, efficient force of differentiation at work among his compatriots. He offers an assessment of his own behavior: "Since Larry died I have realized that my greatest mistake, my biggest shortcoming as a union officer, was not fighting like hell for what I knew was right. I took the passive role too often because I had learned from the past struggles in the Filipino community how bad fights at the top can get. I always sacrificed my personal convictions for what I thought or was convinced was the good of the union, and sometimes I think this was a mistake. I just sacrificed too much" (Scharlin and Villanueva 1992, 78).

When Chavez aligns himself with the U.S.-Marcos dictatorship, the segmentary line of development snaps. The instrumental mode of subjugation and bureaucratic representation ends. Vera Cruz no longer allows himself to be used by the UFW to represent Filipinos—this constituency has both dwindled and fragmented since 1965. He engages in a new form of self-valorization by writing the history of his intellectual formation. Earlier, he has tried to heal the split between the public mask of union officer who sought to present a "united front" to the enemy and the private conscience that operated on the principle of "What I believed I would say to everybody because that's the way I am." When Chavez surrenders Vera Cruz's right to speak to the will of the Marcos dictatorship, when the power indivisible with such a right is suppressed, then Vera Cruz withdraws from the stage of purely union activism and begins his exodus. So far, the narrative has evinced how the productivity/producibility of the Filipino worker-intellectual manifested itself through breaks and distortions in the process of making a living, a process the contour of which has been shaped by the racism of civil society and the state. Chavez's subservience to global capital (instanced by its neocolonial hegemony in the Philippines) reproduced the imperial enemy in the UFW, the target of radicalized Filipino Americans inspired by Vera Cruz's militance. The degeneration of the UFW leadership thus opens the space for the invention of a new subjectivity: Vera Cruz's labor of writing—a recomposition of multiple parts, remembered events, dispersed experience—generates a network of social valorization that affords the evocation of an alternative subject position that dissociates itself from the narrow corporatism of business unionism and rejoins global anti-imperialist alliances.

What has happened, in effect, is a dialectical leap in which the surplus value appropriated by Vera Cruz as union activist is now reprocessed into use value for a new strategy. Vera Cruz assumes the role of "tribune of the people," Lenin's rubric for the communist intellectual. Labor is no longer conceived economistically in its formal subsumption by capital; it has now become a social function of the whole society. This coincides of course with the passing of the generation of Manongs and the supersession of the petty bourgeois Filipino majority by the seventies and eighties (Cariño et al. 1990, 49–53). A recomposition of the Filipino community in the past two decades by a regime of atomistic laissez-faire individualism and a neoliberal program of "sustainable development" demands a new oppositional strategy of social change and redistribution.

The figure of rupture from within a transmogrified institution occupies center stage in Vera Cruz's chronicle of a life assumed without any prior guarantee of intrinsic worth. This rupture implies an adequation of knowledge with the mutable character of social assemblages. If chapter 8 may be regarded as the climax of this narrative of education, a line of escape from the regime of authoritarian rule, then chapter 9 and the Epilog suggest the third use afforded by reading Vera Cruz's narrative. What precisely does Vera Cruz's claim of being an "internationalist" signify? This is the moment when the temptation of succumbing to the fashionable lexicon of postmodernist postality—postcolonial hybridity, immigrant Imaginary, deconstructive aporia, discourses of displacement via borders and margins, and so on—becomes most urgent. Where is the location of the speaking subject, the subject of enunciation, in the text we are trying to make sense of? Vera Cruz refuses the temptation: The locus of engaging sectarian and chauvinist "identity" politics (bourgeois elitism and its resonance in the rank and file) is still the terrain of popular forces in action. The adventure of Vera Cruz as a finite mode of affects (passive and active) becomes contemporaneous with its affiliations and linkages with multitudes around the world seeking national-popular liberation.

Having successfully resisted co-optation by the Establishment, Vera Cruz does not shirk the task of attempting to lay the foundation for articulating a new Filipino subjectivity. Although he accepted the Ninoy Aquino Award in 1987, it was in deference more to the "associated living labor" of the Filipino community than to his ego. Although he constantly invoked his sense of pride as an excuse for not telling the truth about the misfortunes and travails of his life—this is the allegory of pretense played out by "old-timers," as the doxa goes—Vera Cruz has also extinguished this pride in upholding the primacy of the "living productivity of human cooperation," the substantive conatus of popular democracy. Reflecting on the attenuation of the Filipino will for affirming national-popular sovereignty within the U.S. polity, Vera Cruz writes: "Our survival in this country as a minority is determined by how well we learn from the lesson of the past. . . . We need the truth more than we need heroes" (Scharlin and Villanueva 1992, 76). This truth he seeks to provide by delineating its conditions of possibility and its contexts in his life.

What Vera Cruz is engaged in here is a survey of the field that has produced the distinctive sensibility of a Filipino radical and what it signifies for the present. It approximates to what Antonio Negri and Michael Hardt call the ontological act of constructing the alternative to capital and the legitimacy of the commodifying state: "Constructing the names of reality constitutes the cognitive space within which being develops the passage from cupiditas (the desire to live) to cooperation, love, and the incorporation with the living source of being. . . . It is as if the world is unmade and reconstructed on the basis of that set of thoughts, actions, and intuitions established on the individual and collective singularity that organize it through its desire and its power" (1994, 287). By a series of deliberate emancipatory moves, the Filipino actor names the forces and events overdetermining his people's "Babylonian captivity" and their exodus to liberation. Vera Cruz's geopolitical reconstruction of the various strands in his itinerary from the Philippines to the United States may be construed as an endeavor to define the "individual and collective singularity" epitomized by the Filipino in her or his multiple positions as colonial subaltern, radicalized worker, trade union militant, insurgent nationalist, subversive intellectual, and internationalist tribune.

One clear evidence that what Vera Cruz is staging in his narrative of apprenticeship as union organizer and later as theoretician of a counterhegemonic politics is the vicissitudes of the production of a new subject beyond the limits of an ethnic, workerist closure. At first, this effort simulates the Enlightenment archetype of the birth of the autonomous individual, the juridical person with rights based on possession of rational agency. When he was a student at Gonzaga University, Vera Cruz described how he "argued with his classmates who believed in a God who was supposed to be leaned on all the time. For me, to depend on something or someone who's more superior than yourself was a sign of your own weakness and inability to understand what life is all about. . . . I became a bit of a rebel at this time about religion because I didn't think the teachings of the church were really helping the poor people in the realities of life" (Scharlin and Villanueva 1992, 64). Vera Cruz saw the duplicity and hypocrisy of religion in the case of the church in the Philippines, which "had been very much responsible for the exploitation and enslavement of my own people!"

The flight from colonial/feudal subjugation marks the turning point in Vera Cruz's recomposition of his life story, inscribing agency and the power of enunciation in the palimpsest of the disciplined inarticulate body (see San Juan 1994b, 123–25). To refuse dependency, to reject subaltern acquiescence—this conatus explains the impulse to acquire the means to economic independence, to earn not only to survive but also to be free. In this process of fighting for survival, the colonial subjects find their class identity when they locate themselves in the hierarchical structure of social positions in the metropolis. Self-valorization articulates itself here in the voice of the survivor who claims a mother's attachment and who assumes the role of the father in maintaining the kinship network as defensive cultural strategy against imperial racist domination. Self-valorization is witnessed in Vera Cruz's decision "to struggle to make it [America] good, at least for myself." Self-valorization appears when he decides to become a citizen so that he can participate fully in the political process. It appears too when he reflects on the peculiar configuration of the Filipino collective psyche: Filipinos have not expressed themselves politically because (in Vera Cruz's judgment) of "our long tradition of seeing issues and events philosophically and not politically. . . . For many years we had to be content with addressing issues on an abstract level rather than questioning the realities that underlined our present conditions" (Vera Cruz 1992, 28). In the same breath, however, he contradicts this essentialism when he identifies the constituent, spontaneous power of the multitude as the decisive and pivotal event of his life: "When the Filipino farmworkers went on strike in Delano on September 8, 1965, they made that decision on their own without the explicit support of the AWOC director and the AFL-CIO leadership" (Scharlin and Villanueva 1992, 26, 28).

Vera Cruz learned from his white American friends that the struggle for freedom involved everyone, "whatever the color of their skin." His internationalism grew out of the accumulation of practical experiences that enabled him to apprehend the nuanced relation between speech and action, intention and performance, and thereafter calculate the effects of their nonsynchrony and asymmetry. But it was his comprehension of U.S. civil society, the public space where the state recuperates social antagonisms to legitimate its rule and where disciplinary institutions impose the self-serving interest of corporate business as the universal one, that enabled Vera Cruz to escape the corporatist syndrome and embrace a global transformative vision. He poses the rhetorical question concerning the efficient causality and political necessity of a critical, materialist intellect: "But damn it, is Cesar [Chavez] too dumb to see that these U.S. agribusinesses in the Philippines are connected with their counterparts here in California, through the same economic system that exploits U.S. farmworkers for bigger profits?" (Scharlin and Villanueva 1992, 122). In chapter 9, he elaborates on the theme of transnational capitalism and introduces the notion of the world system of globalized capital and the unequal international division of labor: "Third world countries [from which new immigrants to the U.S. originate] have been exploited so much by the multinational corporations that their people, moved by extreme poverty, leave their home countries to seek work in an industrialized country like the United States. The multinationals suck the wealth out of their homeland like a vampire sucks blood. And these same businesses here greet these new immigrants with open arms" (Scharlin and Villanueva 1992, 127).

We confront the anticlimactic last chapter with a sense that no denouement or resolution is possible in a world system where class antagonisms have grown sharper. The encounter with the charismatic Aquino exhibits a pathos suffused with Vera Cruz's disillusionment with Chavez. Understatement, the anxiety of passive waiting, vacuous protocol, and anticlimactic forgetfulness of the purpose of such a meeting surround this episode. When Vera Cruz meets Aquino, the question he remembers asking Aquino is "why the Philippines was allowing pesticides that are banned in first world countries, like the U.S., to be used there" (Scharlin and Villanueva 1992, 144). The question remained unanswered, only to be followed by letters he and his indefatigable comrade Deborah Vollmer wrote to Aquino about the lack of human rights in the Philippines. What makes the text open-ended is this gesture of continuing concern, literally a call of vigilance awaiting a communal response.

Vera Cruz lamented that he could never go home again, but the subject or protagonist of this narrative has virtually made connections with people everywhere across the continents, a network of transnational communication grappling with worldwide issues and concerns, so that the homeland Vera Cruz really belongs to then and now may be where the power (Spinoza's *potentia* [1994]) of multitudes is expressing itself and where a new society is being constituted by subjects whose emergence his own narrative of becoming has unwittingly prophesied. At this point, Vera Cruz's identity has become coeval with the fate of the world's laboring masses today—the scientific, affective, and cooperative energies that can no longer be circumscribed by the old manual/mental dichotomy or the ethnic minority/majority split. We have indeed reached new ground, a "common notion" of solidarity approximating a consensus of collective praxis and desire, after traversing the still-intractable geography of Philip Vera Cruz's life.

Postscript

A short version of this paper was read at the MLA convention at San Diego on December 30, 1994. One listener (white male academic) reacted vehemently to the three panel speakers' application of "high literary theory" on ethnic writing, thus allegedly promoting bourgeois domination over "native" or "indigenous" cultural production. My initial response was to explain that the MLA framework and its specialized audience lends some legitimacy to that conjunctural deployment of the resources of "high theory." Moreover, such a division between "high culture" and plebeian mass culture has a long historical development not due to a simple view of the bourgeoisie imposing its ideas on the peasantry and the proletariat. On second thought, my tack should have been this: I should have emphasized the struggle for popular-democratic hegemony (as Gramsci originally employed it) as one requiring organic intellectuals of people of color to struggle on the same ideological terrain occupied by the ruling classes; a terrain where residual, dominant, and emergent strands of the same cultural-ideological formation are intricately intertwined; and that being so, the situation constrains us to mobilize or refunction versatile tools, the origins of which (whether "high" or "low" depends on specific circumstances and strategic needs) need not necessarily determine their progressive or regressive uses. Furthermore, this struggle for hegemony is a matter of political calculation in which the social energies circulating in "high theory" and plebeian cultural practices can be harnessed for popular-democratic ends. To instruct people of color not to use "high theory" (by which is meant Gramsci, Jameson, Said, Spinoza, and so on) and instead "cultivate their own garden" is, in the light of such a conception of the struggle for hegemony, not only naive, crudely patronizing, and simply out of touch with the complex historical realities of world systemic imperialism, uneven and combined development in the colonies, and so on; it serves chiefly to maintain the unequal international division of labor, transnational corporate hegemony, and so on. In brief, it serves capital's power of oppression and apartheid exploitation.

6

Prophesying a Permanent Cultural Revolution

All humans are equal, for their being is one.

Emilio Jacinto

As that good theologian Lenin said, "History and life is infinitely more complex than even the most class-conscious parties can grasp."

Edicio De La Torre

But our friendship draws its sustenance from the rich soil of people's war.

Maria Lorena Barros

In the issue of the *Philippines Mail* for October 8, 1934, a letter appeared signed by Filipino farm-workers in Salinas, California, petitioning President Franklin D. Roosevelt to redress their grievances: Not entitled to the rights of full citizens and therefore without any representation, they have been subjected to "racial prejudice and discrimination in all social relationships" and suffer these indignities without protection. They proclaim that "We have all emigrated to the United States, stimulated by the high ideals of Americanism and desirous of finding a higher and more worthy means of expression, only to be disillusioned on every hand by the experiences of our unsatisfactory social status." Reality disabused them of their hopes; fictions of colonial ideology stripped them of self-respect. Who can speak for them now? If they cannot be adequately represented, they request immediate repatriation to the Philippine Islands "so that we may work out our destiny and future among our own people, where we hope and trust, that even though it may not afford all the seeming advantages of Western Civilization, it may be more conducive to our future happiness" (Filipino Petitioners 1997, 133–34).

Surveying the labor situation in California, where "Western Civilization" may be found, Carey McWilliams states that "with the exception of the Mexican, the Filipino has been the most viciously exploited of any of the various races" constituting the vast army of "cheap labor" that for a long time suffered brutal treatment—until they began to strike (1997, 138). This time, however, the Filipino petitioners were employing the tactic of demanding peaceful reforms. President Roosevelt's offer to provide free transportation to these workers, however, proved tantamount to permanent exclusion since anyone who accepted it could not reenter the continental United States except within the meager quota (fifty a year) established by the Philippine Independence Act of March 24, 1934. Hence, promising autonomy to the colonized—no longer docile but, on the contrary, veritable troublemakers—coincided with their exclusion. We encounter once again liberalism's subterfuge of preserving its hegemony by smoke and mirrors, by unconscionable ruses, in the era of its worst crisis, the Depression of the thirties.

It is difficult to perceive in the petitioners' apologetic and beseeching tone any hint of attempting to render "delirious the voice of the other within oneself," the deconstructionist formula for self-identification (Harvey 1996, 103). Obviously, the search for a locus of agency cannot proceed outside concrete historical determinations—unless continuing delusion by metaphysics is sought. If the workers do not heed Derrida's invocation of the Leibnizian conceit to internalize discord and gain psychic equilibrium, that is because their "militant particularism" forces them to measure U.S. ideals learned in the colony's schools against the reality of degrading labor and of living in barns torched by white vigilantes. If they also cannot resort to the postmodern route of dispersal, fragmentation, and aporia of irresolvable difference, that is because they cannot dismiss Pollyanna-like the reality of "mob violence, the destruction of our homes by fire" and "unwarranted arrest"—existential truths undermining the "advantages of Western Civilization" that they believed they would forsake if they were repatriated.

Of more than 100,000 Filipinos on the West Coast during the thirties, only a handful survive today. One article in the *New York Times* (May 11, 1993) featured the "Last of the Manongs," two Filipinos who did not accept repatriation and persisted in their "impoverished lives of stoop labor," forbidden to marry whites, own land, and so on. Fred Abad, eighty-two years old, and Narciso Oliver, ninety-three years old, lived in Agbayani Village, the retirement dwelling constructed by the United Farm Workers Union (UFW) for aging Filipinos at the instigation of its then vice president, Philip Vera Cruz. When Abad landed in California in 1929, the image of the Filipino publicized in the mainstream media was that of "the most worthless, unscrupulous, shiftless, diseased semibarbarian that has ever come to our shore" (DeParle 1993, A14). In the halcyon days of the sixties, Royal F. Morales (1974) described as "Sisyphus-like" the adventures of the *sacadas* and "old-timers" in California. All accounts describing the emergence of the UFW, then headed by Cesar Chavez, refer to the inaugural moment when, on September 8, 1965, Filipino members of the Agricultural Workers' Organizing Committee (headed by Larry Itliong and Philip Vera Cruz) called a strike in Delano against the San Joaquin Valley growers to raise their wages by twenty or thirty cents to $1.40 an hour. The Manongs today are in danger of being reduced to mythology, reified in murals, romanticized and museumized in multicultural archives. Willie Barrientos, former resident of Agbayani Village, exhorted young Fil-Am visitors that they "should not only study past events, but apply their lessons to solving the problems of racism and injustice that continue to exist in the present" (Philippine Center 1985, 24). We may ask then how this thematic archetype in the narrative of Filipino lives and ordeals, an ideologeme drawing sustenance from the uninterrupted passage from the Philippines to the United States and back, is actually interpreted and refunctioned in the collective imagination? What potential does it have to serve the long-range goal of liberation from the unrelenting racist-sexist despoliation of capital?

It is instructive to note here three dramatic presentations I am aware of that deal with the Manongs and how they registered the varying standpoints, ambivalences, and contradictions of their political milieu. Consider first *A Song for Manong* (1988) by Marina Feleo-Gonzalez and Behn Cervantes's adaptation of Virgilio Felipe's thesis, *Istoria ni Bonipasyo: Kasla Gloria Ti Hawai'i* (1991); whereas the former links the struggles of the Manongs with the national-democratic revolution in the Philippines, the latter superimposes a plot of reconciliation on an amorphous mass of information in which plantation workers are made to feel compensated by the "rightful pride" that their sacrifices "made Hawaii" into a prosperous state (see Somera 1982). Although both empathize with the individual sufferings and joys of the Manongs, they differ in reinscribing the group within disparate contexts and centers of gravity. These two diametrically opposed approaches to the Manong's plight reflect, in my view, the drastic shift from the militant anti-imperialism of the seventies to the resigned pathos and indifference of Filipinos in the era of the restoration of the comprador-bureaucratic oligarchy. Meanwhile, the third artistic event embodies the resonance of the revolutionary hopes sparked by the peace talks between the Aquino government and the forces of the National Democratic Front in the late eighties. In Chris Millado's *pere-*

griNasyon: Is America in the Heart (1994), we find an attempt to fuse themes of alienation and community that not only offers verisimilitude (popular realism) but also allegorical direction, suturing the episode of the Manong's agon with the unfolding odyssey of the Filipino people's revolution against U.S. imperialism.

One prominent U.S. historian sympathetically reviewed the trials and tribulations of the Manongs and concluded that their lives indicated "something larger that transcends time and nationality" (Stanley 1985, 50). Nomads no more, they provide the raw material for postmodernist bricolage mimicking tired evangelical homilies. Displaced from such mere contingencies, what could they symbolize? In the age of global capitalism, we confront a return of the *sakadas* in the person of women age 50 and above who are predominantly cultivators in the HC and S plantation in Kahului, Maui (Demirbag 1994). Time and nationality are deeply implicated here since this cohort of women came to Hawaii through the "order book," that is, marriage to older Filipino workers who returned to the Philippines to find brides. The Filipina field-workers in Maui thus pursue the immemorial routine their husbands followed for the past twenty years (Sharma 1987)—except that now we are in the era of post-*pax Americana*. Meanwhile, Filipina women who are recent immigrants enter the "new plantations," the service industries (hotels, restaurants), which depend on tourism. Together with the military bases, the tourist industry finances the state institutions and public services of Hawaii. More than half of 85,000 Filipinos working in this sector are women. In a recent study, Rose Churma notes that "poor work hours, uncertainty of continued employment and the need for workers to seek second or third jobs to make ends meet, has placed tremendous strains on the workers' families" (1994, 67), resulting in the rise of Filipino youth gangs and other problems affected by such an inhospitable environment. It seems that despite all the stories of Filipino millionaires and politicians in high office (can this caste of new "peons" clone Benjamin Cayetano?), the lessons from the aborted pilgrimage of the Manongs are still in search of partisan archaeologists.

One such prospector of undiscovered treasure is the poet Al Robles, cofounder of the Kearny Street Asian American Writers' Workshop in San Francisco, who is celebrated by Ishmael Reed as the bearer of the "heart of the Pilipino soul" and by many as "the master of Pilipino American literature." Such essentializing gestures are perversely compromising. The markedly dated use of "Pilipino" during the sixties to designate ancestry betrays the bittersweet fusion of assimilationist complacency and separatist dreams common to Filipinos born in this territory. But the poems dealing with the Manongs in Robles's collection, *Rappin' with Ten Thousand Carabaos in the Dark* (1996), are ob-

sessed not so much with "roots" that "sprout up all over / like wild locust" (9) as with "weeds" that surround them and evoke the sound of
the chthonic Ifugao mountain nose flute. For Robles, his compatriot
Sam Tagatac, and others, primordial and still uncommercialized Ifugao music "tells no lies."

Robles's poetic art demonstrates one way of inventing the inchoate
vernacular speech of the Filipino still undomesticated by white supremacist ideology. In "A Thousand Pilipino Songs: Ako Ay Pilipino,"
the serial montage reads like a mixture of travelogue, reminiscences,
icons and motifs of a precapitalist formation, slogans from tourist
brochures, images of ritual dancing, and so on, all intended to affirm a
generic definition of ethnic/racial identity. Whitman's "democratic
vista" is cross-fertilized by a naive style of surrealist primitivism:

i am pilipino in a graveyard of wallowing shrunken negrito heads. . . .

i am pilipino—manila cafe—san miguel—one thousand drunken nights
watching worn white silk whores trampling their bodies on a ten-cent
lacquered counter—

i am pilipino—young & old—waiting for a new day to rise—to raise my
bolo—to slash down—to hack the chain that binds my pilipino brothers
and sisters— (1996, 11)

To vindicate the futile lives of the Manongs "echoing sadness in the
pit of lonely carabao bellies," the speaking voice here ushers us to the
site of ceremonial feasts redolent with signs of Rabelaisian gusto: Eating and dancing become symbolic acts of recovering humanity, as
Mikhail Bakhtin (1968) reminds us in another context. Meanwhile,
the motions of bodies are translated into convivial practices for the
reaffirmation of community and renewal of tellurian, cosmic energies:

eat fish tails & fish heads & fish eyes & fish eggs—kumain all day with a
thousand pilipino suns in your belly. . . .

dance to the poor peasants dance to the wild ifugao dung-moon-smeared
women—dance to the flowing blood of wild pigs, spilling down from the
minds of pilipinos—dance to autumn-goats' intestines—to the erection of
a thousand pig ears & pig eyes & pig heads . . . wild boar running wild in
the pool halls. . . .

dance to my tatay with fish and rice in his mouth—dance to the burning
castration of magellan & iron crosses pushing down pilipino faces &
minds & bodies—dance to cock fights & to the gods of the seas & skies &
mountains—dance to pregnant ifugao spirits—dance to the manongs
chasing 7th street blondies. . . . (1996, 12–13)

Aside from his sixties counterculture background, Robles's apprenticeship in Zen Buddhism and other nature religions has taught him the technique of synthesizing diverse sensory impressions. This mode of capturing objects in process, in the confluence of events, approximates in effect what Ernst Bloch (1996) calls the "forming-transforming" anticipatory ideal of revolutionary Marxist poetics. A carnivalesque scenario reconciling the Ifugao hunt and the melancholy landscape of the urban United States—"Chilled ifugao bones crack the lucky M cue ball" (1996, 16) as Robles puts it in "International Hotel Night Watch"—affords the modality for rehumanizing commodified migrant labor. Nature and artifice coalesce in the rhythm of meditation and spontaneous discovery. It is a simple technique of juxtaposing the ethnic signature of landscapes and artifacts with the physiognomies of the Manongs to trigger sudden epiphanies and defamiliarizing recognitions:

> *cagayan loincloth*
> *eat with carabao-winter hands*

> *"why i got these for—my hands?*
> *who give them to me?*
> *the rice and fish taste better dat way."*
> ("Manong Jacinto Santo Tomas"; 1996, 21–22)

> *Tino's barbershop*
> *Manila Cafe: adobo rising from carabao plates*
> *Lucky "M" poolhall*
> *Pin stripe, gabardine, english tweed, worsted*
> *Macintosh double-breasted, single-breasted, cara-*
> *Breasted, pinoy-breasted suits*
> *50–60 years of dreams and nightmares*
> *Rising out of mudfish eyes*
> *Shrimp dances hidden in the Louisiana swamps*
> *Brown feet stomping to Bagobo beats*
> *Pinoys left hugging coconut trees*
> *Damp with leftover semen*
> *Brown flesh clinging to Louisiana blondies*
> *Stretched across the velvet cloth pooltables*
> *Her long legs crossed over like a manilatown crucifix*
> *Apoy, apoy between the legs. . . .*
> ("Guadalupe: 'Come to Me My Melancholy Baby'";
>   1996, 41)

These exercises in biographical still-life portraits and witty amalgamations of the Filipino and the Western may be considered pleasurable in themselves and as such they are ephemeral. Robles, however, claims to be a "Pilipino American" poet and this choice of belonging to a beleaguered community decisively marks him as ethically committed, necessarily political, and even dangerous. Despite traits of quietist and solipsist aestheticism, Robles's art transcends the individualist self-indulgence one finds in some New York–based celebrities insofar as it aspires to a project of honoring the memory of the nameless, not just the Manongs of the past but also their successors, the Overseas Contract Workers, who constitute the nascent Filipino diaspora of the present. Robles's testimony is memorably expressed in the first section of "The Wandering Manong" :

> I am not ashamed of the manong, nor do I feel sad by their tragic story in America. The manongs have been on a long journey and I have been one of those wanderers who they have met along the way. What right does anyone have to judge these manongs who have come to America seeking for a new life. They have lived through so many wars and have scars in their hearts to prove it. They were the brown gypsies, the low-down niggers, the brown apache savages, the uncivilized nomads who wandered from place to place in search of their dreams. They left the waterbuffalo at home. Even the waterbuffalo was led home with an iron ring strung around its nose. The manongs threw the ring across the ocean. They lived, as it were, in two worlds—in a world they left behind, and in a dream before their eyes (1996, 30).

The last phrase depicting a Janus-faced position leads me to staking my central argument here. For this historical conjuncture, my interest in the performance of Robles, Hagedorn (more later), and other Filipino artists concerns not so much the question of their aesthetic competence or hermeneutic richness, topics with an elite aura of limited value, but their possible contribution to knowledge about geopolitical history and the transformation of the contemporary milieu of power relations. In particular, how do these artists and intellectuals illuminate the persistent racialization and marginalization of the Filipino in the United States and the worsening dependency of the Philippines on transnational capital? How can they help change this international state of affairs? These questions can be posed even to such celebrities of popular culture as the singer Jocelyn Enriquez, acclaimed 1996 Outstanding Dance Artist; to Manuel Ocampo, the enfant terrible of the trendy avant garde; to the innovative musician Eleanor Academia and film star Tia Carrere; to Mike Hanopol, inventor of Pinoy Rock; and to any number of politicians, corporate moguls, hustlers, and so on. Exchanges on the nature of "Filipino American culture" (see, for example, Fuentebella 1989), or "Pinoy pride," cannot proceed meaningfully without first problematizing the "Americaniza-tion" of the Filipino and the utilitarian discourse of multivocality, hy-bridity, and contingency that underwrites the insidious ontology of U.S. "exceptionalism."

Within the framework of post–Cold War geopolitical alignments, the trends associated with postmodern transculturation and the "poli-tics of identity" have affected Filipinos in the United States in a way that tends to negate all the gains won in the era of civil rights mobi-lization. For example, the theory of Filipinos as "transnational mi-grants," or transmigrants (no relation with the religious idea of rein-carnation of souls), assumes that all nations or sovereign states are equal in power, status, and so on. Like melting-pot assimilationism, this theory combined with the neoliberal idea of the individualist work ethic geared for the competitive market promotes the continu-ing subordination of Filipinos and other racialized minorities. It erases the complex nuances of history and reinforces the continued "Other-ing" of people of color by denying popular memory and their irrepress-ible histories of resistance.

I interpose a reminder, always timely because it is always forgotten in the face of the seductions of consumerist multiculturalism, that re-peats the leitmotif of this book: Filipinos are distinguished from other Asians in the United States because their country of origin was the ob-ject of violent colonization and subjugation by U.S. monopoly capital and its state. It is this inaugural moment, not the settling in French Louisiana of a handful of fugitives from the Spanish galleons in the eighteenth-century, that demarcates the precarious life world of Fil-ipinos in this territory. Without fully comprehending this moment of violence and the internalization of dependency (now mediated through subtle mechanisms of co-optation and sublimation), Filipinos will not be able to claim their own specific historical trajectory here as a dialectical heteroglotic formation—one based on the continuing struggle of Filipinos for national independence and socialist democ-racy in the Philippines, and the other based on the exploitation and oppression of Filipino recruits, exiles, immigrants, and adventurers—from the fabled Manongs to the post-1965-"brain drain" generation to the present diasporic hemorrhage. These two aspects are indivisible in lived experience, but they can be analytically disentangled in order to assign priority of tasks and foci of attention. There are two distinct histories that although geographically separate flow into each other and produce a singular narrative or project that needs articulation at every stage of the struggle. So far, this has not been done because the stereotypes, self-delusions, and other disorders of the collective psyche, abetted by academic functionalist sociology, distort both histories across the domains of lived experience complicated by the dynamics of class, gender, race, nationality, sexual orientation, and so on.[1]

In the days before the census bureaucrats invented categories like "Asian Americans" or "Asian Pacific Islanders," there were only clusters of Chinese, Japanese, Filipinos, Indians, and so on. R. Zamora Linmark comments on how the matter of hyphenating or parentheticizing one's identity started because people in Hawaii, for example, prefer identity markers that will distinguish them from each other, not pluralize them for the sake of a spurious ethics of tolerance. Zamora Linmark disavows the convenient tags and references:

> It is only when I step outside Hawai'i and into the Continental U.S. that I become faced "Asian American," "Asian Pacific Islander," "Filipino-American," "Pil-Am," etc. In the Continental U.S., I become a millefeuille of labels and (im)personae. But to use "Asian American" as a mark of identity? Impossible. Too many different nationalities, ethnicities, races, languages, dialects, dances, impersonations, and coup d'etats. And, besides, not all the melodramas are subtitled in yellow. (1997, 38)

It would be difficult to accuse Zamora Linmark of essentialism, whether strategic or merely ludic, since it is precisely the historical specificity of the colonization of Hawaii and the production of ethnic identity via the political economy of plantation agriculture that enables his protean (not ambivalent) sensibility to apprehend exactly what political forces define inside and outside and police the boundaries.

Although they are full participants in the project of popular-democratic liberation for the Filipino nation-in-the-making, Filipinos in the United States possess their own historical trajectory and their own locus of agency. It is a trajectory the distinctive path of which is that of mediating the two experiences of domination and subjugation. To capture this singular trajectory, we need what Gramsci calls an inventory of all the deposits and traces that history has inscribed in our lives, to reckon with that "necessity which gives a conscious direction to one's activity" (1989, 124). Such an inventory, as one would expect, has been blocked by two pitfalls, the ubiquity of which tends to normalize their perils: first, a tendency to nostalgic essentialism, which, for example, pervades the fetishism of traditional dances, costumes, rituals of Igorots and Moros in Pilipino Cultural Night and other community activities given to the reflex celebration of putative Filipino customs and values; and, second, the way of minstrelsy and tutelage as a means of entitlement: Americanization by default, the staging of exemplary "little brown brothers" and sisters worshipping in the temple of white supremacy.

We might take note of how, for many young Filipino Americans, the event called "Pilipino Cultural Night" has been taken as a phenomenal expression of ethnic or racial pride. It is praised as "an affirmation of our culture" and a mode through which thousands of young students "discover ourselves . . . our identity (Benito and Thornton 1989, 51). In one single marathon cultural event, Filipinos are supposed to discover and rediscover who they are through performing the cultural heritage—folk songs, traditional dances, skits that foreground the richness and depth of something called the "Pilipino" experience. One suspects that the distinctive physiognomy of the Filipino materializes not so much in the fetishized spectacles of dancing and theatrical presentation but in the experience of group trust, solidarity, and cooperation that occurs in undertaking such a collective effort. In other words, it is the form of the project that generates the "family spirit" or quasi-organic affiliation between performers and audience, students and parents, kin and friends and acquaintances, an occasion to which is ascribed the sense of empowerment and unity that people have. It is, in short, an ersatz religious experience in a world devoid of an equalizing, compassionate, and just providence.

Obviously, Pilipino Cultural Night (PCN) is guilty of the pitfalls I mentioned earlier. Theo Gonzalves, the most painstaking aficionado and critic of what is now a viable institution at least on the West Coast, charges the PCN of essentialism and categorical hypostatization. Given its entrepreneurial logic, PCN mandates the *quidditas* of being—more precisely, of becoming—Filipino by reifying the results of cultural production instead of presenting the dynamic, flexible and multiple aspects of Filipino culture. Gonzalves cites the PCN's format and program that evince its essentialist or Orientalizing logic, including the deployment of indigenous languages as "a transnational cultural expression." The inventory of dances in PCN is static and thus dehistoricizes their ethnic import. What is more unforgiveable, Gonzalves continues, is the obsession with technical mastery of performance to produce extravagant spectacles that ultimately become predictable and repetitious. What is needed, however, is to establish a venue for experimenting with contingency, transgression, testimony, and serious "entertainment." His argument targets the narrative that connects the various dance sequences, the quest motif or "reverse exile," in which characters going through the sounds and visions of the dance suites reach

> an epiphanic state of cultural awareness and pride which they take back with them to the U.S. . . . For our young characters, "something" is miss-

ing, that which is re-placed by an "imagined" "return" to the Philippines where the "crisis" of Filipino American identity is "solved." The tacit assertion being made here is that the Philippines is a sturdy repository of "knowledge," a repository of authentic representations of Philippine life which can be accessed and brought back. The exercising of the "reverse exile" motif refuses to acknowledge the fact of cultural change, indeterminacy, and reconstruction at work in both the Philippines and in the U.S. (1995, 136)

Ironically, Gonzalves himself testifies to the fact that given the vicissitudes of Filipino cultural production, modifications and alterations are bound to happen, as witness the San Francisco State University (SFSU) Pilipino American Collegiate Endeavor's 1993 production of "Cultural Evidence" and its presentation of Filipino hip-hop culture. Although his criticism of the PCN's narcotic effect of commodifying Filipino folk dances, costumes, and usages is well taken, one needs to stress that such performances cannot be other than what they are, given the political economy of mass reification. We do not have to read Adorno and Horkheimer's denunciation of the culture industry to bewail the formulaic schemes that foreclose the "multivocality of heterogeneous and conflicting positions," even though the marketing of fluid and ambiguous identities is readily available in local emporiums. Could the pattern of the "reverse exile" be other than a reflection, however mediated, of the present dilemma of Filipinos, a symptom of the need to compulsively repeat something that is painful to accept?

I offer the suggestion that a rigorous symptomatic reading of PCN would in fact reveal those absences, lacunae, and gaps that make the crisis of the awareness of erasure and invisibility impossible to resolve. To put this in another way: Why is "Cultural Evidence" able to deviate from the normative exoticizing formula? What is the political economy of that alternative program that allowed the highlighting of "the process of identity as an unfolding set of contradictions and possibilities, rather than the fixed structure of identity to be (re)presented" (Gonzalves 1995, 139)? One is reminded of the old criticism of religion as an "opium of the people," whether espoused by mechanical materialists or secularizing agnostics, to which Marx responded: You do not blame the victim of these illusions for their malady as though complaining of the effects will remove the cause. Why not find out what specific conditions drive and habituate people to manufacture and have faith in illusions, to crave fetishes and mystifications? This is not to excuse the patent inanities, however entertaining, of PCN and the attendant waste of money, talent, and energies that could have been expended in a more sophisticated theatrical form influenced, say, by Bertolt Brecht, Dario Fo, the San Francisco Mime Troupe, Augusto

Boal, or even by the Philippine Educational Theater Association (PETA)—such examples are probably anathema or presumptuous to the organizers and sponsors of PCN.

Learning the hard way is in many instances the more feasible option. Intervention from outside—but who determines who is outside?—should be a last resort. If change in this cultural practice cannot be ruled out (as Gonzalves himself attests), it would be more useful to engage in proposing more effective and as yet untried modes of fulfilling the quest for identity by young Filipinos and not to succumb to the cult of contingency with its politics of pragmatic calculation that underlie post-Fordist capital accumulation. Instead of "strategic essentialism" which assumes a monadic positionality, I would recall here Marina Feleo-Gonzalez's (1988) project of articulating the trajectory of two histories united by one goal: self-emancipation of the Filipino from the racializing bondage of imperial patriarchy. What is imperative is to refuse the seduction of postcolonial ambiguity, which only reinforces the pluralist liberal consensus, and the other temptation of submerging one's history into a hierarchized Asian American category or any other ethnic absolute. This last possibility in fact violates the historical integrity of the Filipino people's tradition of revolutionary struggle, their outstanding contribution to humankind's narrative to transcend necessity and open up the realm of freedom—free development of all according to each one's needs.

My conviction is simply stated: *What will identify and distinguish us as Filipinos with dignity and worth is the struggle for national-democratic liberation in the Philippines and the struggle for equality and justice here, not the blind pursuit of the American "Dream of Success."* Becoming Filipino is a process of dialectical struggle that posits agency as a function of historical determination. Without a cognitive mapping of the field of battle, the limits and possibilities of historical action, all the cry for agency, creative freedom, and individual responsibility will remain empty moralizing.

Answerability for our present situation, however, cannot be evaded even before such a mapping takes place. The reason for this is that utterance (including writing) as an act of communication lacks definitive closure despite the claims of poststructuralist nihilism. Speech caught in the circuit of communication always demands, always requires interpretation. What is addressed is received and answered, deliberately or by default. One of the more cunning ripostes to the routine fabrication and reproduction of "the Filipino" in Western media and in pedagogical discourse is Zamora Linmark's recent work, *Rolling the R's.* A section of this irreverent picaresque collage is entitled "They Like You Because You Eat Dog," a mimicry-cum-parody and satire of a dislocated people from a gay Filipino Hawaii-based point of view, I quote the beginning and ending lines:

> *They like you because you eat dog, goat, and*
> *pig's blood.*
> *They like you because you grind your women the*
> *way you eat pulutan.*
> *They like you because you drink, play mah-*
> *jongg, and cockfight.*
> *They like you because you go to church every*
> *Sunday. . . .*
> *They like you because you speak broken English,*
> *and always say, Yes.*
> *They like you because you keep it all to yourself.*
> *They like you because you take it in, all the way*
> *down.*
> *They like you because you ask for it, adore it.*
> *They like you because you're a copycat, want to*
> *be just like them.*
> *They like you because—give it a few more*
> *years—you'll be just like them.*
> *And when that time comes, will they like you*
> *more?* (1995, 71–72)

We have in this text an attempt to rehearse the genealogy of the illegitimate, the bastard, the recalcitrant hybrid, a sport not of nature but of history. One of Zamora Linmark's characters recalls an "asphyxiating room" in his school that reminds him "of the colonial history of the Philippines—from Magellan's three-hundred-year old crucifix to President McKinley's hallucinations to Tsuneyoshi's camps to MacArthur's shades" (1995, 49). This syncretism of cultural *disjecta membra*, the signature of the postcolonial quandary, assumes a cosmic malevolence and hilarious absurdity when it is transposed into a setting, a library room of a Filipino family that fled the Marcos dictatorship in the seventies:

Thumbtacked on the wall facing the typewriter are three posters. A blindfolded Jesus wearing a barbed-wire tiara is crucified at the center; his lips are stapled shut. The head of the cross is inscribed with the date 1521. To his right is a map of the Philippine archipelago that is striped in red-white-and-blue and looks like the skeleton of a dog sitting upright; to his left is a cartoon of Mount Rushmore bearing the faces of George Washington, Thomas Jefferson, Ferdinand Marcos, and Charles Manson.

Above their heads, in capital letters, is the phrase ALL IN THE FAMILY. (1995, 59)

Such, then, is the fate of "melting-pot" assimilation and multicultural pluralism so much touted in polite neoliberal conversation.

Can "remembrance of things past" provide a clue to the often grotesque if well-intended misrepresentation of Filipinos? Some historians entertain the belief that the reason why Americans had the notion that Filipinos were dog-eating savages can be traced to the widely publicized ethnographic exhibit of aboriginal tribespeople that the U.S. colonial administration in the Philippines helped to organize for the Louisiana Purchase Exposition at St. Louis, Missouri, in 1904. But I think it is misleading to ascribe to this minor spectacle an exorbitant power that can even overshadow the now-mythical stature of the Iron Butterfly's (Imelda Marcos) shoe fetish that has—for good or ill—put the Philippines in the map of the global bestiary and folklore of mass consumerism. Whatever the deceptive power of these media spectacles may be, if we continue to delude ourselves that we are not objects of racist interpellations—that we are in fact on the way to successful incorporation into the U.S. civil religion of messianic imperialism (Gill 1993)—then history might repeat itself. We might be paraded again as dutiful "little brown brothers" and sisters civilized by U.S. tutelage, a mutant subspecies soon to be made extinct in some proverbial melting pot, a quaint cross between the comic-strip icon of the Mexican *bandido* and those "inscrutable Orientals" who should be shipped back as soon as possible—"go back where you came from" is the taunt often heard—thus restoring the purity of the body politic. A mythical purity as an obsession, the myth of purity feeding on and nourishing the totems of white supremacy. Either be like us or else.

It does not require Superman's x-ray vision for us to know that the paragon of the postcolonial/postmodern "hybrid" often masks an insidious "common culture" premised on differences, not contradictions. Heterogeneity can be the ruse for homogenizing patriotism. The latest version is the theory of "multiple identities" and fluid positions of immigrants straddling two nation-states assumed to be of equal status and ranking in the world system; such identities are unique because they allegedly participate in the political economies of both worlds. This is clearly a paradigm based on the dynamics of market exchange value whereby a third abstract entity emerges and circulates between two incommensurable objects or domains, supposedly partaking of both but identical with neither. The artifactual entity, however, hitherto remains parasitic on the superior nation-state, incapable of autonomous action.

Because of the seductive potential of this speculation, I would like to comment on Yen Le Espiritu's instructive study, *Filipino American Lives* (1995). In it, she applies the new conceptual model of transnationalism. When post-1965 second- and third-generation Filipinos (mostly professionals) devise strategies to construct multiple and overlapping identities, thus ostensibly altering their rank or placing in U.S. society, they succeed in resisting the dominant ideology of subordination by race, class, gender, nationality, and so on. Although the self-interpretation of the Filipino informants does contain indices of flux rather than continuity, multilinear lines of narrative rather than one monologic strand, this is not due to their overall success in elevating their country and culture of origin to equal status with the United States and its hegemonic standard. This is the flagrant mistake of the transnational model despite its gesture of acknowledging it: It assumes the parity of colonized/dominated peoples and the U.S. nation-state in contemporary global capitalism. All kinds of fallacious judgments stem from the error of marginalizing the colonial subjugation of the Filipino people by the United States, directly from 1898 to 1946 and indirectly from 1946 to the present (Kolko 1976; San Juan 1996b).

The resourceful cunning and prudence of Filipino immigrants in trying to survive and flourish in a generally inhospitable environment (San Diego, California, is considered representative of the whole country) should not be unilaterally construed as a sign of postmodern playfulness and inventiveness. Mindful of the historical relationship between subaltern people and colonizing state, one should interpret Filipino ethnic strategies as symptoms of the colonial trauma and the ordeal of enduring its effects in new disabilities, this time in the heartland of the imperial power. Because of this, most Filipinos seek assimilation and welcome acculturation; but experiences of racist insult, discrimination, ostracism, and violence disrupt their modes of adaptation and suspend their psyches in a limbo of symbolic ethnicity if not political indeterminacy. This is not a bipolar state oscillating between nostalgic nativism and coercive assimilation; it is a diasporic predicament born of the division of labor in the world system and the racialization of people of color by capital accumulation (Balibar and Wallerstein 1991).

Without disavowing the limitations of Espiritu's theoretical apparatus and its negligence of contemporary issues (poverty, teen pregnancy, gang violence, AIDS, drug abuse, and so on) for most Filipinos, I take issue with the positivistic reading of the narratives of cultural Americanization that ignore the symptoms I have alluded to. Espiritu's informants Ruby, Armando, and Elaine, for example, all invoke a distinctive Filipino history that belies Espiritu's claim that Filipino ethnicity lacks "a practiced culture" (1994, 265). It is a truism that for colonized, subaltern subjects in the historical conjuncture of post-1965 United States, the process of survival involves constant renegotiation of cultural spaces, revision of inherited folkways, reappropriation of dominant practices, and invention of new patterns of adjustment. This in itself is the cultural practice of a people attempting to transcend subalternity (as evidenced by the pertinacious appeal of Pilipino Cultural Night). What is crucial is how and why this practice is enabled by the structures of society and the varying disposition of the agents themselves. When Filipinos therefore construct the meaning of their lives (whether you label this meaning Filipino American, U.S. Filipino, Americanized Pinoys, the content determines the form), they do not—contrary to Espiritu's claim—simultaneously conform to and resist the dominant racializing ideology. This implies a latitude of free choice that does not exist. Indeed, the construction of a Filipino ethnic identity as a dynamic, complex phenomenon defies both assimilationist and pluralist models when it affirms its antiracist, counterhegemonic antecedent: the revolutionary opposition of the Filipino people to U.S. imperial domination.

In a recently published essay, Espiritu (1996) approaches Filipino ethnic organization, the social location of the group in the host society, by positioning the Philippines in the global racial order. This is a useful corrective to the transmigrant model. Elements of world system theory and the international division of labor complicate the formation of Filipino national consciousness, given the regional and class composition of the immigrant cohorts. This sums up the orthodox wisdom, in particular the stress on objective structures like residential segregation and occupational stratification required by U.S. colonial policies, recruitment practices, and working conditions. Espiritu, however, anticlimactically ventures a hypothesis: "While class and regional differences divide Filipinos in the United States, it is possible that the confrontation with US racism—one that lumps all Filipinos together—will eventually lead to community unity, at least for political purposes" (1996, 43). Positivism vitiates her thesis by attributing the origin of agency to the given reified milieu, ignoring Filipino initiatives in political mobilization. As for cultural practices immanent in the bewildering array of social clubs and regional associations, Espiritu holds that this is positive because it will link Filipinos to "multiple levels of solidarity." The fetish of heterogeneity rears up its head here. The most poignant example of this ideological reflex I can think of is the desperate if audacious plea of the speaker in Evelina Galang's sketch "Mix Like Stir Fry" from *Her Wild American Self:*

Finally, after all the voices, hear your own and know, you are one of a kind. An anomaly. . . . This is your life. It is enough for you to know you are not white, you are not from China or Japan or even, you're not even from the Philippines, the place where your parents are from. You are from the Mid-West. You are an American. You're what they call American-born-Filipina. . . . Get on with your day—changing lanes on east-coast highways, rubbing Buddha bellies everywhere, planting basil in milkbox gardens or cracking jokes in your sweet, sweet lover's bed. Get on with it. Look in the mirror. See. At last, your voice rises above the others and speaks to you, guides you, brings you to this place where you can find your wild American self, a woman who speaks out with nasal twang, drinks beer with brats and rice, and dances when no one's looking. (1996, 184)

The formula of "mix fast like stir fry" can yield only a trivial pot-pourri or hodgepodge, an essentialism of whatever goes in market cap-italist society. Instead of challenging the racist-sexist syndrome of the majority, this attitude supposedly exalts chance, subjective freedom, gratuitous happenings. But, in actuality, it accepts the designs of a commodifying technocracy of profiteers who manipulate the institu-tions of civil society and state structures for their benefit. The "wild American self" is, in the last analysis, circumscribed by territory and genetics, not by the erotic unconscious or subliminal daemonic self. In the end, we are still left disarmed and alienated, deprived of that in-ventory of ourselves necessary to plot the next seditious attack, the next insurrection.[2]

Given the unprecedented fact of 6 million Filipinos scattered around the world as "contract workers" (including "hospitality" women in Japan and elsewhere), the neocolonial (not postcolonial) im-passe of Filipino society has not suffered attenuation. On the contrary, the whole country has been refeudalized as a Western enclave in the cartography of global, transnational capitalism. This change demands a new historically grounded analysis, properly a collective and open-ended enterprise, one that would ideally be informed by an emancipa-tory and counterhegemonic praxis.

Within this horizon of exploring the terrain of the possible, adjacent to the embattled zone of subaltern metanarratives, I would like to consider here the recent novel by Jessica Hagedorn entitled *The Gang-ster of Love* (1996). One might remember that her first novel *Dog-eaters* (1990) enjoyed a brief notoriety as an afterimage of the Marcos-dictatorship interlude in our history. This is the pretext to pose questions that have now occupied center stage in the debate on multi-culturalism, identity politics, the existence of a "common culture," nationalism, racialized ethnicities, and globalized borderlands— themes and motifs rehearsed in the resurgent tide of "political correct-ness." The commentator Russell Jacoby (1995) censures postcolonial discourse for its obscure and solipsist grandiosity, its banal politics, its jargonized language, its tiresome and infantile self-obsession. Lest someone mistake me for Jacoby's target—he is actually referring to Gayatri Spivak, Homi Bhabha, and their epigones—I hasten to assure the reader that I do not consider myself a postcolonial critic if by that is meant someone from the Commonwealth countries that formed part of the nearly all-encompassing British Empire—a diasporic writer like Salman Rushdie or a successful "Third World" intellectual in a first-world institution of higher learning. But certain questions raised by Edward Said and others about the Orientalized construction of the Other by Western knowledge-power (to use Foucault's term), about the legitimacy of representations of indigenous and subaltern subjects and their capacity to speak for themselves, about the nature of agency and the possibilities of critique and transformation of world-historical inequalities—these questions rather than purely formal questions of aesthetic form will serve as the framework around which I offer the following observations on the themes and motivations of *The Gangster of Love* (1996).

The story is simple: Brought by her mother to the United States in the year Jimi Hendrix died, Raquel Rivera (together with her brother Voltaire, who eventually returns to the Philippines) grows up in the milieu of the sixties, meets a felicitously named partner Elvis Chang, and forms a band with him called "The Gangster of Love." She then befriends a versatile woman, Keiko Van Heller, and plunges into a series of somewhat déjà vu adventures with her as well as with a host of other idiosyncratic characters like her uncle Marlon Rivera. She then moves to New York City from California; teams up with Jake Montano, with whom she has a child; goes through grotesque and tragicomic scenes of her mother's death—a turning point in her life. She then returns to Manila to visit her dying father (the concluding episode is named after him) whose philandering—an index of the patriarchal regime she is revolting against but also elegizing—led to the dissolution of the family. Does the ending imply a return of the "prodigal" daughter, a reconciliation? Or does it prefigure a bridging of the gap between the homeland that had just witnessed the turmoil of the February 1986 uprising against the U.S.-backed Marcos dictatorship and the imperial power that offered a refuge to the despot in its Pacific outpost, Hawaii? Even if that is so, the dead Jimi Hendrix cannot be resurrected so easily and "The Gangster of Love" remains defunct.

Part 4 indeed carries the heading "To Return." But that rubric is a provocative alibi. It is undermined by the duplicitous connotation of the yo-yo, the toy that serves here as an icon of Filipino ethnicity, which (Hagedorn instructs us) means not just "to return" but also "to cast out." At the beginning of part 1, Hagedorn provides the slang definition of the yo-yo—a person regarded as not only stupid and ineffectual but also eccentric. More apropos of the narrative design of the novel—a bricolage interweaving of scenes using interior monologue, stream of consciousness, parody, lyric transcripts of memories and dreams, a thesaurus of trendy code words, and so on—is the colloquial sense of yo-yo: fluctuating, variable, but also automatic. If the postcolonial text is usually categorized as a pastiche of styles and idiom, a montage of heterogeneous materials that syncopate linear plot with a polyphony of voices, tones, and rhythms, then Hagedorn's invention fits the bill.

We are in the presence of a classic postmodern artifice: The causal narrative of the modern realistic novel inherited from nineteenth-century bourgeois Europe is here articulated with a picaresque mode reminiscent of feudal times, recurrent snapshots of grotesque characters symptomatic of an atomized industrial society, scenes of ribald festivity, sexual encounters, tableaux of recollections, quotations from the mass confections of Hollywood and the pop music industry, all interwoven with introspective diarylike notations. This highly stylized fabrication tries not only to dovetail the past and present in a meaningful configuration but also to intimate the emergence of the new, of future forms of life that escape the fatal cycle of the yo-yo and the reproduction of the seemingly eternal round of the "return of the repressed." What I am trying to get at is that this work attempts to render the experience of transition, of what it means to live in and through the collision of contradictory modes of production in a historically determinate social formation defined by the colonial nexus between the Philippines and the United States. What is privileged here is the process of transition, not the terminals of origin and destination. That experience of uprooting, the subsequent struggle for survival translated here as the reconstitution of "family" or some analogue of traditional consanguinity in an alien environment, and with it the construction of a new identity, is usually designated as the archetype of the postcolonial experience.

My own argument, however, is that this is not postcolonial but anticolonial or, if you like, counterhegemonic and oppositional in motive and telos. This is not the surface intent of the novel, of course. I call it the "political unconscious" (after Jameson 1981) of the text, which goes beyond the exposure of the spurious "civilizing mission" of Anglo-Saxon white supremacy. I suggest a reconstructive reading here. What makes Hagedorn's text transgressive is its supersession of the countercultural cult of the superstars of the sixties and its alignment with the social memory of the Filipinos in California crystallized by her mother's illness and death. In this itinerary of exile, the narrative begins to shape a modality of resistance to the commodifying power of late-capitalist culture and ideology. One may even suggest that its "unconscious" project, sublated in the variegated texture of the prose and its melange of genres, is to mobilize the submerged and hidden resources of indigenous forms of life for the goal of popular-national liberation. This paramount objective is indivisible with sexual and gender emancipation.

To illustrate my thesis, let me point to the fundamental contradiction expressed on the level of thematic detail. Rocky Rivera, a Filipina woman of mixed ancestry, seeks to chart her life in a society dominated by the instrumentalizing rigor of business and individualist competition. What is her point of departure? Two things are insinuated in terms of native resources: food and language. Although the temper of postmodernist art is to refuse universals and exalt particulars, we discern here a fascination with spatial ordering that becomes a surrogate means of cognitive reconnaissance. There seems to be a fetishism of place (a metaphoric geography of culture, moods, and enigmatic personalities) that tries to compensate for the secular uniformities of industrialized society. Hagedorn knows that a rupture has taken place—her body and psyche have been transported in time and space—but pretends that it has not happened: Her mother and relatives cook and eat the native foods, talk the same language (now exoticized or defamiliarized), and carry on their customary ways, with some minor adjustments. But all the same this pretense is grounded on the recognition of the truth of separation, of unequivocal distance: The brother's return confirms this. I locate this fetishism in the "Prologue," a testimony that celebrates the sheer incongruities, absurd juxtapositions, seemingly gratuitous coexistence of idioms, lifestyles, artifacts, and tastes the resonance of which dramatize the variegated temporal/spatial stratification of Philippine social life:

> There are rumors. Surrealities. Malacañang Palace slowly sinking into the fetid Pasig River, haunted by unhappy ghosts. Female ghosts. Infant ghosts. What is love? A young girl asks.
>
> Rumors. Malicious gossip, treacherous tsimis. Blah blah blah. Dire predictions, arbitrary lust. The city hums with sinister music. Scandal, innuendo, half-truths, bald-faced lies. Adulterous love affairs hatched, coups d'etat plotted. A man shoots another man for no apparent reason. A jealous husband beats his wife for the umpteenth time. The Black Nazarene collapses in a rice paddy, weeping.
>
> I love you, someone sings on the omnipresent radio. Soldiers in disguise patrol the countryside.
>
> Love, love, love. Love is in the air.
>
> Background, foreground, all around.

But what is love? A young girl asks.
A fatal mosquito bite, the nuns warn her.

Rumors. Eternal summers, impending typhoons. The stink of fear un-
mistakable in the relentless, sweltering heat. (1996, 1)

At first glance, this opening landscape strikes us as a multimedia
composite of elements with dissonant matrices and contexts. Location is not random or contingent but deliberate. Organized around a
metonymic axis are the seat of government (the mention of Mala-
canang Palace fixes the historic determinateness of the narrative); the
Pasig River, which threads through Manila, the urban center; news of
domestic violence carried by newspapers and radio; the religious icon
of the Black Nazarene suffering an accident; the presence of the military in the countryside, and so on. This collage is cut through by a re-
frain, a deflated query about love. What sutures this series is the
metaphoric cluster of "rumors" and the extremities of the climate.
How to make sense of this seemingly unintelligible conjuncture of
features of the natural and artifactual surroundings, of ubiquitous rumors, the reverberation of which is punctuated with violence, and religious codes trying to put a lid on the explosive mixture—this crux,
this bundle of contradictions, is what the novel will try to resolve on
an imaginary plane. In other words, Hagedorn will attempt to grasp
the deformed, uneven, fractured social landscape of the Philippines
with the apparatus of a self-reflexive aestheticizing consciousness, one
which is itself a product of the phenomenon of imperial violence it is
trying to grapple with and master.

In my opinion, this attempt fails—and that may be the intent of the
"political unconscious." In the section "Tropical Depression," toward
the end of the novel, Hagedorn restages the landscape with a revealing
dramatic variation: The appearance of a mythical Black Virgin functions to sublimate all the incongruities and discordances, permitting
the force of nature to normalize the phenomena of crisis. This occurs
at the time of her return after her mother's death, an event signifying
the loss of the pre-Oedipal anchor or center for her self-identifying ex-
plorations. On the terrain of chaos and unpredictability emerges a unifying and centralizing image. After the August typhoon subsides, the
city is ravaged by epidemics:

Strange scenes of violence and grieving occur without warning. Grown
men weep uncontrollably. Women run amok, hacking at everyone in
their path with any weapon they can find—bolo knives, scissors. Infants
are born with webbed feet. The general mood of despair is alleviated by
frequent sightings of the Black Virgin. She wanders the countryside, seek-

ing to comfort those who cannot be comforted. A young woman wearing a blond wig has herself crucified in a public ceremony. Her spectacle of sacrifice draws thousands of believers, showy penitents flogging their own, mildewed flesh with dainty, custom-made whips. Blood flows, the only vibrant color in this black sea of waterlogged depression. In Manila, phosphorescent crocodiles and moray eels lurk in the aquatic ruins of a submerged mega-shopping mall on Epifanio de los Santos. (290)

The sight of the flooded megamall on the highway where the February 1986 revolution took place may suggest either the inchoate level of industrialization, symptom of the inadequacy of the Filipino comprador bourgeoisie, or the irresistible power of the past, the archaic, what escapes rational and systematic control. In any case, the presence of the Black Virgin may be interpreted as symbolic of the enduring hold of mythical and magical thinking in the neocolony amid a rationalizing, secularized business environment. Ironically, this ruse is available precisely because Weberian disenchantment and commodity fetishism have not completely dominated, something that escapes the narrator's avant-garde sensibility and secretly assists its desire to ground the self (the imagination) in the field of mutual and reciprocal recognition. The author wants to have it both ways: affirm both primordial ethnicity and its antithesis, bureaucratized individualism. This anarchist politics of representation can also be read as a pretext for vindicating the status quo, business as usual. I think that is the point of the meeting of father and estranged daughter, a strange encounter of self and other, at the end of the novel.

On the level of political significance, this staging of hybridity and "in-between" confluence of signs, objects, happenings signifies the most fundamental characteristic of the kind of experience shared by subjects in most colonial formations: uneven and combined development. Although a preponderant number of characters here may be viewed as walking cyborgs or amphibians, there are two characters that function as microcosms of unevenness: Keiko and Marlon. This unevenness prevails in the sociocultural level as an effect of the diverse modes of production (and their corresponding social relations) coexisting together. Underlying the complex social formation of a peripheral, dependent region, we find the juxtaposition of various precapitalist or archaic modes of production, the tributary or feudal and artisanal spliced together with assorted capitalist modes, the most visible of which are mercantile or trading and comprador business. Absent of course is an industrial fraction—that is the space preempted by the transnational corporations as well as the World Bank and the International Monetary Fund. What is dominant, however, is a combination of bureaucratic and comprador capitalisms to which everything else—semifeudal and petty bourgeois operations and class fractions— is subordinate. This nonsynchronic combination produces specific effects on the diachronic plane that explain the concrete, quotidian forms of behavior assumed by the juridicopolitical institutions and ideological-cultural practices of all classes.

I think it is within this perspective of geopolitical unevenness and overdetermination that we can grasp the singularity of the literary/ aesthetic mode of production epitomized by Hagedorn's work. In spite of the fact that Hagedorn produces chiefly for a First World audience and more narrowly for a limited multicultural audience in urban zones, the practice she exemplifies is defined by the uneven social formation that is precisely the condition of possibility for her kind of writing. What do I mean by this?

Postcolonial orthodoxy mandates that essentialism or any quest for roots be proscribed in the same breath as syncretism and hybridity are valorized and made obligatory. Gayatri Spivak, for example, congratulates herself for reopening the "epistemic fracture of imperialism without succumbing to a nostalgia for lost origins" (1991, 272) and urges us to attend to the "archives of imperialist governance." Refusing to perform such a hermeneutic task, Hagedorn instead presents an anatomy of the Filipino colonized formation. Her style of cognitive mapping delivers an archaeology of multifarious signs alluding to several periods or stages of the development of the capitalist world system. I do not mean here a recapitulation of the evolutionary phases of the transition from feudal or precapitalist structures to modern industrial capitalism. What seems to transcend the binary opposites of the politics of blame and the politics of compassion—for Sara Suleri (1995), the "commonality of loss" that masks colonizer and colonized as complicitous binary opposites—is precisely the novel's drive to curb the vertiginous excess of heterogeneity by putting into question its feasibility for the Filipino subject-on-trial. That would mean perpetuating uneven development, even glorifying the hybrid and syncretic wretchedness produced and sustained by global capitalism and its local agencies.

The route of egocentric delirium finally arrives at a cul de sac. I have already noted the text's offering of postmodernist options addressed to Rocky Rivera's search for a community that would substitute for the neocolonial extended family her mother's departure repudiated: First is Keiko with her chameleonic masks—"one day she's Japanese and black, the next day she's Dutch and Hawaiian" (Hagedorn, 1996, 44). She mimics the role of the performative self, as in some kind of unintended parody that harbors a half-serious and half-mocking resonance: "Yesterday I was Josephine Baker. . . . Tonight I'm Edith Sitwell, and Rocky's

Marpessa Dawn. We can be them forever. Anytime we want" (117). The second option is Marlon Rivera, a Filipino gay who claims to have played "Elvis Presley's happy-go-lucky sidekick in *Blue Hawaii* and also as a nonspeaking waiter in a Chinese restaurant in Samuel Fuller's *Pickup on South Street.*" In the section "Film Noir," Marlon Rivera, who rechristened himself after seeing the film *The Wild One*, proves to be the only character that grasps his niece's implacable obsession: "She was reinventing herself moment to moment, day by day" (87). Rocky Rivera can only make sense of the craziness of Isabel L'Ange and oddities like her by juxtaposing them with movie stars and celebrity films of the past: Marlene Dietrich, Greta Garbo, Dorothy Dandridge, Anna May Wong. This is self-identification achieved by metonymy and metaphor, the effect of linguistic mechanisms working on commercial, mass-produced culture in the United States and substituting for kinship and community devalued in the periphery.

We are in the realm of simulations and mass-mediated images, a space like New York that, aside from being a real place, is for Rocky "a source of intense inspiration, a daily barrage of worthy movie moments" (98). The move from San Francisco to New York signals a shift from the mother/kin-centered milieu that mediates between the semi-feudal periphery and the core metropolis to the arena of anomic individualism, between the locus of ascription and the site of performance and social action. Before the second migration eastward, the breakup of Rocky's relation with Elvis Chang prompts Rocky's rejection of the two options as incapable of dealing with pain: "Maybe I'd rather fuck in my imagination. I allow myself to run wild and wallow in my own private kitsch. I dream of hermaphrodite angels with bronze skin floating alongside the naked, bleeding perfection of my tormented Saint Sebastian. . . . My mother's right. I am just like everyone else in my family. I believe in heaven and hell, the pleasures of denial, and the rewards of sin. . . . I enjoy this only because it's forbidden" (129–30).

Whatever the seductions of border crossings and other boundary violations, the protean pleasures of the cyborg, and the free-floating hubris of indeterminacy afforded by consumerism and the liberal marketplace, Rocky Rivera knows that it will be an ordeal to shed the markers of subordination and dependency. The stigma of Otherness persists. She cannot put aside "unbearable questions" such as "What's Filipino? What's authentic? What's in the blood?" Before she moves east and separates from her mother, Rocky meditates on this reprise of the first uprooting. The interrogative mood is displaced by the subjunctive:

I am unable to leave, overcome by helplessness in the face of family, blood, and the powerful force of my own reluctant love. Family sickness, homesickness. Manila, our dazzling tropical city of memory. The English language confuses me. What is at the core of that subtle difference between homesick and nostalgic, for example? .... "Ties to the spirit world, fierce pride, wounded pride, thirst for revenge, melodrama, fatalism, weeping and wailing at the graveside. We're blessed with macabre humor and dancing feet—a floating nation of rhythm and blues," Voltaire answers, repeating what this old guy known as the Carabao Kid used to say: "We're our own worst enemy." (57–58)

This passage reveals both the allure of imperial exoticism and the impulse of critique, skepticism, and sentimentality, the presence of the Manichean duality once described by Frantz Fanon (1968) in the period of the Algerian revolution. Evocation of the neocolony as the archetypal locus of incongruities and dissonances, a microcosm of opposites like the sadomasochistic figure of St. Sebastian, may be a tactic of eliding the discrepancy between the homeland and the place of exile. This may be called for by the yo-yo trope that seeks to define the method and architectonics of the whole narrative. But the tactic is not an endorsement of postcolonial multiplicity or "interactive mutuality" between master and servant. It is, on the contrary, an attempt to transcend the symbolic economy of fetishism that denies what is absent and by that token affirms it.

A telling instance of the novel's allegorical rendering of conflated modes of production may be found in the treatment of the Carabao Kid, a figure as legendary as the grandfather who invented the yo-yo. The section describing Rocky's encounter with the Carabao Kid is a recollection that occurs after the birth of Venus, Rocky's child. The Carabao Kid serves here as the character that links the first generation of Filipino farm-workers, the Manongs (whom Carlos Bulosan wrote about in *America Is in the Heart* [1946] 1973) , and the post-1965 influx of professionals. He was then considered the "unofficial spiritual leader" of the Pilipino arts movement in San Francisco, the emblem for which was the water buffalo. Even though the Carabao Kid was leading civil rights demonstrations and rallies against the Vietnam War, he was still a migrant worker (he dies before the start of a shrimping expedition in Louisiana); his residence, Watsonville, evokes the anti-Filipino riots of the thirties. Rocky asserts at the end that she does not need him anymore—for her, he symbolizes the mawkish sentimentalism, humility, and need to suffer that afflicts the Filipino sensibility—so that the snapshot of the community at the end of part 2 turns out to be the sacrifice of the father at the altar of the pre-Oedipal mother. We confront here the petty bourgeois Filipinos of the sixties and seventies (still mired in the barbarity of Cold War anticommunism) using a pretext for dissociating themselves from the working-class struggles of Bulosan, Chris Mensalvas, and Philip Vera Cruz. Hagedorn's tribute to this generation is instructive as a gesture of solidarity and of demarcation:

Ah, the Carabao Kid and what he taught us. How to be a F(P)ilipino. Voltaire's idealized father figure. And mine too, I suppose. He was this Pinoy poet from Watsonville with the sleepy, wise face of a water buffalo, a man totally obsessed with the Philippines who'd never been there. In hushed tones, he'd describe the fiery sunsets, swaying coconut trees, and white sand beaches, sounding like some romantic tourist brochure. Kinda ironic and laughable, except the Kid thought it was funny too. "Oh yeah, sister, I forgot—I've never been there." America was here: vast, inhospitable, and harsh. The Philippines was there: distant, lush, soulful, and sexy. He made constant jokes out of what he called his "carabao dreaming" and wrote a series of self-deprecating haikus called "Existential Pinoy Paralysis," questioning his fears about returning to the homeland. "Maybe I just don't want to be disappointed, went one of the more quotable lines of his poem 'Maybe.' Another ditty was called 'EXpat vs. EXile.' The fact that Voltaire and I had actually been born in the Philippines had earned us his lasting admiration." (1996, 199)

This portrait explodes the model of postcolonial "sly civility" as one based on a fabric of fetishes, half-truths, and fraudulent mystifications. The dreaming carabao cannot distance itself from the illusion that the Philippines and the United States are on equal footing, autonomous, geopolitically independent from each other. References to the colonial situation abound (one example is the scene with the Puerto Rican taxi driver Eduardo Zuniga). The sections "Lost in Translation" seem like satiric spoofs on the postcolonial idea of translation as a way of negotiating the distance between oppressed and oppressor, a gap acerbically brought home by the "Joke Not So Lost in Translation": "Why did the Filipino cross the road? Because he thought America was on the other side" (70).

One hypothesis may be introduced here. The enunciation of apparent similarities and affinities as deceptive may be Hagedorn's warning that postcolonial erasure of conflict may be a disservice to people of color, not praise for their adaptive resourcefulness. Crossing the "road" from the Philippines to the United States is an act of cognitive mapping of present-day neocolonialism, also called globalization. For Hagedorn, the symbolic yo-yo enacts this orientation in terms of an easy compromise between exile and return: She visits the Philippines in 1992 to say goodbye to her father, who has endured his terminal cancer for at least ten years. The yo-yo as "jungle weapon" also reaffirms a certain native ingenuity and resilience that distinguishes his life under Western surveillance and diktat. This implicit nationalism, however, finds itself sublimated in the themes of youth revolt, the vicissitudes of the artist's education, and her endeavor to forge an identity outside of the ethnic/racial and class determinations of her origin.

The figure of Jimi Hendrix finally offers us the key to specify the project of this anti-postcolonial text—if one may so categorize it in its generic impulse. Hendrix (together with Janis Joplin and later Jim Morrison) may be construed as emblems for the rock festival of the sixties, the occasion providing the experience of community that the music expressed aesthetically. This experience is a renewal if not recreation of trust, of the sense of possibility, the harmony between public and private life, the sense of honesty and authenticity—what Pilipino Cultural Night adumbrates via parody, excess, and commodification. Simon Frith comments on the value of this event for its audience: "Rock performance . . . came to mean not pleasing an audience (pop style) nor representing it (folk style) but, rather, displaying desires and feelings rawly, as if to a lover or friend. The appeal . . . of Jimi Hendrix rested on the sense that his apparently uninhibited pursuit of pleasures was on show, for all of us to see and share" (1984, 66). Hendrix was one of the cult stars who proclaimed a utopia without struggle, founded on the immediacy of pleasure and solidarity. In this context, Rocky Rivera's band "The Gangster of Love" seeks to imitate that politics of aestheticism, though now informed with a somewhat cynical toughness and punk's psychedelic playfulness: "Congo today, money tomorrow" (1996, 245).

In "Our Music Lesson #1" in the first part, Hendrix is worshipped as a historical charismatic figure. Rocky salutes him with "flames bursting out your skull. Salvation funky. Redemption funky." But here Rocky also confesses a certain distance. When Hendrix begs her to "Fuck me, then. Save my soul," Rocky retorts: "I know all about you. I was fourteen when you died, but I'm not stupid" (77). She would not —as she puts it—"suck King Kong's dick" to get to him. In "Our Music Lesson #2," Hendrix's ironic pathos is "appropriated and dissolved in 'Pilipino blood,'" so that his "LSD-laced, corny cosmi-comic mythology" becomes indigenized, so to speak. For Hagedorn's generation, Hendrix represents the young martyr dying young, the doomed outsider who performs the ritual sacrifice to propitiate the gods of order. After Hendrix's death (at which point Hagedorn's narration begins), Todd Gitlin observes the decline of youth counterculture into the monadic narcissism of John Lennon: "Woodstock Nation's symbols peeled away from their Aquarian meanings and became banal with popularity" (1987, 429). In a sense, Hagedorn's novel is one long elegy to the demise of rock culture's internationalism as a strategy for overthrowing U.S./Western imperial hegemony over the oppressed and exploited masses of the planet.

After fifteen years, Rocky Rivera dismantles her band and bids farewell to the illusions of the sixties. "We F(P)ilipinos can imitate, but this audience [in Zamboanga, a city in southern Philippines] prefers the real thing" (1996, 245). Considered "postmodern, postcolonial punks," Rocky's band had to flee the irate natives, "condemned to exile as second-rate, Western imperialist, so-called artists," seeking refuge in the "safety of Motown memory" (246). Deprived of that ersatz community, Rocky Rivera, now a mother, recuperates the memory of her mother's life before her move to the United States—a labor of unfolding the genealogy of her deracination so as to derive meaning from that process. It is an act of constituting experience that is coeval with the narrative (for Hagedorn's reflection on the substance of this experience, see Aguilar–San Juan 1994).

When she returns to the Philippines, Rocky Rivera is no longer just an isolated individual. She becomes a collective presence, holding in a composite and synthesizing trope the dispersed and fragmented lives of generations of Filipinos whose chief claim to distinction is (to paraphrase the Carabao Kid) their unrelenting pursuit of happiness and their equally inexhaustible capacity to suffer. We are already beyond the postcolonial economy of complicity and guilt, of narcissism and paranoia, of Manichean dualism and the metaphysics of difference and ambivalent identity that Hagedorn syncopated in the adventures of her group, "The Gangster of Love." There is no nostalgia for the return of an idyllic and innocent past. There is no easy route to Arcadia or a remote classless utopia. We are in the zone of accounting for difference as a symptom of unequal power relations between the hegemonic imperial power and the colonized, this time transcoded into the decline of patriarchal authority (emblematized here by the dying Francisco Rivera) and the anticipated empowerment of the "mothers." This eventuality takes place in the "weak links" of uneven development, precisely where the layers of temporalities do not coincide, where ruptures and breaks and discontinuities persist in reproducing conflicts that open up the space for grassroots intervention. This novel presents us with an allegory of how such a space can materialize in the interstices of alienation, displacement, and defeats. The carnival of the dispossessed and the conquered is just beginning.

In the introduction to her collection *Danger and Beauty* (1993), Hagedorn outlines the genealogy of her vocation in the sixties, citing not only Hendrix but also George Jackson and Angela Davis aside from "water buffalo shamans" like Al Robles. She recalls their anxiety to celebrate "our individual histories, our rich and complicated ethnicities ... borders be damned" (ix). At about the time the socialist Salvador Allende was overthrown by the CIA-backed junta in Chile,

Hagedorn marks a turning point in her life: "The year 1973 is when I begin discovering myself as a Filipino-American writer. What does this newfound identity mean? The longing for what was precious and left behind in the Philippines begins to creep in and take over my work" (x). In the year she formed her band "The West Coast Gangster Choir" and Ho Chi Minh finally drove the Americans out of Indochina, she returned to the Philippines after an absence of many years. Apart from her musical experimentation, it was her journey back home that inspired much of her later work. In the process, she believes her volatile voice "has hardened, become more dissonant and fierce" (Hagedorn 1993, xi). It was during the precipitous decline of the Marcos dictatorship, the 1986 February insurrection, and the return of the oligarchs and warlords in the Aquino regime that she composed this novel, her "love letter to my motherland: a fact and a fiction borne of rage, shame, pride . . . and most certainly, desire" (xi). It is the politics of this ludic "desire," the "playful and deadly serious" trajectory of Hagedorn's performance, that I have tried to assay here, searching for clues to that permanent cultural revolution that Marx, Lenin, Emilio Jacinto, Edicio de la Torre, and Maria Lorena Barros spoke of beyond the vigil of Pilipino Cultural Night and the elegiac farewells of *balikbayans* and other peregrine exiles.

7

Fragments from
an Exile's Journal

. . . but shall be overtaken unawares.

The Rubaiyat of Omar Khayyam

It has been almost forty years now, to this longest day 21 June 1996, of my sojourn here in the United States ever since we left Manila. The time of departure can no longer be read in the number of passports discarded, visas stamped over and over again. A palimpsest to be deciphered, to be sure. But you can always foretell and anticipate certain things. For example, when someone meets you for the first time, this Caucasian—in general, Western—stranger would irresistibly and perhaps innocently (a reflex of commonsensical wisdom) always ask: "And where are you from?" Alas, from the red planet Mars, from the volcanic terra of the as yet undiscovered satellite of Andromeda, from the alleys of Tondo and the labyrinths of Avenida Rizal. . . .

The sociologist Zygmunt Bauman (1996) delineates the possible life strategies that denizens of the postmodern era can choose: stroller, vagabond, tourist, player. In a world inhospitable to pilgrims, I opt for the now obsolete persona of the exile disguised as itinerant and peripatetic student without credentials or references, sojourning in places where new experiences may occur. No destination nor destiny, only a succession of detours and displacements.

Apropos of the sojourner, Cesar Vallejo (1976) writes during his exile in Paris, November 12, 1937: "*Acaba de pasar sin haber venido*" ("He just passed without having come"). A cryptic and gnomic utterance. One can interpret this thus: For the sake of a sustained bliss of journeying, the "passenger" (the heroine of the passage) forfeits the grace or climax of homecoming. But where is home? Home is neither on the range nor in the valley nor on the distant shores—it is no longer a "place" but rather a site or locus to which you can return no more, as Thomas Wolfe once elegized. We have not yet reached this stage, the desperate act of switching identities (as in Michelangelo Antonioni's *The Passenger*, in which the protagonist's itinerary ends in the ad hoc, repetitious, inconsequential passage into anonymous death) so as to claim the spurious originality of an "I," the monadic ego a.k.a. the foundation of all Western metaphysics. Our postdeconstructionist malaise forbids this detour, this escape. Antonioni's existential "stranger" forswears the loved one's offer of trust, finding danger even boring and trivial. After all, you are only the creature—not yet a cyborg—shunted from one terminus to another, bracketed by an amethodical doubt and aleatory suspicion.

So here we are, "here" being merely a trope, a figure without referent or denotation. To such a denouement has Western consumerized technological society come, trivializing even Third World revolutions and violence as cinematic fare. *Beyond Rangoon* is the latest of such commodities in the high-cultural supermarket of the Western metropolis. The setting is no longer Burma but Myamar. The names do not matter; what is needed is some exotic location to which to transplant a white U.S. woman's psyche suffering a horrendous trauma: discovering the murdered bodies of her husband and son upon coming home from work. Desperate to put this horror behind her, she and her sister then join a tour to Myamar. Soon, she gets involved in the popular resistance against a ruthless military dictatorship. So what happens? Carnage, melodramatic escapades, incredible violence and slaughter, until our heroine begins to empathize with the unruly folk and arguably finds her identity by rediscovering her vocation, as physician, at the end of the film. She begins to attend to the victims without thought of her own safety or pleasure. She is reconciled with the past, finding substitutes for the dead in "Third World" mutilated bodies. And so white humanity redeems itself again in the person of this caring, brave, daring woman whose "rite of passage" is the thematic burden of the film. It is a passage from death to life, not exactly a transmigration from scenes of bloodletting to moments of peace and harmony; nonetheless, strange "Third World" peoples remain transfixed in the background, waiting for rescue and redemption. So, for the other part of humanity, there is no movement but simply a varying of intensity of suffering, punctuated by resigned smiles or bitter tears.

So the "beyond" is staged here as the realization of hope for the West. But what is in it for us who are inhabiting (to use a cliché) the "belly of the beast"? But let us go back to Vallejo, or to wherever his imagination has been translocated. Come to think of it, even the translation of Vallejo's line is an escape: There is no pronoun there.

Precisely the absence of the phallus (if we follow our Lacanian guides) guarantees its infinite circulation as the wandering, nomadic signifier. Unsettled, traveling, the intractable vagrant. . . .

Lost in the desert or in some wilderness, are we looking for a city of which we are unacknowledged citizens? Which city, Babylon or Jerusalem? St. Augustine reminds us: "Because of our desire we are already there, we have already cast our hope like an anchor on these shores" (quoted in Kristeva 1991, 83). By the logic of desire, the separation of our souls from our bodies is finally healed by identification with a figure like Christ who, in Pauline theology, symbolizes the transit to liberation from within the concrete, suffering body. What is foreign or alien becomes transubstantiated into a world-encompassing Ecclesia, a new polis in which we, you and I, find ourselves embedded.

Stranger no more, I am recognized by others whom I have yet to identify and know. Instead of Albert Camus's *L'Etranger* (which in my youth served as a fetish for our bohemian revolt against the provincial Cold War milieu of the Manila of the fifties), Georg Simmel's "The Stranger" (1977) has become of late the focus of my meditation. It is an enigmatic text, the profound implications of which cannot really be spelled out in words, only in lived experiences, in praxis. Simmel conceives "the stranger" as the unity of two opposites: mutating between "the liberation from every given point in space" and "the conceptual opposite to fixation at such a point," hence the wanderer defined as "the person who comes today and stays tomorrow." Note that the staying is indefinite, almost a promise, not a certainty. But where is the space of staying, or maybe of malingering?

Simmel's notion of space tries to bridge potentiality and actuality: "Although he has not moved on, he has not quite overcome the freedom of coming and going. He is fixed within a particular spatial group, or within a group whose boundaries are similar to spatial boundaries." The wanderer is an outsider, not originally belonging to this group, importing something into it. Simmel's dialectic of inside/outside spheres is tricky here; it may be an instance of wanting to have one's cake and also eat it:

> The unity of nearness and remoteness involved in every human relation is organized, in the phenomenon of the stranger, in a way which may be most briefly formulated by saying that in the relationship to him, distance means that he, who is close by, is far, and strangeness means that he, who also is far, is actually near. For, to be a stranger is naturally a very positive relation; it is a specific form of interaction. The inhabitants of Sirius are not really strangers to us, at least not in any sociologically relevant sense: they do not exist for us at all; they are beyond far and near. The stranger, like the poor and like sundry "inner enemies," is an ele-

ment of the group itself. His position as a full-fledged member involves both being outside it and confronting it. (1977, 14)

And so, following this line of speculation, the query "Where are you from?" is in effect a token of intimacy. For the element that increases distance and repels, according to Simmel, is the one that establishes the pattern of coordination and consistent interaction that is the foundation of coherent sociality.

Between the essentialist mystique of the *Volk*/nation and the libertarian utopia of laissez-faire capitalism, the "stranger" subsists as a catalyzing agent of change. In other words, the subversive function of the stranger inheres in his or her being a mediator of two or more worlds. Is this the hybrid and in-between diasporic character of postcoloniality? Is this the indeterminate species bridging multiple worlds? Or is it more like the morbid specimens of the twilight world of Antonio Gramsci (1957), languishing in prison, once alluded to, caught between the ancien régime slowly dying and a social order that has not yet fully emerged from the womb of the old. We are brought back to the milieu of transition, of vicissitudes, suspended in the proverbial conundrum of the tortoise overtaking the hare in Zeno's paradox. This may be the site where space is transcended by time. The stranger's emblematic message may be what one black musician has already captured in this memorable manifesto: "It ain't where you're from, it's where you're at" (Gilroy 1990).

Historically, the stranger in Simmel's discourse emerged first as the trader. When a society needs products from outside its borders, an intermediary is then summoned who will mediate the exchange. (If a god is needed, as the old adage goes, there will always be someone to invent him or her.) But what happens when those products coming from outside its territory begin to be produced inside, when a middleman role is no longer required, that is, when the economy is closed, land divided up, and handicrafts formed to insure some kind of autarky? Then the stranger, who is the supernumerary (Simmel cites European Jews as the classic example), becomes the settler whose protean talent or sensibility distinguishes him or her. This sensibility springs from the habitus of trading "which alone makes possible unlimited combinations," where "intelligence always finds expansions and new territories," because traders are not fixed or tied to a particular location; they do not own land or soil or any ideal point in the social environment. Whence originates their mystery? From the medium of money, the instrument of exchange:

Restriction to intermediary trade, and often (as though sublimated from it) to pure finance, gives him the specific character of mobility. If mobil-

ity takes place within a closed group, it embodies that synthesis of nearness and distance which constitutes the formal position of the stranger.
For the fundamentally mobile person comes in contact, at one time or another, with every individual, but is not organically connected, through
established ties of kinship, locality, and occupation, with any single one.
(1977, 14)

From this paradoxical site of intimacy and detachment, estrangement and communion, is born the quality of "objectivity" that allows
the fashioning of superior knowledge. This does not imply passivity
alone, Simmel argues: "It is a particular structure composed of distance and nearness, indifference and involvement." For instance, the
dominant position of the stranger is exemplified in the practice of
those Italian cities that chose judges from outside the city because "no
native was free from entanglement in family and party interests."
Could the courts in the Philippines ever contemplate this practice,
courts that are literally family sinecures, nests of clan patronage and
patriarchal gratuities? Only when there is a threat of interminable
feuds, a cycle of vindictive retribution. Otherwise, legitimacy is always based on force underwritten by custom, tradition, the inertia of
what is familiar. So, strangeness is subversive when it challenges the
familiar and normal, the hegemony of sameness.

On the other hand, this persona may also be conservative. The
stranger, then, like Prince Myshkin in Dostoevsky's *The Idiot* (1971),
becomes the occasion for a public display of intimacies. He or she becomes the hieratic vessel or receiver of confessions performed in public, of confidential information, secrets, rumors, and so on; the bearer
of guilt and purgation, the stigmata of communal responsibility and
its catharsis. His or her objectivity is then a full-blown participation
that, obeying its own laws, thus eliminates—Simmel theorizes—"accidental dislocations and emphases, whose individual and subjective
differences would produce different pictures of the same object" (1977,
15). From this standpoint, the prince is a stranger not because he is not
Russian but because he "idiotically" or naively bares whatever he
thinks—he says it like it is. Which does not mean he does not hesitate
or entertain reservations, judgments, and so on. Dostoevsky invents
his escape hatch in the prince's epileptic seizures, which become
symptomatic of the whole society's disintegrated totality.

We begin to become more acquainted with this stranger as the spiritual ideal embedded in contingent reality. Part of the stranger's objectivity is his or her freedom: "The objective individual is bound by no
commitments which could prejudice his perception, understanding,
and evaluation of the given"(1977, 15). Is this possible: a person without commitments, open to every passing opportunity? Spinoza, G. E.

Moore, Mikhail Bakhtin are not wanted here. Ethics be damned. I think here Simmel is conjuring up the image of the value-free sociologist who has completely deceived himself or herself even of the historical inscription of his or her discipline, finally succumbing to the wish fulfillment of becoming the all-knowing scientist of historical laws and social processes. Simmel is quick to exonerate the stranger, the middleman-trader, from charges of being a fifth columnist, an instigator or provocateur paid by outsiders. On the other hand, Simmel insists that the stranger "is freer, practically and theoretically; he surveys conditions with less prejudice; his criteria for them are more general and more objective ideals; he is not tied down in his action by habit, piety, and precedent." The stranger has become some kind of omniscient deity, someone like the god of Flaubert and Joyce paring his fingernails behind the clouds while humanity agonizes down below.

Finally, Simmel points out the abstract nature of the relation of others to the stranger. This is because "one has only certain more general qualities in common," not organic ties that are empirically specific to inhabitants sharing a common historical past, culture, kinship, and so forth. The humanity that connects stranger and host is precisely the one that separates, the element that cannot be invoked to unify the stranger with the group of which he or she is an integral part. So, nearness and distance coalesce again: "To the extent to which the common features are general, they add, to the warmth of the relation founded on them, an element of coolness, a feeling of the contingency of precisely this relation—the connecting forces have lost their specific and centripetal character"(1977, 16).

One may interpose at this juncture: Why is Simmel formulating the predicament of the stranger as a paradox that too rapidly resolves the contradictions inherent in it? The dialectic is shortcircuited, the tension evaporated, by this poetic reflection: "The stranger is close to us, insofar as we feel between him and ourselves common features of a national, social, occupational, or generally human, nature. He is far from us, insofar as these common features extend beyond him or us, and connect us only because they cannot connect a great many people"(1977, 16). What generalizes, estranges; what binds us together, individualizes each one.

We witness an immanent dialectical configuration shaping up here. Every intimate relationship then harbors the seeds of its own disintegration. The aborigine and the settler are fused in their contradictions and interdependencies. For what is common to two, Simmel continues to insist, "is never common to them alone but is subsumed under a general idea which includes much else besides, many possibilities of commonness." This, I think, applies to any erotic relationship, which, in the beginning, compels the lovers to make their relationship unique, unrepeatable, even idiosyncratic. Then estrangement ensues; the feeling of uniqueness is replaced by skepticism and indifference, by the thought that the lovers are only instances of a general human destiny. In short, the lovers graduate into philosophers reflecting on themselves as only one of the infinite series of lovers in all of history. These possibilities act like a corrosive agent that destroys nearness, intimacy, communal togetherness:

> No matter how little these possibilities become real and how often we forget them, here and there, nevertheless, they thrust themselves between us like shadows, like a mist which escapes every word noted, but which must coagulate into a solid bodily form before it can be called jealousy. . . . Similarity, harmony, and nearness are accompanied by the feeling that they are not really the unique property of this particular relationship. They are something more general, something which potentially prevails between the partners and an indeterminate number of others, and therefore gives the relation, which alone was realized, no inner and exclusive necessity. (1977, 16)

Perhaps in Gunnar Myrdal's (1974) "America," where a universalistic creed, once apostrophized by that wandering French philosophe de Tocqueville, prevails, this privileging of the general and the common obtains. But this "perhaps" dissolves because we see, in the history of the past five decades, that cultural pluralism is merely the mask of a "common culture" of market individualism, of class war inflected into the routine of racial politics. Witness the victims of the civil rights struggles, the assassination of Black Panther Party members, violence inflicted on Vincent Chin and other Asians, and so on.

As antidote to the mystification of hybridity and in-betweenness, we need therefore to historicize, to come down to the ground of economic and political reality. What collectivities of power/knowledge are intersecting and colliding? In a political economy where racial differentiation is the fundamental principle of accumulation, where profit and the private extraction of surplus value is the generalizing principle, it is difficult to accept Simmel's concept of strangeness as premised on an initial condition of intimacy and mutual reciprocity. Simmel is caught in a bind. He says that the Greek attitude to the barbarians illustrates a mind frame that denies to the Other attributes that are specifically human. But, in that case, the barbarians are not strangers; the relation to them is a nonrelation. For the stranger is "a member of the group," not an outsider. Simmel arrives at this concluding insight:

> As a group member, the stranger is near and far at the same time as is characteristic of relations founded only on general human commonness. But between nearness and distance, there arises a specific tension when

the consciousness that only the quite general is common stresses that which is not common. [Here is the kernel of Simmel's thesis.] In the case of the person who is a stranger to the country, the city, the race, etc., however, this non-common element is once more nothing individual, but merely the strangeness of origin, which is or could be common to many strangers. For this reason, strangers are not really conceived as individuals, but as strangers of a particular type: the element of distance is no less general in regard to them than the element of nearness. (1977, 17)

Examples might illuminate this refined distinction. Simmel cites the case of the categorization of the Jew in medieval times, which remained permanent, despite the changes in the laws of taxation: The Jew was always taxed as a Jew, his or her ethnic identity fixed by social position, whereas the Christian was "the bearer of certain objective contents" that changed in accordance with the fluctuation of his or her fortune (ownership of property, wealth). If this invariant element disappeared, then all strangers by virtue of being strangers would pay "an equal headtax." In spite of this, the stranger is "an organic member of the group which dictates the conditions of his existence"— except that this membership is precisely different in that, while it shares some similarities with all human relationships, a special proportion and reciprocal tension produce the particular, formal relation to the "stranger."

An alternative to Simmel's hypothesis is the historical case of Spinoza, the archetypal exile. A child of the Marrano community of Jews in Amsterdam, Holland, who were driven from Portugal and Spain in the fourteenth and fifteenth centuries, Spinoza was eventually excommunicated and expelled by the elders of the community. Banned as a heretic, Spinoza became an "exile within an exile." It was, however, a *felix culpa* since that became the condition of possibility for the composition of the magnificent *Ethics* (1994), a space of redemption in which *deus/natura* becomes accessible to ordinary mortals provided they can cultivate a special form of rationality called *scientia intuitiva*. The "impure blood" of this "Marrano of Reason" (Yovel 1989) affords us a created world of secular reason that, if we so choose, can become a permanent home for the diasporic intellect. Unfortunately, except for a handful of recalcitrant spirits, Filipinos have not yet discovered Spinoza's *Ethics*.

So where are we now in mapping this terra incognita of the nomadic monster, the deviant, the alien, the stranger?

We are unquestionably in the borderline, the hymen, the margin of difference that is constituted by that simultaneous absence and presence that Jacques Derrida was the first to theorize as a strategy of suspicion. It is, one might suggest, an epileptic seizure that is regularized, as the character of Prince Myshkin demonstrates. When asked by that unforgettable mother, Mrs. Yepanchin, what he wrote to her daughter Aglaya—a confession of need of the other person, a communication of desire for the other to be happy as the gist of the message, Prince Myshkin replied that when he wrote it, he had "great hopes." He explains: "Hopes—well, in short, hopes of the future and perhaps a feeling of joy that I was not a stranger, not a foreigner, there. I was suddenly very pleased to be back in my own country. One sunny morning I took up a pen and wrote a letter to her. Why to her, I don't know. Sometimes, you know, one feels like having a friend at one's side."

Dear friend, where are you?

Since we are in the mode of a "rectification of names," a semantic interlude is appropriate here. Just as our current hermeneutic trend seeks etymologies and obsolete usages for traces of the itinerary of meanings, let us look at what Webster offers us for the word "exile": It means banished or expelled from one's native country or place of residence by authority, and forbidden to return, either for a limited time or for life; abandonment of one's country by choice or necessity. "The Exile" originally refers to the Babylonian captivity of the Jews in the sixth century B.C.

The Latin *exilium* denotes banishment; the Latin *exilis* denotes slender, fine, thin; "exilition," now obsolete, "a sudden springing or leaping out." This "sudden springing or leaping out" offers room for all kinds of speculation on wandering strangers inhabiting borderlines, boundaries, frontiers, all manner of refusals and evasions. But the movement involved in exile is not accidental or happenstance; it has a telos underlying it. It implicates wills and purposes demarcating the beginning and end of movement. As Spinoza teaches us, everything can be grasped as modalities of rest and motion, of varying speed. Even here ambiguity pursues us: Rest is relative to motion, motion to rest. If everyone is migrating, then who is the native and who the settler?

Another word should supplement "exile" and that is "migration." The movement from place to place that this word points to in one usage is quite circumscribed: It is the movement from one region to another with the change in seasons, as many birds and some fishes follow, for example, "migratory locust." "Migratory" worker is "one who travels from harvest to harvest, working until each crop is gathered or processed," to wit, the Filipino "Manongs" and their Mexican counterparts. The species of *homo sapiens* pursues the line of flight instinctively followed by bird and fish, but this calibration of the instinct itself is drawn by the rhythm of the seasons, by earth's ecological mutation. So exile betrays political will, whereas migration still

obscures or occludes the play of secular forces by the halo of natural-
ness, the aura of cosmic fate and divine decree. The fate of Bulosan
and compatriots of the "warm body export" trade today—all 5 million
bodies—offers the *kairos* of an exemplum.

The life history of the national hero Jose Rizal offers one viable paradigm for Filipino intellectuals in exile. When this leading anticolonial
propagandist-agitator was banished to Dapitan, in the southern island
of Mindanao, in 1892, he assured his family that "Wherever I might go
I should always be in the hands of God who holds in them the destinies
of men" (Guerrero 1969, 341). Despite this unabashed deistic faith,
Rizal immediately applied himself to diverse preoccupations: horticul-
ture, eye surgery, collecting butterflies for study, teaching, civic construction, composing a multilingual dictionary, and so on. He also
maintained a voluminous correspondence with scientists and scholars
in Europe and Manila. Even though the Spanish authorities were le-
nient, Rizal had no utopian illusions: "To live is to be among men, and
to be among men is to struggle. . . . It is a struggle with them but also
with one's self, with their passions, but also with one's own, with errors and with anxieties" (Guerrero 1969, 345). The anguish of Rizal's
exile was assuaged somewhat by his mistress, Josephine Bracken, an
Irish Catholic from Hong Kong. But he could not deny that his being
transported to Dapitan was demoralizing, given "the uncertainty of the
future." This is why he seized the opportunity to volunteer his medical
skills to the Spanish army engaged in suppressing the revolution in
Cuba. Amplifying distance and alienation, he could resign himself to
the demands of duty, of the necessity "to make progress through suffering." Fatalism and service to the cause of humanity coalesced to distinguish the ethos of this exile at a time when rumblings of popular dis-
content had not yet climaxed in irreversible rupture. When Rizal was
executed in December 1896, the revolution had already exploded, con-
centrating scattered energies in the fight against a common enemy,
first Spain and then the United States.

In the context of globalized capitalism today, the Filipino diaspora
acquires a distinctive physiognomy and temper. It is a fusion of exile
and migration: the scattering of a people, not yet a fully matured nation, to the ends of the earth, across the planet throughout the sixties
and seventies, continuing up to the present. We are now a quasi-wan-
dering people, pilgrims or prospectors staking our lives and futures all
over the world—in the Middle East, Africa, Europe, North and South
America, Australia and all of Asia; in every nook and cranny of this
seemingly godforsaken earth. No one yet has performed a "cognitive
mapping" of these movements, their geometry and velocity, across national boundaries, mocking the carnivalesque borderland hallucinations glorified by academics of color.

Who cares for the Filipino anyway? Not even the Philippine government does—unless compelled by massive demonstrations of anger at
the execution of Flor Contemplacion in Singapore. We are a nation in
search of a national-democratic sovereign state that will care for the
welfare of every citizen. When Benigno Aquino was killed, the slogan
"The Filipino is worth dying for" became fashionable for a brief inter-
val between the calamity of the Marcos dictatorship and the mendacity of Corazon Aquino's rule. But today Filipinos are dying—for what?

In 1983 alone, there were 300,000 Filipinos in the Middle East. I met
hundreds of Filipinos, men and women, in the city park in Rome, in
front of the train station, during their days off as domestics and semi-
skilled workers. I met Filipinos hanging around the post office in
Tripoli, Libya, in 1980. And in trips back and forth, I have met them in
London, Amsterdam, Madrid, Barcelona, Florence, Montreal, and of
course everywhere in the United States—a dispersed nationality, perhaps a little better than Philip Vera Cruz and his compatriots during
the thirties and forties, field hands and laborers migrating from harvest to harvest from California through Oregon to Washington and
Alaska. A whole people dispersed, displaced, dislocated. A woman
from Negros watched her husband flying to Saudi Arabia in 1981:
"Even the men cry on leaving and cling to their children at the airport.
When the airplane lifted off, I felt as though my own body was being
dislocated." Like birth pangs, the separation of loved ones generates a
new experience, a nascent "structure of feeling," for which we have
not yet discovered the appropriate plots, rhetorical idioms, discursive
registers, and architectonic of representation. Indeed, this late-capitalist diaspora demands a new language and symbolism for rendition.
Should it be rendered as narrative? or as spectacle?

The cult hero of postcolonial postmodernity, Salman Rushdie, offers
us a harvest of ideas on this global phenomenon in his novel *Shame*
(1983). The migrant has conquered the force of gravity, Rushdie
writes, the force of belonging; like birds, he has flown. Roots that have
trammeled and tied us down have been torn. The conservative myth
of roots (exile, to my mind, is a problem of mapping routes, not dig-
ging for roots) and gravity has been displaced by the reality of flight,
for now to fly and to flee are ways of seeking individual freedom:

> When individuals come unstuck from their native land, they are called
> migrants. When nations do the same thing (Bangladesh), the act is called
> secession. What is the best thing about migrant peoples and seceded na-
> tions? I think it is their hopefulness. Look into the eyes of such folk in
> old photographs. Hope blazes undimmed through the fading sepia tints.
> And what's the worst thing? It is the emptiness of one's luggage. I'm
> speaking of invisible suitcases, not the physical, perhaps cardboard, vari-
> ety containing a few meaning-drained mementoes: we have come un-

stuck from more than land. We have floated upwards from history, from memory, from Time. (1983, 91)

Rushdie finds himself caught not only in the no-man's-land between warring territories but also between different periods of time. He considers Pakistan a palimpsest souvenir dreamed up by immigrants in Britain, its history written and rewritten, insufficiently conjured and extrapolated. Translated into a text, what was once a homeland becomes a product of the imagination. Every exile or deracinated subaltern shares Rushdie's position, or at least his invented habits: "I, too, like all migrants, am a fantasist. I build imaginary countries and try to impose them on the ones that exist. I, too, face the problem of history: what to retain, what to dump, how to hold on to what memory insists on relinquishing, how to deal with change" (1983, 92).

And so this is the existential dilemma. For all those forced out of their homeland—by choice or necessity, it does not really make a difference—the vocation of freedom becomes the act of inventing the history of one's life, which is equivalent to founding and inhabiting that terra incognita that only becomes known, mapped, named as one creates it partly from memory, partly from dream, partly from hope. Therefore, the stranger is the discoverer of that region that becomes home in the process the termination of which coincides with the life of the planet Earth or with our galaxy.

At this juncture, we can also learn from the mentor of the Palestinian diaspora, Edward Said, who has poignantly described the agon of exile. Caught in medias res and deprived of geographical stability or continuity of events, the Palestinian narrator of the diaspora has to negotiate between the twin perils of fetishism and nostalgia:

> Intimate mementoes of a past irrevocably lost circulate among us, like the genealogies and fables severed from their original locale, the rituals of speech and custom. Much reproduced, enlarged, thematized, embroidered and passed around, they are strands in the web of affiliations we Palestinians use to tie ourselves to our identity and to each other. . . . We endure the difficulties of dispersion without being forced (or able) to struggle to change our circumstances. . . . Whatever the claim may be that we make on the world—and certainly on ourselves as people who have become restless in the fixed place to which we have been assigned—in fact our truest reality is expressed in the way we cross over from one place to another. We are migrants and perhaps hybrids in, but not of, any situation in which we find ourselves. This is the deepest continuity of our lives as a nation in exile and constantly on the move. (quoted in Bowman 1994, 152–153)

Said's hermeneutic strives to decipher the condition of exile as the struggle to recover integrity and reestablish community not in any viable physical location but in the space of cultural production and exchange. Despite its cogency and the eloquence of its truth-bearing signs, Said's discourse can only articulate the pathos of a select few.

We Filipinos need a cartography and a geopolitical project for the masses in diaspora, not for the elite in exile. Many of our fellow expatriates, however, are obsessed with beginnings.

Speaking of who arrived here first on this continent, our "born-again" compatriots are celebrating the first men from the archipelago who landed one foggy morning of October 21, 1587 at Morro Bay, California. These sailors from the Spanish galleon *Nuestra Señora de Buena Esperanza* were of course colonial subjects, not "Filipinos," a term that in those days only referred to Spaniards born in the Philippines (in contrast to the Peninsulars, those born in the European metropolis). But no matter, they have become symbolic of the renewed search for identity.

Such "roots" seem to many a prerequisite for claiming an original and authentic identity as a people. After all, how can the organic community grow and multiply without such attachments? Margie Talaugon of the Filipino American Historical National Society points to Morro Bay as the spot "where Filipino American history started" (*Sacramento Bee*, May 19, 1996). If so, then it started with the Spaniards expropriating the land of the Indians for the Cross and the Spanish crown. Under the command of Pedro de Unamuno, "a few Luzon Indians" acting as scouts (because of their color) accompanied the exploring party into the California interior until they were set upon by the natives who failed to correctly interpret their offerings. In the skirmish born of misrecognition, one Filipino lost his life and Unamuno withdrew. Other expeditions followed—all for the purpose of finding out possible ports along the California coast where galleons sailing from Manila to Acapulco could seek refuge in case of attack from pirates. When the Franciscan missionaries joined the troops from Mexico mandated to establish missions from San Diego to Monterey that would serve as way stations for the Manila galleons, Filipinos accompanied them as menials in colonizing Indian territory in what is now California (Crouchett 1982, 9–17).

Anxiety underlying the claim to be first in setting foot on the continent also accounts for the revival of interest in the "Manillamen." The rubric designates the Malay subjects of the archipelago who allegedly jumped ship off Spanish galleons and found their way into the bayous of Louisiana as early as 1765. In contrast to the early Luzon "Indians," these were rebels protesting brutal conditions of indenture; they were not knowing accomplices or accessories to colonial rampage. There is even a rumor that they signed up with the French buccaneer Jean Laffite and thus took part in the Battle of New Orleans during the War of 1812. These fugitives settled in several villages outside New Orleans, in Manila Village on Barataria Bay. They engaged chiefly in shrimp fishing and hunting.

The best-known settlement (circa 1825) was St. Malo, which was destroyed by a hurricane in 1915 (Hearn 1883). The Filipino swamp settlers of St. Malo were memorialized by one of the first "Orientalists," Lafcadio Hearn, whose life configuration appears as amphibious and rhizomatic as the transplanted Malays he sought to romanticize. Here is an excerpt from his article, "Saint Malo: A Lacustrine Village in Louisiana":

> For nearly fifty years, there has existed in the southern swamp lands of Louisiana a certain strange settlement of Malay fishermen—Tagalas from the Philippine Islands. The place of their lacustrine village is not precisely mentioned upon maps, and the world in general ignored until a few days ago the bare fact of their amphibious existence. Even the United States mail service has never found its way thither, and even in the great city of New Orleans, less than a hundred miles distant, the people were far better informed about the Carboniferous Era than concerning the swampy affairs of the Manila village. . . .
>
> Out of the shuddering reeds and grass on either side rise the fantastic houses of the Malay fishermen, poised upon slender support above the marsh, like cranes watching for scaly prey. . . . There is no woman in the settlement, nor has the treble of a female voice been heard along the bayou for many a long year. . . . How, then, comes it that in spite of the connection with civilized life, the Malay settlement of Lake Borgne has been so long unknown? perhaps because of the natural reticence of the people.

What is curious is that Hearn, in another "take" of this landscape (in the *Times-Democrat*, March 18, 1883), shifts our attention to the mood and atmosphere of the place to foreground his verbal artistry. The need to know these strange swamp dwellers is now subsumed into the program of a self-indulgent aestheticizing drive; the will to defamiliarize turns the inhabitants, the "outlandish colony of Orientals," into performers of fin-de-siècle decadence. Voyeurism feeds on invidious contrasts and innuendoes that weakly recall Baudelaire's worldly ennui:

> Louisiana is full of mysteries and surprises. Within fifty miles of this huge city, in a bee line southwest, lies a place as wild and weird as the most fervent seekers after the curious could wish to behold,—a lake village constructed in true Oriental style, and equally worthy of prehistoric Switzerland or modern Malacca. . . . The like isolation of our Malay settlement is due to natural causes alone, but of a stranger sort. It is situated

in a peculiarly chaotic part of the world, where definition between earth and water ceases,—an amphibious land full of quiverings and quagmires, suited rather to reptile life than to human existence,—a region wan and doubtful and mutable as that described in "The Passing of Arthur," where fragments of forgotten peoples dwell ... a coast of ever shifting sand, and, far away, the phantom circle of a moaning sea.

... Nature, by day, seems to be afraid to speak in a loud voice there; she whispers only. And the brown Malays,—for ever face to face with her solitude,—also talk in low tones as through sympathy,—tones taught by the lapping of sluggish waters, the whispering of grasses, the murmuring of the vast marsh. Unless an alligator show his head;—then it is a shout of "Miro! cuidado!" (quoted in Tinker [1924] 1970, 170–72)

Since the voices captured are in Spanish, we know that these brown peoples have been Hispanized and estranged from their original surroundings. But never mind: The sounds blend with the other creatures of the bayous, a cacophony of organic life orchestrated by Hearn's precious craft. St. Malo's miasma is domesticated for the elegant French salons of New Orleans and the adjoining plantations. Unlike the foggy, damp, and rainy Siberia of Chekhov's 1892 story "In Exile," which becomes the site of epiphanic disclosures and cathartic confessions, Hearn's theater affords no such possibility. Old Semyon, Chekhov's choric observer, can demonstrate his toughness and fortitude all at once in the face of Czarist inhumanity: "Even in Siberia people can live—can li-ive!" (Chekhov 1979, 96).

The repressed always returns, but in serendipitous disguise. Hearn would be surprised to learn that St. Malo's descendants, now in their eighth generation, are alive and well, telling their stories, musing: "Well, if we don't know where we come from how do we know where we are going?" The indefatigable filmmaker Renee Tajima interviewed the Burtanog sisters in New Orleans and notes, "There are no mahjongg games and trans-Pacific memories here in the Burtanog household. The defining cultural equation is Five-card Stud and six-pack of Bud (Lite). The talk is ex-husbands, voodoo curses, and the complicated racial design of New Orleans society" (1996, 270–71). Out of the mists exuding from Hearn's prose, the Burtanog sisters speak about antimiscegenation and Jim Crow laws, the hierarchical ranking and crossing-over of the races in Louisiana. These exuberant women certainly do not belong to Bienvenido Santos's tribe of "lovely people"—a patronizing epithet—whose consolation is that they (like artists) presumably have ready and immediate access to the eternal verities. No such luck. Not even for internal exiles like Mikhail Bakhtin, Ann Akhmatova, or Ding Ling or for "beautiful" souls like Jose Garcia Villa.

Why this obsessive quest for who came first? Is precedence a claim to authenticity and autochthonous originality? What if we came last, not "fresh off the boats," clinging to the anchors or even floating on driftwood? Does this entitle us less to "citizenship" or the right to be here? Who owns this land, this continent anyway—the "natives" before the cartographer Amerigo Vespucci was recast as the name given to a whole continent?

In his semantic genealogy, Raymond Williams traces the etymology of "native" to the Latin *nasci* (to be born); *nativus* means innate, natural; hence, "naive" as artless and simple. After the period of conquest and domination, "native" became equivalent to "bondman" or "villein," born in bondage. This negative usage—the ascription of inferiority to locals, to non-Europeans—existed alongside the positive usage when applied to one's own place or person. Williams observes further: "Indigenous has served both as a euphemism and as a more neutral term. In English it is more difficult to use in the sense which converts all others to inferiors (to go indigenous is obviously less plausible than to go native). In French, however, indigenes went through the same development as English natives, and is now often replaced by autochthones" (1983, 215–16).

We may therefore be truly naifs if we ignore the advent of U.S. power in Manila Bay (not Morro Bay) in 1898. This is the inaugural event that started the process of deracination, the primordial event that unfolded in the phenomena of *pensionados* and the recruits of the Hawaiian sugar plantations up to the "brain drain" of the seventies, the political opportunists who sought asylum during the Marcos dictatorship, and the present influx of this branch of the Filipino diaspora. To shift to the romance of the Spanish galleons is to repress this birth of the Filipino in the womb of the imperial body, a birth that—to invoke the terms in which Petrarch conceived of his exile as the physical separation from the mother's body—implies liberation. This is probably why Jose Marti, the revolutionary Cuban who lived in exile in the United States while Spain tyrannized over his motherland, spoke of living in the "belly of the beast."

Here, the metaphor becomes fertile for all kinds of movements, of embarkations and departures. For Petrarch, "Exile was the primary fantasy of discontinuity that allows the poet some relief from the tremendous anxiety he seemingly felt because of his 'belatedness'— that is, his exile" (Wojciehowski 1972, 19–20). Petrarch was "wounded" by his Greek precursors; he resolved to heal the wound by conceiving the act of writing as a process of digestion, of engulfing, regurgitating, and absorption. We find analogous strategies of sublimation in Virgil and Dante, in Gramsci in his *Prison Notebooks* (1971), and so on. This displacement of the original trauma, which assumed earlier Gnostic resonance as the imprisonment of the soul within the body, may perhaps explain the preponderance of oral and gustatory images, eating and digesting activities, in the fiction of Hagedorn, Zamora Linmark, and others.

Are Filipinos condemned to this fantasy of cannibalism as a means of compensation for the loss of the mother? Are we in perpetual mourning, unable to eject the lost beloved that is still embedded in the psyche and forever memorialized there? Are we, Filipinos scattered throughout the planet, bound to a repetition compulsion, worshipping fetishes (like aging veterans of some forgotten or mythical battle) that forever remind us of the absent, forgotten, and unrecuperated Others?

That is perhaps the permanent stance of the exile, the act of desiring what is neither here nor there. This paradigm is exemplified in the last speech of Richard Rowan, the writer-hero of James Joyce's *Exiles*, addressing Bertha but also someone else, an absent person: "I have wounded my soul for you—a deep wound of doubt which can never be healed. I can never know, never in this world. I do not wish to know or to believe. I do not care. It is not in the darkness of belief that I desire you. But in restless living wounding doubt. To hold you by no bonds, even of love, to be united with you in body and soul in utter nakedness—for this I longed" (1951, 112). The quest for the mother as the cure for jealousy, for the illness accompanying the discovery that one cannot completely possess the body of the loved one (the mother surrogates), is given an ironic twist by Joyce's meditation on women's liberation in his notes to *Exiles:* "It is a fact that for nearly two thousand years the women of Christendom have prayed to and kissed the naked image of one who had neither wife nor mistress nor sister and would scarcely have been associated with his mother had it not been that the Italian church discovered, with its infallible practical instinct, the rich possibilities of the figure of the Madonna" (1951, 120–21).

Come now, are we serious in all these melancholy reflections? Was Jose Rizal indulging in this canny interlude when, in exile at Dapitan, he was preoccupied not just with Josephine Bracken but with a thousand projects of cultivation, teaching, polemical arguments with his Jesuit mentors, correspondence with scholars in Europe, ophthalmological practice, and so on? "What do I have to do with thee, woman?" Or Isabelo de los Reyes—our own socialist forebear—hurled not into the Heideggerian banality of our quotidian world but into the dark dungeon of Montjuich prison near Barcelona for his anarchist and subversive connections (Scott 1982, 279): Was he troubled by porous and shifting boundaries? and that perchance he was not really inside but outside? Or for General Artemio Ricarte, self-exiled in Japan after the victory of the Yankee invaders, is imagining the lost nation a labor of mourning too?

Let us leave this topos of Freudian melancholia and ground our speculations on actual circumstances. Such postmodern quandaries concerning the modalities of displacement of time by space, of essences by contingencies, could not have budged the tempered will of Apolinario Mabini ([1974] 1989) into acquiescence. A brilliant adviser to General Emilio Aguinaldo, president of the first Philippine Republic, the captured Mabini refused to swear allegiance to the sovereign power of the United States. This "sublime paralytic" conceived of deportation as a crucible of his insurrectionary soul. Intransigent, he preferred the challenge of physical removal to Guam, where he was incarcerated for two years. Contemplating from the shores of Guam the remote islands of *las islas Filipinas* across the Pacific Ocean, Mabini felt that we needed to bide our time because surrender/defeat was not compromise but a strategy of waiting for the next opportunity. He envisioned a long march, a protracted journey, toward emancipation. One can only surmise that Mabini's shrewd and proud spirit was able to endure the pain of banishment because he was busy forging in his mind "the conscience of his race," writing his memoirs of the revolution, his cunning deployed to bridge the distance between that melancholy island and the other godforsaken islands he was not really able to leave.

Exile then is a ruse, a subterfuge of the temporarily weak subaltern against the master. It is a problem of deploying time against space—the classic guerilla stratagem against superior firepower. It is the cunning of conviction, of hope. We have a replay of Hegel's choreography of master and slave in a new context. Long before Foucault and Michel de Certeau came around to elaborate the performance of everyday resistance, Bertolt Brecht had already explored in his *Lehrstücke* the theme of Schweikian evasions and underminings. The moment of suspended regularity, the interruption of the normal and habitual, becomes the occasion to vindicate the sacrifices of all those forgotten, invisible, silenced. In Peter Weiss's play *Trotsky in Exile*, in the scene before his execution Trotsky expresses this hope amid setbacks, defeats, losses of all kinds: "I can't stop believing in reason, in human solidarity. . . . Failures and disappointments can't stop me from seeing beyond the present defeat to a rising of the oppressed everywhere. This is no Utopian prophecy. It is the sober prediction of a dialectical materialist. I have never lost my faith in the revolutionary power of the masses. But we must be prepared for a long fight. For years, maybe decades, of revolts, civil wars, new revolts, new wars" (1973, 156). In times of emergency, Trotsky's waiting in exile proves to be the time of pregnancy, of gestation and the emergence of new things.

After the Jewish diaspora in the sixth century B.C., the captivity in Babylon ... now we have the Palestinians, deprived of their native habitat, finally on the way, in transit, to—we do not know yet. A nation-state: Is that the harbor, the terminal, of the passage from darkness to light? Unless the transnational bourgeoisie conspire together in this post–Cold War era of intercapitalist rivalry, I hazard that after so much sacrifice the new social formation will not be a simple mimicry of the bourgeois nation-state. Let us hope not. For so many years after World War II, the Palestinians were the "wandering Jews," also known as "terrorists" by their enemies. One of the most eloquent poets of this diaspora, Fawaz Turki, described how Palestinians in exile signify to "the transcendence ... in the banal," how they agonized "over who is really in exile:/they or their homeland,/who left who/who will come back to the/other first/where will they meet" (1978, 20–21). Exiles are like lovers then who yearn not for homecoming but for a meeting, another tryst, the long-awaited encounter and reunion. At first, the land was the loved one; later on, the land metamorphoses into events, places, encounters, defeats, and victories.

For Edward Said, however, exile is the space of the "extraterritorial" where the Baudelairean streetwalker of modernity finally arrives. Said celebrates exile with a vengeance. In *After the Last Sky*, he recognizes the pain, bitter sorrow, and despair but also the unsettling and decentering force of the exile's plight, its revolutionary potential. Even though Said believes that "The pathos of exile is in the loss of contact with the solidity and the satisfaction of earth: homecoming is out of the question," he seems to counterpoint to it a Gnostic, even neo-Platonic, response by invoking Hugh of St. Victor, a twelfth-century monk from Saxony:

> It is, therefore, a source of great virtue for the practiced mind to learn, bit by bit, first to change about in visible and transitory things, so that afterwards it may be able to leave them behind altogether. The person who finds his homeland sweet is still a tender beginner; he to whom every soil is as his native one is already strong; but he is perfect to whom the entire world is as a foreign place. The tender soul has fixed his love on one spot in the world; the strong person has extended his love to all places; the perfect man has extinguished his. (quoted in Said 1994, 335)

But this asceticism may be culture bound, or it may be peculiar to a continental mentality overshadowed by surrounding mountains. Like our brothers and sisters in the Caribbean, we Filipinos are archipelagic creatures trained to navigate treacherous waters and irregular shoals. Our epistemic loyalty is to islands with their distinctive auras, vibrations, trajectory, fault lines. John Fowles was one of the few shrewd minds that can discern the difference between the continental and the archipelagic sensorium: "Island communities are the original alternative societies. That is why so many islanders envy them. Of their nature they break down the multiple alienations of industrial and suburban man. Some vision of Utopian belonging, of social blessedness, of an independence based on cooperation, haunts them all" (1978, 17).

With this Utopian motif, we may recall Shevek in Ursula K. Le Guin's *The Dispossessed* (1975) for whom exile is the symbol for inhabiting an unfinished, incomplete world where fulfillment (happiness, reunion, homecoming) is forever postponed. This sustained deferral is what exile means: "There was process: process was all. You could go in a promising direction or you could go wrong, but you did not set out with the expectation of ever stopping anywhere" (268). Meanwhile, consider the fate of partisans of the South African struggle now allowed reentry into their homeland. Exile for them always entailed a return to exercise the rights of reclamation and restitution. Yet, when the "rendezvous of victory" arrived in 1992, we find "translated persons" and partisans of *métissage* at the entry points. Commenting on Bessie Head's achievement, Rob Nixon considers the exiles as an invaluable asset for the construction of a new South Africa: "Reentering exiles should thus be recognized as cross-border creations, incurable cultural misfits who can be claimed as a resource, rather than spurned as alien, suspect, or irrelevant" (1995, 163).

Toward the predicament of uprooting, one can assume polarized stances. One is the sentimental kind expressed poignantly by Bienvenido Santos: "All exiles want to go home. Although many of them never return, in their imagination they make their journey a thousand times, taking the slowest boats because in their dream world time is not as urgent as actual time passing, quicker than arrows, kneading on their flesh, crying on their bones" (1982, 11). The other is the understated, self-estranged gesture of Bertolt Brecht. Driven from Europe by Hitler's storm troopers, the pathbreaking dramatist found himself a refugee, neither an expatriate nomad nor border-crossing immigrant. Crossing the Japanese Sea, he watched "the grayish bodies of dolphins" in the gaiety of dawn. In "Landscape of Exile," Brecht cast himself in the role of the fugitive who "beheld with joy . . . the little horse-carts with gilt decorations / and the pink sleeves of the matrons / in the alleys of doomed Manila" (1976, 363–64). Situated on the edge of disaster, he discovered that the oil derricks, the thirsty gardens of Los

Angeles, the ravines and fruit market of California "did not leave the messenger of misfortune unmoved." By analogy, were the Pinoys and other Asians at the turn of the century messengers of a messianic faith, underwriting visions of apocalypse long before Brecht sighted the coast of the North American continent?

From these excursions into delinquent and wayward paths, we return to the idea of transit, passage, a movement of reconnaissance in search of a home everywhere, that is, wherever materials are available for building a shelter for work and community. This may be the ultimate philosophical mission in our time, the most provocative and poignant prophet of which is John Berger. Berger's meditations on home, migration, and exile in *And our faces, my heart, brief as photos* (1984) deserve careful pondering. By way of provisional conclusion to these notes, I can only summarize a few of his insights on the complex phenomenology of exile here.

You can never go home again, Thomas Wolfe counseled us. But what do you mean by home? we respond. Berger speculates on what happens after the loss of home when the migrant leaves, when the continuity with the ancestral dead is broken. The first substitute for the lost, mourned object (kin, home) is passionate erotic love that transcends history. Romantic love unites two displaced persons, linking beginnings and origins, because it predates experience and allows memory and imagination free play. Such passion inspired the project of completing what was incomplete, of healing the division of the sexes—a substitute for homecoming. But romantic love, like religion and the sacramental instinct, has suffered attenuation and transmogrification in the modern world of secular rationality. It has been displaced by commodity fetishism, the cash nexus, and the cult of simulacra and spectacles. Meanwhile, Berger expounds on the other alternative historical hope of completion:

> Every migrant knows in his heart of hearts that it is impossible to return. Even if he is physically able to return, he does not truly return, because he himself has been so deeply changed by his emigration. It is equally impossible to return to that historical state in which every village was the center of the world. One hope of recreating a center is now to make it the entire earth. Only world-wide solidarity can transcend modern homelessness. Fraternity is too easy a term; forgetting Cain and Abel, it somehow promises that all problems can be soluble. In reality many are insoluble— hence the never-ending need for solidarity.
>
> Today, as soon as very early childhood is over, the house can never again be home, as it was in other epochs. This century, for all its wealth and with all its communication systems, is the century of banishment. Eventually perhaps the promise, of which Marx was the great prophet,

will be fulfilled, and then the substitute for the shelter of a home will not just be our personal names, but our collective conscious presence in history, and we will live again at the heart of the real. Despite everything, I can imagine it.

Meanwhile, we live not just our own lives but the longings of our century. (1984, 11–12)

Revolution, then, is the way out through history. It is Walter Benjamin's *Jetzt-Zeit,* now time, that will blast the continuum of reified history, an ever-present apocalypse, the presiding spirit of which in the past, Joachim da Fiore, finds many incarnations in the present: for one, the Filipino overseas contract worker and his or her unpredictable, unlicensed peregrinations. Meanwhile, look, stranger, on this planet Earth belonging to no single individual, our mother whom no one possesses. We find solidarity with indigenous peoples an inexhaustible source of comfort, inspiration, and creative renewal. The aboriginal American Indians, dispossessed of their homelands and victimized by those merchants—agents of Faust and Mephistopheles—obsessed by private ownership and solitary hedonism, express for us also what I think can be the only ultimate resolution for human exile and diaspora: "We and the earth, our mother, are of one mind" (Wilden 1980, 487).

Notes

Introduction

1. Contrary to Sucheng Chan (1991), who alleges that Filipinos organized fraternal associations because U.S. culture influenced them to do so, Masonic-like groups named after Rizal testify to the residual revolutionary culture among these early immigrants.

2. For a refreshing response to this practice of blaming Filipinos for their lack of culture or their "damaged" culture (advanced by James Fallows 1989), see Miguel Gonzalez's (1990) article. Gonzalez reminds us that "There is no such thing as a damaged culture any more than there is a perfect culture. ... Culture is, to say the least, dynamic and always shifting" (1990, 9).

3. A recent event may vindicate the homogenized, unitary culture predicated of Filipinos everywhere; see the item titled "Knowledge of Filipino culture helped L.A. cops nab fugitive" (Phillipine News 1996).

4. On the problem of a common culture, Mike Featherstone writes, "It becomes impossible to talk about a common culture in the fuller sense without talking about who is defining it, within which set of interdependencies and power balances, for what purposes, and with reference to which outside culture(s) have to be discarded, rejected or demonified in order to generate the sense of cultural identity" (1990, 11).

Chapter One

1. Occeña's pioneering effort can be supplemented and corrected by regional studies made by Barbara Posadas (1986–1987), Edwin Almirol (1985), Theo Gonzalves (1995–1996), and original archival work now being done by younger scholars.

2. Although the term "Asian American" as an operational bureaucratic designation is misleading (because of the now widely disparate historical experiences of the groups concerned) and tends to covertly privilege one or two of its elements (as in the Modern Language Association surveys published so far; Kitano and Daniels 1988; Schaefer 1996), Occeña points out that the self-recognition and societal recognition of the peoples involved stem from their integration into U.S. society "on the bases of inequality vis-à-vis whites; subjected

to various forms of racial and national discrimination and constituted as an oppressed strata of U.S. society" (1985, 29). But because the Asian and Pacific peoples from their arrival up to now have not amalgamated to form one distinct nationality, it is best to discard the label "Asian American" and use the particular names of each nationality to forestall homogenizing ascriptions like "superminority."

3. Until 1946, Filipinos did not have the right to be naturalized. Nor, in California, could they marry whites until 1948 or own land until 1956. In 1933, Salvador Roldan was tried in Los Angeles for marrying a white woman (see Chan 1991; Takaki 1989).

4. This trend is discernible in the Flips' statement of identity politics. The Flips mainly descend from the relatively conservative formation of the second wave of Filipino immigrants (about 30,000) comprising war veterans enjoying some privileges (Catholic Institute 1989). Their code words registering anxiety toward "melting pot" miscegenation are found in phrases like "cathartic stage of ethnic awareness" and "maintaining ethnic awareness." But by juxtaposing inside/outside, they replicate what they want to negate: including the Same/excluding the Other.

5. Does this then explain why Fred Cordova, in his pictorial essay *Filipinos: Forgotten Asian Americans* (1983, 221), insists: "An estimated one million innocent Filipino men, women and children died while defending Americanism during World War Two from 1941 to 1945"? Indeed, one may ask: Have all these many Filipinos been really screwed up all their lives to make that sacrifice? One million natives defending the cause of the Lone Ranger and Charlie Chan—ugly racist stigmata cited by Fred Cordova—whom he lumps together with Florence Nightingale and Martin Luther King Jr.? One million dark-skinned natives sacrificing their lives for Americanism? As for celebrating Filipino "firsts" to generate ethnic pride, what does it signify if we learn that Filipinos were the first this and that, to wit, the first Asians to cross the Pacific Ocean to the North American continent, and that their descendants in New Orleans, Louisiana, fought with the pirate Jean Laffite and the Americans during the War of 1812? Would such knowledge relieve the lostness or sublimate the grim pathos of a situation bewailed so often by Bienvenido Santos, inventor of the myth of Filipinos as "lovely people": "Think of the impotence of Filipino exiles in America who are displaced and uprooted wandering in strange cities" (Alegre and Fernandez 1984, 227).

Chapter Two

1. It might be useful to note here how Marx, in *Capital*, criticized bourgeois political economists for taking Robinson Crusoe as their theoretical model of the "natural man" or *homo economicus*—the classic ideological move to claim universal objectivity for a particular interest (see Tucker, 1978, 324–28).

2. Eugene Genovese (1971), among others, has substantively demonstrated the presence of an autonomous, counterhegemonic culture of the African slave in the antebellum South.

3. See, for example, Werner Sollors (1986). In the work of Sollors and other ethnicity experts, the whole Asian American experience and its prototypical expressions exist as gaping lacunae. For a critique of the prevailing ethnicity paradigm, see Alan Wald (1987).

4. The debate on the relevance of poststructuralist theory for the study of ethnic writing has been going on for some years now primarily among African American scholars. I find the controversy surrounding the critical practice of Henry Louis Gates Jr. provocative and useful in weighing the strengths and liabilities of poststructuralist methodology for a research program investigating racist discourse and practices.

5. I paraphrase here statements from Hazel Carby (1980).

6. The category of the ethnic intellectual is still open to further analytic specification for which the most suggestive beginning has been made by Georg Simmel's (1977) essay "The Stranger." For germinal insights on the phenomenology of immigration and homelessness, see John Berger (1984).

7. A provisional example of the "and/or" strategy of disruption may be exemplified by David Henry Hwang's *M Butterfly* (1986) in which the mystique of the exotic Oriental and its material base is exploded and the binary opposites East/West deconstructed within certain limits. But I question the "We" of the playwright's statement in the "Afterword": "We have become the 'Rice Queens' of realpolitik." As for Brecht's *Verfremdungeffekt* and his anti-Aristotelian poetics, see John Willett (1964) and Walter Benjamin (1978, 203–38).

8. *Katipuneros* refers to members of the *Katipunan*, the revolutionary organization founded by Andres Bonifacio in 1896 that spearheaded the anticolonial revolt against Spain; *Colorum* refers to peasant millennial groups in the twenties and thirties that staged insurrections in various provinces. For an account of some of these groups and also an interview with Pedro Calosa, a Filipino strike leader in Hawaii in the twenties, consult David Sturtevant (1976).

9. This can begin by taking note of basic facts of U.S. political economy with respect to the Filipino community: See Amado Cabezas and Gary Kawaguchi (1989).

10. I am thinking here of Brecht's alienation effect in his epic dramaturgy and chiefly his theory of theatrical production contained in "A Short Organum for the Theater" (Willet 1964, 179–208). See Walter Benjamin, "The Author as Producer" in his *Reflections* (1978, 220–238). Kristevan semiotics can also be used as antidote to reactionary postmodernism; see her *Desire in Language* (1980) and also the application of poststructuralist semiotics to popular culture by Dick Hebdige (1979).

Chapter Three

1. Eric Chock, another name listed by Amy Ling, identifies himself as a Hawaiian writer and resident (Ruoff and Ward 1990, 362). The Filipinos in Hawaii, condemned to almost castelike conditions, constitute a community significantly different from Filipinos in the mainland. For a survey of the writing by Hawaiian Ilocanos, see Rene Somera (1982).

2. Aside from serving as director of the Peace Corps in the Philippines (1961–1963), Fuchs was executive director of the Select Commission on Immigration and Refugee Policy under President Carter. Another mode of recuperation is exemplified by Peter Stanley (1974, 4), who insists on the "relatively libertarian character of U.S. rule."

3. In 1946, 6,000 Filipino workers were imported to Hawaii to counter the industrywide strike—proof once more that the Philippines is an "inside" factor in the U.S. imperial polity (Philippine Center 1985, 6).

To the early contingents of Filipino workers belong the honor of spearheading the first and most resolute labor militancy in Hawaii in modern U.S. history. According to Sucheng Chan, after the 1882 Chinese Exclusion Act and the Gentlemen's Agreement of 1908 limiting the entry of Japanese labor, Filipinos became the predominant agricultural labor force in Hawaii: "Not surprisingly, they became the main Asian immigrant group to engage in labor militancy. Moreover, as Beechert has noted, they did so in politically repressive environments with criminal syndicalist laws" (1991, 87). Although Bulosan does not claim to describe, for instance, the epic strikes of 1924 in Hawaii's Hanapepe plantation and of 1937 in Puunene, the scenes of union organizing and strikes in *America* function as an allegorical emblem of all such instances of the sporadic or organized resistance of masses of people of color. Bulosan's life covers four major episodes in the Filipino workers' history: the action of the Agricultural Workers Industrial Union–Trade Union Unity League in 1930, the formation of the Filipino Labor Union in 1933, the affiliation of the Alaska Cannery Workers Union with the CIO in 1937, and the establishment of the Filipino Agricultural Workers Association in 1939.

In the late 1930s, 25 percent of Filipinos were service workers, 9 percent were in the salmon canneries, and 60 percent in agriculture (Takaki 1989, 316–18; Catholic Institute 1987, 36).

4. Aside from Sam Tagatac's experimental "The New Anak" (Peñaranda's "Dark Fiesta" deals with native rituals and folk beliefs in the Philippines), the Flips will only include the Flip poets—some of those in *Without Names* (Ancheta et al., 1985), and some in Bruchac's collection. I will not repeat here the bibliographic data of Filipino American authors found in King-kok Cheung and Stan Yogi's (1988) excellent reference guide.

In fairness to the Flips, I should state here that Serafin Malay Syquia's poems and his essay "Politics and Poetry" (Navarro 1974, 87–89) represent a crucial intervention that seeks to reclaim an "America" reconstituted by people of color. At a time when leaders of the community were rejecting Bulosan's socialist vision and the legacy of the Manongs, Syquia and his comrades were striving to reconnect via their ethnic rebellion with the insurgency in the neocolony—an emancipatory project of opening up the space prematurely closed by Santos's conciliatory acceptance of the status quo, Gonzalez's myths of restoration, and Villa's patrician withdrawal.

5. I take issue with the bias of functionalist, positivist social science in my book *Racial Formations/Critical Transformations* (1992a). The assimilationist doctrine of the ethnic paradigm, with its ahistorical empiricism, has vitiated practically most studies of the Filipino community in the United States.

Typical is Antonio Pido's *The Pilipinos in America* (1986), littered with blanket pronouncements like "Pilipinos fear alienation" (35) and so on. Far more insightful are articles such as Aurora Fernandez, "Pilipino Immigrants," *East Wind* (Fall/Winter 1982): 34–36, and Teresita Urian (written by Mila de Guzman), "Into the Light," *Katipunan* 4.7 (October 1991): 10–11.

6. Although S. E. Solberg is correct in pointing out the interdependence of Filipino American writing and indigenous Filipino writing in English, his ascription of a mythmaking function to Bulosan and others (which explains, for instance, Buaken's failure to produce a unified narrative out of his own fragmented life) is misleading since the myth's regime of truth turns out to be a discourse of co-optation as "the Filipino dream of independence fades into the American dream of equality and freedom" (1991, 56).

7. Gonzalez's subaltern mentality typically contrives an apologia for the Cordova volume (1983, xi) when he cites the white master's endorsement of his servant: "My servant was a Manilla man." In this way the stereotype of Filipinos in the thirties as "wonderful servants" (Takaki 1989, 317) is repeated and reinforced.

8. To illumine the deceptive stoicism of Santos's closure in his stories "The Day the Dancers Came" or "Scent of Apples," it would be instructive to compare the ending of J. C. Dionisio's "Cannery Episode" (1936, 413) in which the narrator captures the discipline and strength of the "Alaskeros" in the face of a horrible mutilation of one of their compatriots. We also find in Pete's character (reflected by the choric narrator) an embodiment of revolt against the inhumane system, a subject position typically absent in Santos's and Gonzalez's fiction.

9. Elaine Kim dismisses Villa as nonethnic (1982, 288). Bulosan's judgment of Villa reflects my own earlier polemical evaluation (1984, 73–76). For Bulosan, Villa "is somewhat in line with Baudelaire and Rimbaud, for these two appeared when French poetry had already reached its vortex and was on the downgrade. Naturally they were great apostles of the poetry of decay. When we speak of literature as a continuous tradition, a growing cultural movement, Villa is out of place and time"; Villa does not represent "the growth of our literature," rather he "expresses a declining culture after it has reached its height" (1979, 151).

10. Here, I approximate the first mode of incorporation via commodity form that Dick Hebdige outlines (1979, 94–96); the ideological mode of incorporation I exemplify in my remarks on Bulosan, Santos, and Villa.

11. Only 2 of over 200 photos depict Filipinos on strike (pages 76 and 81). Most are photos of families and relatives of the editor and the kin-related staff of the Demonstration Project. If one compares the text of the section "Alaska Canneries" with a contemporary account of the dismal conditions by Emeterio Cruz (1933), one will notice the textual and iconographic techniques of neutralization and obfuscation deployed by Cordova's album, the cutoff point of which is 1963, a revealing date that marks the initiation of radical activism in the Filipino community. In featuring Hilario Moncado (183), Cordova commits an act of partiality and censorship, one of many, when he fails to mention Moncado's notorious opposition to Filipino workers' demands for justice (Chan 1991, 76, 89).

Cordova's inadequacies include his false generalizations on religion (167) and his eulogy for one million Filipinos who died during World War II for the sake of "Americanism" (221). But these amateurish mistakes descend to unwitting racism when he lumps inter alia Lincoln, the Lone Ranger, Superman, Charlie Chan, and Martin Luther King Jr. together (230).

A similar reservation can be made of otherwise instructive documentaries like *In No One's Shadow*, in which the cinematic sequence focuses on the normal adjustment of the Filipino immigrant despite all odds. This selective method of fetishizing individual success stories conceals the institutional structures and historical contingencies that qualified and limited such individual lives. The ideology of the image and its system of verisimilitude needs to be elucidated and criticized as a determining apparatus producing a deformed Filipino subjectivity ripe for hegemonic reproduction.

12. A modest attempt has been made by the Philippine Center for Immigrant Rights in New York City to revive the example of *Letters in Exile* with the publication of the pamphlet *Filipinos in the USA* (1985). But no major initiative has been taken to organize the Filipino community on the basis of its nationality and its unique response to continuing U.S. domination since the demise of various socialist formations with Filipino leadership in the eighties.

13. Puerto Ricans are an exception. In another essay, I argue that the cultural history of the United States cannot be fully inventoried and assayed without registering the symptomatic absence in it of Filipinos and Puerto Ricans as colonized subjects. Operating in the field of American English, the Filipino interruption of U.S. monologism is unique insofar as it demarcates the limits of the imperial episteme, its canonical inscriptions, and its reflexive frame of reference.

14. A play directed by Behn Cervantes, who adapted materials from Virgilio Felipe's M.A. thesis, "What You Like to Know: An Oral History of Bonipasyo," presented in Hawaii in late 1991. The assimilationist rationale for this event may be perceived from this statement in the program notes: "The Hawaii [the chief protagonist] was lured to as 'paradise' seems harsh and full of hardships, but is compensated for by Bonipasyo's rightful pride in the conviction that his toil and sacrifice made Hawaii." Whose Hawaii?

15. Fermin Tobera, a 22-year-old worker, was killed during the anti-Filipino riot in Watsonville, California, on January 22, 1930; his body was interred in the Philippines on February 2, marked as "National Humiliation Day" (Quinsaat 1976, 55, 57; for a contemporary estimate of the Watsonville situation, see Buaken (1946, 97–107). Silme Domingo and Gene Viernes were anti-Marcos union activists and officials of the International Longshoremen's and Warehousemen's Union, Local 37, in Seattle, Washington, whose 1952 yearbook Bulosan edited. They were slain on June 1, 1981, by killers hired by pro-Marcos elements and corrupt union operatives. It is also alleged that the FBI and CIA were involved in this affair (Churchill 1995).

16. By "anticanon," I mean a mode of resisting standardization by the dominant EuroAmerican ideology and by the conservative aura of a compradorbourgeois Filipino tradition. On the problematic of the canon, see the last chapter of my *Hegemony and Strategies of Transgression* (1996a) and my *Beyond Postcolonial Theory* (1997).

17. Berger inflects the theme of exile in this century of banishment by suggesting, "Only worldwide solidarity can transcend modern homelessness" (1984, 67).

Chapter Four

1. Except where otherwise specified, all quotes from Bulosan's letters interspersed throughout this chapter are taken from Carlos Bulosan, *Sound of Falling Light*, edited by Dolores Feria (1960). See also Bulosan's (1980) *Selected Works* for the "Letters to an American Woman [Dorothy Babb]."

2. See Emeterio Cruz (1933), Carey McWilliams (1964), Roland Takaki (1989).

3. Bulosan furnishes us a veridical substantiation of the matrix of this story in his letter to Babb dated January 20, 1938; see *Bulosan: An Introduction with Selections* (1983a, 66–69). For an extended commentary, see San Juan (1992a).

4. An example of how Bulosan allowed his editor or publisher to revise parts and rewrite whole passages of his work may be instanced by comparing the original text of "I Am Not a Laughing Man" in the University of Washington Archives and its published version in *The Writer* (1946). Documentation of this practice awaits further scholarly investigation. One can hypothesize that this is what happened to the manuscript of *America*, and I suspect that it occurred chiefly toward the concluding chapters. Given the euphoria of the Allied victory against Japan and the beginning of the Cold War, the publisher would certainly want to cash in and obtain the maximum profit by pandering to the media sentiment with the imprimatur of official ideology.

5. Contrary to what has been alleged by Evangelista, Kim, and others, Bulosan and his friend Chris Mensalvas did not organize the United Cannery, Agricultural, Packing and Allied Workers of America (UCAPAWA), which was set up in 1933 in Seattle. Note that it was only in 1930 that the nineteen-year old Bulosan arrived in the United States. UCAPAWA affiliated later with the ILWU, which invited Bulosan to edit its 1952 yearbook. Kim's error is repeated by Amy Ling in her prefatory note to the Bulosan selection in Paul Lauter's *Heath Anthology of American Literature* (1990).

6. When I visited the University of Washington Archives sometime in the early seventies to examine the papers left by Bulosan and his friends, I stumbled on a long typescript of a novel titled *The Cry and the Dedication*. As far as I can recall, there is only a passing allusion to this novel in his letters. In a letter dated November 2, 1949, Bulosan mentioned his "secret dream of writing here a 1,500-page novel covering thirty-five years of Philippine history." But this is only one of a series of four novels covering one hundred years of Philippine history, and the one he had been working on at the time spans the period 1915–1950. Another book was intended to cover the period from the birth to the death of Rizal; another, from Rizal's death to the outbreak of World War I. A fourth one (partly fulfilled by *The Cry and the Dedication*) was to deal with the period 1951–1961, the events of which Bulosan then estimated as constituting "a great crisis in Philippine history." Although he ac-

knowledged the pressure of "historical currents and crosscurrents," what he really wanted to write was "a novel covering the ideal friendship, courtship and marriage of a Pinoy and an American white woman." This topic of Filipino male/American woman contact has been somewhat idealized in *America* in the chivalric handling of such maternal figures as Marian, Mary, Alice, and Eileen Odell, and instrumentalized to recuperate the pathos of a feminine sublime, as in stories like "Silence," "The Soldier," and others. This topic of miscegenation (in the light of its legal prohibition) definitely obsessed Bulosan for quite a long time, but his energies in the terminal years of his life were preoccupied in writing this novel, which, in projecting a sequel to the interrupted revolution of 1896, is quite a formidable achievement.

7. For a full discussion of the novel, see chapter 6 of my book *Reading the West/Writing the East* (1992b) and my introduction to the novel published by Temple University Press (1995b). Because of his incisive critique of U.S. imperialist hegemony, Bulosan at present has become a battlefield of political contestation. Were he alive today, he might have relished this position of being the medium through which life-and-death questions formerly muted or sidetracked are released into the public sphere for debate. In a Third World formation like the Philippines, however, what preponderates in this sphere is not so much reason as hope and fear, the twin passions of the modality of finite existence that Spinoza considered barriers for enjoying freedom. We often see intellectuals and journalists who, pandering to their reactionary patrons, insist that Bulosan is minor and negligible, that he was too ignorant of actual happenings in the Philippines for his writings to be relevant, and so forth. No one of course is claiming that Bulosan's body of work has no weaknesses or inadequacies; his limitations I have myself pointed out in my pioneering study, *Carlos Bulosan and the Imagination of the Class Struggle* (1972) and in numerous essays. But whatever the real motivations of the anti-Bulosan camp, it is the most self-serving kind of crass narrow-mindedness to charge that this novel is inaccurate and therefore does not reproduce the received dogmas about the Huk uprising. It seems to me too late in the day to remind ourselves again that literary production, as Althusser, Macherey, and others have argued, is far more complex and overdetermined than what a simplified Lukácsian realism allows. In any case, Lukács himself would not have endorsed the easy positivist reflection theory of infantile leftism that still plagues sectarian critics entrenched in their "mountain stronghold." To apply a mechanical criterion based on the inadequate superstructure/base grid is to show insensitivity to the contextual intricacies of Bulosan's practice in the fifties, a situation somewhat analogous to the persecution of the seditious playwrights by the U.S. colonial authorities in the first decade of this century. It is not that Bulosan was trying to fabricate an ingenious Aesopian discourse to outwit the police. His effort to craft a cross-cultural, ecumenical allegory had no past models or traditional precedents; hence its novelty startles conformist taste. The conventional mode of reception is certainly blind to the way Bulosan, for example, transforms the motif of the journey in Goethe's *Wilhelm Meister* into an allegorical mapping (in Walter Benjamin's sense) of the vicissitudes of U.S.-Philippine relations. Nor is it sensitive to the way Bulosan interweaves

the more subtle ideological "war of position" with the largely economistic conception of the "war of maneuver" rendered by doctrinaire realism. This is understandable because the problem of hegemony that preoccupies Bulosan's major texts has not really been addressed by Western critics until the recent discovery of the significance of Gramsci's thought and of Bakhtin's inquiry into popular/folk expression. We need a truly historicizing approach to texts like Bulosan's that would be cognizant of the specific audience for whom he was writing, the sociohistorical field of forces overdetermining his consciousness, and the limits and possibilities of the semiotic genres and conventions within which he was operating. This chapter is a contribution toward shaping such a materialist approach.

8. The letters are reproduced in Campomanes and Gernes (1988). Although these two writers expound the thesis that "This strategy, this conscious retrieval of what at face value appears to be trivial, configures the aesthetic design of *America* and of Bulosan's other work" (1988, 17), they unfortunately undermine their case by overvalorizing textuality at the expense of other nonverbal signifiers. They ascribe "absence of viable symbols, the scarcity of cultural capital" to impoverished Filipinos; they privilege an epistolary form of writing linked to capitalist modes of transport and communication and thus legitimize such hegemony. To unfold their emancipatory potential, one could argue that Bulosan's texts are better read as betrayals of sexuality, focusing on gaps, interruptions, silences, the symptoms of which are grammatical distortions, breakdown of syntax and written communication itself, incomplete utterances, non sequiturs, the salience of music and sounds of nature and bodies, nonlinear plots, and other estrangement effects that disrupt an organic unity imposed by Western disciplinary regimes.

9. This was the context in which I wrote the first book-length study of the published writings of Bulosan, *Carlos Bulosan and the Imagination of the Class Struggle*, launched a day before the fateful declaration of martial law in 1972. It was a belated and modest response to such a rediscovery and to the nationalist mobilization in the Philippines following the First Quarter Storm of 1970. The renewed interest in Bulosan was initially sparked by the explosion of strikes by Filipino farmworkers in the sixties, in particular by the Delano grape strike of 1965 led by Larry Itliong and Philip Vera Cruz. My book was then followed by the reissuing of *America* in 1973 by the University of Washington Press with a substantial introduction by a Bulosan contemporary, Carey McWilliams, who was then editor of the *Nation*. In 1977, I undertook the task of arranging the publication of The *Cry and the Dedication* by Tabloid Books, based in Guelph, Ontario, Canada (this edition, which retitled the novel *The Power of the People*, was reissued by National Book Store, Manila, in mid-1986, and published in the United States in 1995 by Temple University Press with its original title). This was followed by a collection of Bulosan's unpublished stories (most of which revolved around the figure of Uncle Sator) that I assembled for New Day Publishers in Quezon City, Philippines, entitled *The Philippines Is in the Heart* (1978) and by the special Bulosan number of *AmerAsia Journal* (1979) which I helped edit. When the New Day anthology appeared, the Bolshoi Ballet, Van Cliburn, and other Western celebrities were

lording it over indigenous expression in the Cultural Center of the Philippines with the blessings of the conjugal dictatorship. A limited edition of Bulosan's writings was issued in 1980 by the Friends of the Filipino People, Honolulu, Hawaii, containing a selection of Bulosan's hitherto unpublished letters to Dorothy Babb. All these efforts finally culminated in the 1983 publication of my *Bulosan: An Introduction with Selections* by National Book Store. In due time, I expect a reprinting of the neglected classic *The Laughter of My Father* and a volume of critical essays by various authors that would establish Bulosan's stature as an indispensable Third World writer in the vanguard of the multicultural revaluation of the U.S. literary canon now proceeding.

10. Licerio Lagda and a few other students share Morantte's dogmatic stance against any serious, intelligent analysis of Bulosan's fiction, a symptom of philistine "know-nothingism." This bias should be distinguished from the naive empiricism discernible in the tart comment of Fr. Miguel Bernad in his review of *The Laughter.*

11. See the celebration of multimillionaire Loida Nicolas Lewis and Hawaii Governor Benjamin Cayetano in the pages of *Filipinas*, the *Philippine News*, and other periodicals. Meanwhile, the transplantation of recent Filipino immigrants to the urban sprawl of Los Angeles, San Francisco, Chicago, New York, and Seattle has impelled younger writers to valorize the alleged urban sensibility born from the "uneasy encounter" with the West, adoptive and adaptive at the same time (Aguilar–San Juan 1994). Consequently, Bulosan is rejected as "rural," collapsing the trajectory of his generation's history—from California's Imperial Valley to Washington's Yakima Valley and the Alaska canneries—to a geographical triviality. This is more a symptom of anxiety than a critical analysis of the conditions of subalternity. Ascribing an essentialist "archaeology" of visions to Filipino writing based on universal folklore motifs (themes of combat, quest, and so on) will not salvage Serafin Malay Syquia, or Villa for that matter, from the "backwaters" or canonize the *agon* of the Manongs and the Hawaiian *sakadas* for use by a new generation of Filipinos inventing history from below.

Chapter Five

1. Philip Vera Cruz died on June 10, 1994. In the early eighties, I had the good fortune to visit him in his home in Bakersfield, California, and interview him about our common struggle against the U.S.-Marcos dictatorship. I promised then to write about it, but other things intervened. Now, after more than a decade, I am fulfilling my promise in this form and I hope his spirit likes this metacommentary and memorial to the future, a homage to his intransigent lifework.

Chapter Six

1. Last year, a furor was caused by the dismissal of a Filipino professor from the faculty of the University of California, Berkeley. Filipinos bewailed the

"enforced invisibility of Filipinos" at that privileged campus, the limited number of Filipinos admitted, and the withdrawal of affirmative action as a major
cause for the gradual exclusion of Filipinos from the university (see also
Almirol 1988). Although the largest minority in California, Filipinos are se-
verely underrepresented in the student body, the faculty, and the curriculum.
More scandalous is the fact that the Department of Ethnic Studies and its
Asian American component at UC Berkeley have never involved any tenured
faculty of Filipino descent in the twenty years of its existence, this in an institution that constantly brags of diversity. In an open letter, I shared my experience of being "tokenized" by the ethnic faculty and used for the ignoble purpose of pacifying angry Filipino students at the firing of Professor Amado
Cabezas. This is an unforgettable example of people of color doing a "contract"
on subaltern Pinoys/Pinays, betraying the putative enlightenment rationale of
their profession, succumbing to bourgeois *Realpolitik* for petty rewards.

2. An alternative to the route of the "wild American self" can be found in
Jeffrey Arellano Cabusao's installation art, a work in progress, entitled "Balikbayan Dreams, Balikbayan Realities . . . Remembering My Lola," exhibited at
Oberlin College in 1996–1997. In an inscription on one of the boxes he uses,
Cabusao explains his project of articulating a Filipino trajectory in anti-
mimicry of the cargo cults of certain Pacific peoples and in the process distills
the thrust of what I have been trying to communicate in this chapter:

"This work uses two Balikbayan boxes. Balikbayan boxes are filled with U.S.
goods—candies, fruits (like gigantic apples and bunches of grapes, which would
almost never reach their destination), canned foods as well as clothes (old and
new)—which our relatives and family friends in the Philippines may be able to
use. As a child growing up in San Diego, CA, the packing of a Balikbayan box
to be shipped or to be carried on the plane by a relative going home was one of
my vital links to the Philippines. I used to wonder why we had to send these
things to the Philippines. My mother and father would tell me that these items
are usually difficult to obtain in the Philippines—they were too expensive or
just inaccessible. This is only scratching the surface of the unequal global
power relations between the U.S. and its neocolony, the Philippines.

"This work is also meant to be an altar of remembrance—remembering my
Lola Mommy, Teresita de Leon Arellano 1928–1988. It was my Lola who began to plant seeds in my consciousness about the necessity of never being
ashamed of my Filipino heritage—especially in the U.S. Although I struggled
as a child to turn my back on my 'Filipino-ness,' American racism never made
me forget my reality as a Filipino American, as a person of color living in the
'belly of the beast.' Lola was giving me weapons to raise my consciousness—
so as to eventually call upon the collective consciousness of militant Filipino
resistance to Spanish colonization and U.S. and Japanese neocolonialism.

"Do we as a Filipino American community . . . remember our rich heritage
of resistance to oppression (some examples): beginning with Chief Lapu-
Lapu's slaying of Magellan in 1521 on Mactan Island; to the mobilization of
Filipinos against Spanish colonial oppression by Gabriela Silang in 1764; to
the bloody war of resistance against U.S. colonization in 1898; to the Filipino
resistance against Japanese colonization in the early 1940s; to the militant la-

bor organizing of Filipino farmworkers in Hawai'i in the 1920s as well as in California and Alaska (the cannery industry) in the 1930s; to the establishing of the foundation for the United Farmworkers Union ... to the organizing of Filipinos and Filipino Americans against the Marcos dictatorship ... to the present day organizing of Filipino men and women for the civil rights of Filipinos who are scattered all over the diaspora ... as nurses, domestics, and mail order brides? How do we use this history to inform our present day struggles against U.S. and Japanese neocolonialism? to contribute to an agenda for liberatory collective social change?"

References

Adorno, Theodor. 1974. "Lyric Poetry and Society." *Telos* 20 (Summer):56–71.

Agbayani-Siewert, Pauline, and Linda Revilla. 1995. "Filipino Americans." In *Asian Americans*. Ed. Pyong Gap Min. Thousand Oaks: Sage.

Aguilar, Delia. 1988. *The Feminist Challenge*. Manila: Asian Social Institute.

_____. 1989. "The Social Construction of the Filipino Woman." *International Journal of Intercultural Relations* 13:527–51.

_____. 1995. "Gender, Nation, Colonialism: Lessons from the Philippines." In *Women, Gender and Development*. Eds. Lynn Duggan et al. London: Zed Books.

_____. 1996. "Servants to the Global Masters." *Against the Current* 11 (March-April):21–23.

_____. 1997. "Behind the Prosperous Facades." *Against the Current* (March-April):17–20.

Aguilar–San Juan, Karin. 1994. "The Exile Within/The Question of Identity." Interview with Jessica Hagedorn. In *The State of Asian America*. Ed. Karin Aguilar–San Juan. Boston: South End.

Ahmad, Aijaz. 1992. *In Theory: Classes, Nations, Literatures*. London: Verso.

_____. 1995. "The Politics of Literary Postcoloniality." *Race and Class* 36.3:1–19.

Ahmad, Eqbal. 1982. *Political Culture and Foreign Policy: Notes on American Interventions in the Third World*. Washington, DC: Institute for Policy Studies.

Alegre, Edilberto, and Doreen Fernandez. 1984. *The Writer and His Milieu*. Manila: De La Salle University Press.

Alexander, Jeffrey. 1992. "Citizen and Enemy as Symbolic Classification: On the Polarizing Discourse of Civil Society." In *Cultivating Differences: Symbolic Boundaries and the Making of Inequality*. Eds. Michele Lamont and Marcel Fournier. Chicago: University of Chicago Press.

Allen, James S. 1993. *The Philippine Left on the Eve of World War II*. Minneapolis: MEP Publications.

Almirol, Edwin B. 1985. *Ethnic Identity and Social Negotiation: A Study of a Filipino Community in California*. New York: AMS Press.

_____. 1988. "The Filipino Experience in the American University System." *Asian Profile* 16.3 (June):283–91.

Alquizola, Marilyn. 1989. "The Fictive Narrator of *America Is in the Heart*." In *Frontiers in Asian American Studies*. Eds. Gail Nomura et al. Pullman: Washington State University Press.

_____. 1991. "Subversion or Affirmation: The Text and Subtext of *America Is in the Heart.*" In *Asian Americans: Comparative and Global Perspectives.* Eds. Shirley Hune et al. Pullman: Washington State University.

Althusser, Louis. 1971. *Lenin and Philosophy and Other Essays.* London: New Left Books.

Amin, Samir. 1989. *Eurocentrism.* New York: Monthly Review Press.

_____. 1995. *Re-Reading the Postwar Period: An Intellectual Itinerary.* New York: Monthly Review Press.

Ancheta, Shirley, et al., eds. 1985. *Without Names.* San Francisco: Kearney Street Workshop.

Anderson, Bridget. 1993. *Britain's Secret Slaves.* London: Anti-Slavery International.

Anderson, Robert. 1984. *Filipinos in Rural Hawaii.* Honolulu: University of Hawaii Press.

Appadurai, Arjun. 1994. "Disjuncture and Difference in the Global Cultural Economy." In *Colonial Discourse and Post-Colonial Theory.* Eds. Patrick Williams and Laura Chrisman. New York: Columbia University Press.

Appel, Benjamin. 1951. *Fortress in the Rice.* New York: Bobbs-Merrill.

Ashcroft, Bill, Gareth Griffiths, and Helen Tiffin. 1989. *The Empire Writes Back.* New York: Routledge.

_____, eds. 1995. *The Post-Colonial Reader.* London: Routledge.

Attali, Jacques. 1985. *Noise.* Minneapolis: University of Minnesota Press.

Baker, Houston, Jr. 1984. *Blues, Ideology, and Afro-American Literature.* Chicago: University of Chicago Press.

Bakhtin, Mikhail. 1968. *Rabelais and His World.* Tr. Helene Iswolsky. Cambridge: MIT Press.

Balibar, Etienne. 1989. "Spinoza, the Anti-Orwell: The Fear of the Masses." *Rethinking Marxism* 2.3 (Fall):104–139.

_____. 1990. "Paradoxes of Universality." In *Anatomy of Racism.* Ed. David Goldberg. Minneapolis: University of Minnesota Press. Pp. 283–94.

Balibar, Etienne, and Pierre Macherey. 1981. "On Literature as Ideological Form." In *Untying the Text.* Ed. Robert Young. New York: Routledge & Kegan Paul.

Balibar, Etienne, and Immanuel Wallerstein. 1991. *Race, Nation, Class.* London: Verso.

Ball, Terence. 1991. "History: Critique and Irony." In *The Cambridge Companion to Marx.* Ed. Terrell Carver. Cambridge: Cambridge University Press.

Banks, James A. 1991. *Teaching Strategies for Ethnic Studies.* Boston: Allyn & Bacon.

Banton, Michael. 1987. *Racial Theories.* New York: Cambridge University Press.

Banton, Michael, and Robert Miles. 1984. "Racism." In *Dictionary of Race and Ethnic Relations.* Ed. E. Ellis Cashmore. London: Routledge. Pp. 225–29.

Bataille, Georges. 1985. *Visions of Excess: Selected Writings, 1927–1939.* Minneapolis: University of Minnesota Press.

Baudrillard, Jean. 1984a. "The Precession of Simulacra. In *Art After Modernism.* Ed. Brian Wallis. New York: Museum of Contemporary Art.

———. 1984b. "The Structural Law of Value and the Order of Simulacra." In *The Structural Allegory.* Ed. John Fekete. Minneapolis: University of Minnesota Press.

Bauer, Otto. 1970. "National Character and the Idea of the Nation." In *Essential Works of Socialism.* Ed. Irving Howe. New York: Bantam.

Bauman, Zygmunt. 1996. "From Pilgrim to Tourist—or a Short History of Identity." In *Questions of Cultural Identity.* Eds. Stuart Hall and Paul Du Gay. London: Sage. Pp. 18–36.

BAYAN International. 1994. *The Truth About the Ramos Regime: Facts and Figures About the Philippines.* Los Angeles: Author.

Belkin, Lisa. 1996. "Showdown at Yazoo Industries." *New York Times Magazine* (January 21):27–31, 38, 62, 64, 67, 69.

Bello, Walden. 1987. *Creating the Third Force: U.S.-Sponsored Low Intensity Conflict in the Philippines.* San Francisco: Institute for Food and Development Policy.

Beltran, Ruby, and Aurora Javate De Dios, eds. 1992. *Filipino Women Overseas Contract Workers . . . At What Cost?* Manila: Goodwill Trading.

Benito, Ted, and Meg Malpaya Thornton. 1989. "Pilipino Cultural Night." *East Wind* (Spring-Summer):51–54.

Benjamin, Walter. 1969. *Illuminations.* New York: Schocken.

———.1978. *Reflections.* New York: Harcourt.

Bennis, Phyllis, and Michael Moushabeck, eds. 1993. *Altered States: A Reader in the New World Order.* New York: Olive Branch Press.

Beraquit, Annie. 1983. "As One Regime Totters, a Consciousness Is Born." *Hartford Courant* (September 12):4.

Berger, John. 1984. *And our faces, my heart, brief as photos.* New York: Pantheon.

Berreman, Gerald. 1990. "The Incredible 'Tasaday': Deconstructing the Myth of the 'Stone-Age' People." *Cultural Survival Quarterly* 15:3–25.

Beveridge, Albert. 1987. "Our Philippine Policy." In *The Philippines Reader.* Ed. D. B. Schirmer and Stephen Shalom. Boston: South End.

Bhabha, Homi. 1990. *Nation and Narration.* New York: Routledge.

———. 1992. "Postcolonial Criticism." In *Redrawing the Boundaries.* Eds. Stephen Greenblatt and Giles Gunn. New York: Modern Language Association of America.

Blauner, Robert. 1972. *Racial Oppression in America.* New York: Harper.

Bloch, Ernst. 1996. "Marxism and Poetry." In *Marxist Literary Theory: A Reader.* Eds. Terry Eagleton and Drew Milne. Cambridge, MA: Blackwell.

Blount, James H. 1913. *The American Occupation of the Philippines, 1898–1912.* New York: Putnam.

Bock, Deborah, et al., eds. 1979. *Pearls.* Springfield, VA: Educational Film Center.

Bogardus, Emory S. 1976. "Anti-Filipino Race Riots." In *Letters in Exile.* Ed. Jesse Quinsaat. Los Angeles: UCLA Asian American Studies. Pp. 51–62.

Bourdieu, Pierre. 1986. *Distinction.* New York: Routledge & Kegan Paul.

_____. 1993. *The Field of Cultural Production*. New York: Columbia University Press.

Bowman, Glenn. 1994. "'A Country of Words': Conceiving the Palestinian Nation from the Position of Exile." In *The Making of Political Identities*. Ed. Ernesto Laclau. London: Verso. Pp. 138–70.

Boyce, James K. 1993. *The Philippines: The Political Economy of Growth and Impoverishment in the Marcos Era*. Honolulu: University of Hawaii Press.

Brecht, Bertolt. 1964. *Brecht on Theater*. Tr. John Willett. New York: Hill & Wang.

_____. 1976. *Poems 1913–1956*. Eds. John Willett and Ralph Manheim. New York: Methuen.

Bresnahan, Mary. 1991. *Finding Our Feet: Understanding Crosscultural Discourse*. New York: University Press of America.

Bresnan, John, ed. 1986. *Crisis in the Philippines: The Marcos Era and Beyond*. Princeton: Princeton University Press.

Brewer, Anthony. 1990. *Marxist Theories of Imperialism*. London and New York: Routledge.

Buaken, Manuel. 1940. "Where Is the Heart of America?" *The New Republic* 103 (23 September):410–11.

_____. 1946. *I Have Lived with the American People*. Caldwell, ID: Caxton Printers.

Buell, Frederick. 1994. *National Culture and the New Global System*. Baltimore: Johns Hopkins University Press.

Bulosan, Carlos. 1943. "Freedom from Want." *Saturday Evening Post* (March 6).

_____. 1944. *The Laughter of My Father*. New York: Harcourt.

_____. 1946. "I Am Not a Laughing Man." *The Writer* (May): 143–145.

_____. 1952. "Editorial" and "Terrorism Comes to the Philippines." In *1952 Yearbook, ILWU Local 37*. Seattle: International Longshoremen's and Warehousemen's Union.

_____. 1960. *Sound of Falling Light*. Ed. Dolores Feria. Quezon City: University of the Philippines Press.

_____. 1973 [1946]. *America Is in the Heart*. Seattle: University of Washington Press.

_____. 1978. *The Philippines Is in the Heart*. Quezon City, the Philippines: New Day Press.

_____. 1979. "Writings of Carlos Bulosan." *AmerAsia Journal* [Special Issue] 6.1 (May).

_____. 1980. *Selected Works and Letters*. Eds. E. San Juan Jr. and Ninotchka Rosca. Honolulu, HI: Friends of the Filipino People.

_____. 1983a. *Bulosan: An Introduction with Selections*. Ed. E. San Juan Jr. Manila: National Book Store.

_____. 1983b. *If You Want to Know What We Are*. Minneapolis: West End Press.

_____. 1995a. *The Cry and the Dedication*. Philadelphia: Temple University Press. (Published as *The Power of the People*, Manila: National Book Store, 1986)

_____. 1995b. *On Becoming Filipino*. Ed. E. San Juan Jr. Philadelphia: Temple University Press.

Burke, Kenneth. 1964. *Perspectives by Incongruity*. Ed. Stanley Edgar Hyman. Bloomington: Indiana University Press.

Burma, John. 1954. *Spanish-Speaking Groups in the United States*. Durham, NC: Duke University Press.

Buruma, Ian. 1989. *God's Dust*. New York: Farrar Straus Giroux.

Bush, Ray, Gordon Johnston, and David Coates, eds. 1987. *The World Order: Socialist Perspectives*. London: Polity.

Buss, Claude A. 1987. *Cory Aquino and the People of the Philippines*. Stanford: Stanford Alumni Association.

Cabezas, Amado, and Gary Kawaguchi. 1989. "Race, Gender and Class for Filipino Americans." In *A Look Beyond the Model Minority Image*. Ed. Grace Yun. New York: Minority Rights Group.

Caldwell, Malcolm. 1970. "Problems of Socialism in Southeast Asia." In *Imperialism and Underdevelopment*. Ed. Robert I. Rhodes. New York: Monthly Review Press. Pp. 376–403.

Callari, Antonio, Stephen Cullenberg, and Carole Biewener, eds. 1995. *Marxism in the Postmodern Age*. New York: Guilford.

Callinicos, Alex. 1989. *Against Postmodernism: A Marxist Critique*. New York: St. Martin's.

Campomanes, Oscar V. 1992. "Filipinos in the U.S.A. and Their Literature of Exile." In *Reading the Literatures of Asian America*. Eds. Shirley Lim and Amy Ling. Philadelphia: Temple University Press.

_____. 1995. "The New Empire's Forgetful and Forgotten Citizens: Unrepresentability and Unassimilability in Filipino-American Postcolonialities." *Critical Mass* 2.2 (Spring):145–200.

Campomanes, Oscar V., and Todd Gernes. 1988. "Two Letters from America: Carlos Bulosan and the Act of Writing." *Melus* 15.3(Fall):15–46.

Carbo, Nick. 1995. *El Grupo McDonald's*. Chicago: Tia Chucha Press.

Carby, Hazel. 1980. "Multi-Culture." *Screen Education* 34 (Spring):62–70.

_____. 1990. "The Politics of Difference." *Ms.* (September-October):84–85.

Cariño, Benjamin, James Fawcett, Robert Gardner, and Fred Arnold. 1990. *The New Filipino Immigrants to the United States: Increasing Diversity and Change*. Honolulu, HI: East-West Center.

Casper, Leonard. 1965. "Philippine Poetry." In *Encyclopedia of Poetry and Poetics*. Ed. Alex Preminger. Princeton: Princeton University Press.

_____. 1966. *New Writing from the Philippines*. Syracuse, NY: Syracuse University Press.

_____. 1979. "Introduction." In *Scent of Apples* by Bienvenido Santos. Seattle: University of Washington Press.

Catholic Institute for International Relations. 1987. *The Labour Trade*. London: Author.

_____. 1989. *Comment: The Philippines*. London: Author.

Césairé, Aime. 1972. *Discourse on Colonialism*. New York: Monthly Review Press.

Chan, Sucheng. 1991. *Asian Americans: An Interpretive History*. Boston: Twayne.

Chapman, William. 1987. *Inside the Philippine Revolution*. New York: Norton.

Chekhov, Anton. 1979. *Anton Chekhov's Short Stories*. New York: Norton.

Cheung, King-kok, and Stan Yogi, eds. 1988. *Asian American Literature*. New York: Modern Language Association of America.

Chin, Frank, et al., eds. 1975. *Aiiieeeee! An Anthology of Asian American Writers*. New York: Doubleday.

Chomsky, Noam. 1989. *Necessary Illusions: Thought Control in Democratic Societies*. Boston: South End.

Churchill, Thomas. 1995. *Triumph over Marcos*. Seattle: Open Hand Press.

Churma, Rose Cruz. 1994. "Filipinas in the 'New Plantation.'" In *Filipina: Hawaii's Filipino Women*. Honolulu, HI: FAUW Productions.

Constantino, Renato. 1966. "The Miseducation of the Filipino." In *The Filipinos in the Philippines and Other Essays*. Quezon City, Philippines: Malaya Books.

_____. 1975. *A History of the Philippines*. New York: Monthly Review Press.

_____. 1978. *Neocolonial Identity and Counter-Consciousness*. New York: M. E. Sharpe.

Cordova, Fred. 1983. *Filipinos: Forgotten Asian Americans*. Dubuque, IA: Kendall/Hunt.

_____. 1984. "Challenge to Pro- and Anti-Marcos Groups." *Philippine News* (February 15–22):4, 8.

Covi, Giovanna. 1995. "The Slow Process of Decolonizing Language: The Politics of Sexual Differences in Postmodern Fiction." Doctoral dissertation. State University of New York (Binghamton).

_____. 1996. "Jessica Hagedorn's Decolonialization of Subjectivity: Historical Agency Beyond Gender and Nation." In *Nationalism and Sexuality: Crises of Identity*. Eds. Yiorgos Kalogeras and Domna Pastourmatzi. Thessaloniki, Greece: Hellenic Association of American Studies/Aristotle University.

Crouchett, Lorraine Jacobs. 1982. *Filipinos in California: From the Days of the Galleons to the Present*. El Cerrito, CA: Downey Place Publishing House.

Cruz, Emeterio C. 1933. "Filipino Life in the Alaskan Fish Canneries." *Philippine Magazine* (June):45–48.

Daniels, Roger, and Harry Kitano. 1970. *American Racism*. Englewood Cliffs, NJ: Prentice-Hall.

Daroy, Petronilo. 1968. "Carlos Bulosan: The Politics of Literature." *St. Louis Quarterly* 6 (June):193–206.

Davis, Leonard. 1989. *Revolutionary Struggle in the Philippines*. London: Macmillan.

Davis, Mike. 1984. "The Political Economy of Late-Imperial America." *New Left Review* 134 (January-February):6–37.

_____. 1987. "From Fordism to Reaganism: The Crisis of American Hegemony in the 1980s." In *The World Order: Socialist Perspectives*. Eds. Ray Bush, Gordon Johnston, and David Coates. London: Polity.

De Dios, Aurora Javate, Petronilo Daroy, and Lorna Kalaw-Tirol, eds. 1988. *Dictatorship and Revolution: Roots of People's Power.* Quezon City, Philippines: Conspectus.

De la Torre, Ed. 1986. *Touching Ground, Taking Root.* London: CIIR/British Council of Churches.

Deleuze, Gilles. 1993. *The Deleuze Reader.* Ed. Constantin Boundas. New York: Columbia University Press.

Deleuze, Gilles, and Felix Guattari. 1986. *Kafka: Toward a Minor Literature.* Minneapolis: University of Minnesota Press.

_____. 1987. *A Thousand Plateaus.* Minneapolis: University of Minnesota Press.

Demirbag, Jocelyn Romero. 1994. "Filipinas in the Cane Fields, 1994." In *Filipina: Hawaii's Filipino Women.* Honolulu, HI: FAUW Productions.

DeParle, Jason. 1993. "Last of the Manongs: Aging Voices of a Farm-Labor Fight Find an Audience." *New York Times* (May 11):A14.

Deutsch, Babette. 1962. "Critical Essay." In *Poems 55* by Jose Garcia Villa. Manila: Alberto Florentino.

Dewitt, Howard. 1978. "The Filipino Labor Union: The Salinas Lettuce Strike of 1934." *AmerAsia Journal* 5.2:1–21.

Diokno, Jose W. 1987. *A Nation for Our Children.* Quezon City, Philippines: Claretian.

Dionisio, J. C. 1936. "Cannery Episode." *Philippine Magazine* (August):397, 412–13.

Dirlik, Arif. 1994a. *After the Revolution.* Hanover, NH, and London: Wesleyan University Press.

_____. 1994b. "Third World Criticism in the Age of Global Capitalism." *Critical Inquiry* 20 (Winter):328–56.

_____. 1997. *The Postcolonial Aura: Third World Criticism in the Age of Global Capitalism.* Boulder: Westview.

Dostoevsky, Fyodor. 1971. *The Idiot.* Middlesex, UK: Penguin.

Eggan, Fred. 1991. "The Philippines in the Twentieth Century: A Study in Contrasts." *Reviews in Anthropology* 20:13–23.

Erikson, Erik. H. 1980. *Identity and the Life Cycle.* New York: Norton.

Escoda, Isabel Taylor. 1989. *Letters from Hong Kong.* Manila: Bookmark.

Espina, Marina E. 1971. "Filipinos in New Orleans." *Louisiana Academy of Sciences* 38:117–121.

Espiritu, Yen Le. 1994. "The Intersection of Race, Ethnicity, and Class: The Multiple Identities of Second-Generation Filipinos." *Identities* 1:249–273.

_____. 1995. *Filipino American Lives.* Philadelphia: Temple University Press.

_____. 1996. "Colonial Oppression, Labour Importation and Group Formation: Filipinos in the United States." *Ethnic and Racial Studies* 19.1 (January):29–48.

Evangelista, Susan. 1985. *Carlos Bulosan and His Poetry.* Quezon City, Philippines: Ateneo de Manila University Press.

Evasco, Marjorie, Aurora Javate de Dios, and Flor Caagusan, eds. 1990. *Women's Springbook.* Quezon City, Philippines: Women's Resource and Research Center.

Fabian, Johannes. 1983. *Time and the Other.* New York: Columbia University Press.

Fallows, James. 1989. *More Like Us.* Boston: Houghton Mifflin.

Fanon, Frantz. 1967. *Black Skin, White Masks.* New York: Grove.

_____. 1968. *The Wretched of the Earth.* New York: Grove.

Featherstone, Mike, ed. 1990. "Introduction." In *Global Culture.* London: Sage.

Feleo-Gonzalez, Marina. 1988. *A Song for Manong.* Daly City, CA: Likha Promotions.

Feria, Dolores, ed. 1960. "Sound of Falling Light: Letters in Exile (by Carlos Bulosan)." *The Diliman Review* 8.1–3(January-September):185–277.

Feria, Mike. 1988. "A Kidlat Tahimik Retrospective." *Kultura* 1:33–36.

Filipino Petitioners. 1997 [1934]. "A Plea for Filipino Repatriation." In *Asian Americans: Opposing Viewpoints.* Ed. William Dudley. San Diego, CA: Greenhaven.

Fischer, Ernst. 1996. *How to Read Karl Marx.* New York: Monthly Review Press.

Foster, Nellie. 1994. "Legal Status of Filipino Intermarriages in California." *Asian Americans and the Law.* Ed. Charles McClain. New York: Garland.

Foucault, Michel. 1980. *Power/Knowledge: Selected Interviews and Other Writings 1972–1977.* New York: Pantheon.

Fowles, John. 1978. *Islands.* Boston: Little, Brown.

Francia, Luis, ed. 1993. *Brown River, White Ocean.* Brunswick, NJ: Rutgers University Press.

Francisco, Luzviminda. 1987. "The Philippine-American War." In *The Philippines Reader.* Eds. Daniel B. Schirmer and Stephen Shalom. Boston: South End. Pp. 8–19.

Francisco, Luzviminda, and Jonathan Fast. 1985. *Conspiracy for Empire.* Manila: Foundation for Nationalist Studies.

Franklin, Bruce. 1986. *War Stars.* New York: Oxford University Press.

Fraser, Nancy, and Linda Nicholson. 1990. "Social Criticism Without Philosophy: An Encounter Between Feminism and Postmodernism." In *Feminism/Postmodernism.* Ed. Linda Nicholson. New York: Routledge.

Freire, Paulo. 1972. *Pedagogy of the Oppressed.* New York: Herder & Herder.

Friend, Theodore. 1986. "Philippine-American Tensions in History." In *Crisis in the Philippines.* Ed. John Bresnan. Princeton: Princeton University Press.

_____. 1989. "Latin Ghosts Haunt an Asian Nation." *Heritage* (December):4.

Frith, Simon. 1984. "Rock and the Politics of Memory." In *The 60s: Without Apology.* Eds. Sohnya Sayres, Stanley Aronowitz, and Fredric Jameson. Minneapolis: University of Minnesota Press.

Fuchs, Lawrence. 1991. *The American Kaleidoscope.* Hanover, NH: University Press of New England.

Fuentebella, Cielo. 1989. "What Is Filipino American Culture?" *Philippine News* (August 9–15):12.

Fuss, Diana. 1989. *Essentially Speaking.* New York: Routledge.

Gaborro, Allen. 1997. "Essay on Filipino-Americans." <http://www.europa.com/ ~ria/essay.html>

Galang, M. Evelina. 1996. *Her Wild American Self.* Minneapolis, MN: Coffee House Press.

Genovese, Eugene. 1971. *In Red and Black.* New York: Pantheon.

Gill, Stephen. 1993. "Epistemology, Ontology, and the 'Italian School." In *Gramsci, Historical Materialism and International Relations.* New York: Cambridge University Press.

Gilroy, Paul. 1990. "It Ain't Where You're From, It's Where You're At . . . ": The Dialectics of Diasporic Identification." *Third Text*:3–16.

Gitlin, Todd. 1987. *The Sixties: Years of Hope/Days of Rage.* New York: Bantam.

Gochenour, Theodore. 1990. *Considering Filipinos.* Yarmouth, ME: Intercultural Press.

Goethe, Johann Wolfgang von. 1962. "Conversations with Eckermann." In *Modern Continental Literary Criticism.* Ed. O. B. Hardison Jr. New York: Appleton.

Goldberg, David. 1994. *Racist Culture.* New York: Blackwell.

Gompers, Samuel. 1908. *Meat vs. Rice: American Manhood Against Asiatic Coolieism.* San Francisco: Asiatic Exclusion League.

Gonzales, Juan L. 1993. *Racial and Ethnic Groups in America.* Dubuque, IA: Kendall/Hunt.

Gonzalez, Miguel M. 1990. "Culture of Poverty, Poverty of 'Culture': Colonizing Philippine Images." *Philippine Resource Center Monitor* 9 (November):1, 6–7, 9.

Gonzalez, N.V.M. 1990. "The Long Harvest." *Midweek* (May 23):25–26.

Gonzalves, Theo. 1995. "'The Show Must Go On': Production Notes on the Pilipino Cultural Night." *Critical Mass* 2.2 (Spring):129–44.

_____. 1995–1996. "'We Hold a Neatly Folded Hope': Filipino Veterans of World War II on Citizenship and Political Obligation." *AmerAsia Journal* 21.3 (Winter):155–74.

Gramsci, Antonio. 1957. *The Modern Prince.* New York: International Publishers.

_____. 1971. *Selections from the Prison Notebooks.* New York: International Publishers.

_____. 1989. "The Study of Philosophy." In *An Anthology of Western Marxism.* Ed. Roger Gottlieb. New York: Oxford University Press.

Grigulevich, I. R., and S. Y. Kozlov, eds. 1974. *Races and Peoples.* Moscow: Progress Publishers.

Grow, L. M. 1995. "*The Laughter of My Father:* A Survival Kit." *MELUS* 20 (Summer):35–46.

Guerrero, Leon Maria. 1969. *The First Filipino: A Biography of Jose Rizal.* Manila: Jose Rizal National Centennial Commission.

Guillaumin, Colette. 1995. *Racism, Sexism, Power and Ideology.* London and New York: Routledge.

Hagedorn, Jessica. 1990. *Dogeaters.* New York: Pantheon.

_____. 1993. *Danger and Beauty.* New York: Penguin.

_____. 1994. "The Exile Within/The Question of Identity." In *The State of Asian America*. Ed. Karin Aguilar–San Juan. Boston: South End.

_____. 1996. *The Gangster of Love*. Boston: Houghton Mifflin.

Hall, Stuart. 1986. "Gramsci's Relevance for the Study of Race and Ethnicity." *Journal of Communication Inquiry* 10.2 (Summer):5–27.

_____. 1993. *Danger and Beauty*. New York: Penguin.

_____. 1996a. *Critical Dialogues in Cultural Studies*. New York: Routledge.

_____. 1996b. "New Ethnicities." In *Critical Dialogues in Cultural Studies*. Eds. David Morley and Kuan-hsing Chen. New York: Routledge.

Hall, Stuart, David Held, and Tony McGrew, eds. 1992. *Modernity and Its Futures*. London: Polity.

Hamamoto, Darrell Y. 1994. *Monitored Peril*. Minneapolis: University of Minnesota Press.

Hardt, Michael. 1995. "Spinoza's Democracy: The Passion of Social Assemblages." In *Marxism in the Postmodern Age*. Eds. Antonio Callari, Stephen Cullenberg, and Carole Biewener. New York: Guilford.

Hart, Donn V. 1982. "The Contributions of Filipinos to American Culture." *Silliman Journal* (3rd and 4th quarters):163–168.

Harvey, David. 1989. *The Condition of Postmodernity*. Oxford, UK: Basil Blackwell.

_____. 1996. *Justice, Nature and the Geography of Difference*. Cambridge, MA: Blackwell.

Haug, W. F. 1986. *Critique of Commodity Aesthetics*. Minneapolis: University of Minnesota Press.

_____. 1987. *Commodity Aesthetics, Ideology and Culture*. New York: International General.

Hearn, Lafcadio. 1883. "Saint Malo: A Lacustrine Village in Louisiana." *Harper's Weekly* (March 31):146–52.

Hebdige, Dick. 1979. *Subculture: The Meaning of Style*. London: Methuen.

Hidalgo, Cristina Pantoja, and Priscelina Legasto, eds. 1993. *Philippine Post-Colonial Studies*. Quezon City: University of the Philippines Press.

Hofstadter, Richard. 1967. *The Paranoid Style in American Politics and Other Essays*. New York: Vintage.

Hwang, David Henry. 1986. *M. Butterfly*. New York: New American Library.

Jackson, George. 1970. *Soledad Brother*. New York: Bantam.

Jacoby, Russell. 1995. "Marginal Returns." *Lingua Franca* (September-October):30–37.

James, C.L.R. 1993. *American Civilization*. New York: Blackwell.

Jameson, Fredric. 1981. *The Political Unconscious*. Ithaca, NY: Cornell University Press.

_____. 1986. "Third-World Literature in the Era of Multinational Capitalism." *Social Text* 15:65–88.

_____. 1991. *Signatures of the Visible*. Bloomington: Indiana University Press.

Johnson, Lawrence. 1988. "Filipinos." *Rice Magazine* (July):24–25.

Jones, Gareth Stedman. 1970. "The Specificity of U.S. Imperialism." *New Left Review* (March-April):1–23.

Joyce, James. 1951. *Exiles*. New York: Viking.

Kaplan, Amy, and Donald Pease, eds. 1993. *Cultures of United States Imperialism*. Durham, NC: Duke University Press.

Karnow, Stanley. 1989. *In Our Image: America's Empire in the Philippines*. New York: Random House.

Kerkvliet, Benedict J., and Resil Mojares. 1991. *From Marcos to Aquino*. Quezon City: Ateneo de Manila University Press.

Kim, Elaine. 1982. *Asian American Literature*. Philadelphia: Temple University Press.

Kingston, Maxine Hong. 1989. *China Men*. New York: Vintage.

Kitano, Harry, and Roger Daniels. 1988. *Asian Americans: Emerging Minorities*. 2nd ed. Englewood Cliffs, NJ: Prentice Hall.

Klare, Michael T., and Peter Kornbluh, eds. 1988. *Low Intensity Warfare*. Quezon City, Philippines: Ken.

"Knowledge of Filipino Culture Helped L.A. Cops Nab Fugitive." 1996. *Philippine News* (May 29–June 4):A12.

Kolko, Gabriel. 1976. *Main Currents in Modern American History*. New York: Pantheon.

Kristeva, Julia. 1980. *Desire in Language*. New York: Columbia University Press.

_____. 1991. *Strangers to Ourselves*. New York: Columbia University Press.

Krupat, Arnold. 1989. *The Voice in the Margin*. Berkeley: University of California Press.

Kunitz, Stanley, ed. 1955. *Twentieth Century Artists*. New York: H. W. Wilson.

Kushner, Sam. 1971. *Long Road to Delano*. New York: International Publishers.

Lauter, Paul, ed. 1990. *The Heath Anthology of American Literature*. Boston: Heath.

Lee, Thea. 1991. "Trapped in a Pedestal." *Dollars and Sense* (March):12–15.

Lefebvre, Henri. 1966. *The Sociology of Marx*. New York: Vintage.

_____. 1971. *Everyday Life in the Modern World*. New York: Harper.

_____. 1976. *The Survival of Capitalism*. London: Allison & Busby.

Le Guin, Ursula K. 1975. *The Dispossessed*. New York: Avon.

Lenin, Vladimir. 1939. *Imperialism: The Last Stage of Capitalism*. New York: International Publishers.

Libretti, Timothy. 1995. "U.S. Literary History and Class Consciousness: Rethinking U.S. Proletarian and Third World Minority Literatures." Doctoral dissertation. University of Michigan.

Lim-Wilson, Fatima V. 1984. "Where i am from." *Caracoa V* (November):44.

_____. 1995. *Crossing the Snow Bridge*. Columbus: Ohio State University Press.

Lingis, Alphonso. 1994. *Foreign Bodies*. New York: Routledge.

Lott, Juanito Tamayo. 1989. "Growing Up, 1968–1985." In *Making Waves*. Ed. Asian Women United of California. Boston: Beacon.

Lowe, Lisa. 1995. "On Contemporary Asian American Projects." *AmerAsia Journal* 21.1 & 2:41–52.

Lu, Hsun. 1975. "Some Thoughts on Our New Literature." In *Marxists on Literature*. Ed. David Craig. New York: Penguin.

Lukács, Georg. 1973. *Marxism and Human Liberation: Selected Essays*. Ed. E. San Juan Jr. New York: Dell.

Lyotard, Jean-Francois. 1984. *The Postmodern Condition: A Report on Knowledge*. Minneapolis: University of Minnesota Press.

Mabini, Apolinario. 1989 [1974]. "The Struggle for Freedom." In *Filipino Nationalism*. Ed. Teodoro A. Agoncillo. Quezon City, Philippines: R. P. Garcia.

Manalansan IV, Martin. 1995. "Speaking of AIDS: Language and the Filipino 'Gay' Experience in America." In *Discrepant Histories*. Ed. Vicente Rafael. Philadelphia: Temple University Press.

Mandel, Ernest. 1979. *Introduction to Marxism*. London: Links.

Mangiafico, Luciano. 1988. *Contemporary American Immigrants*. New York: Praeger.

Mao Tse-tung. 1960. *Selected Works of Mao Tse-tung*. Vol. 3. Beijing: Foreign Languages Press.

Marx, Karl. 1973. *Early Writings*. Ed. Quintin Hoare. New York: Vintage.

Marx, Karl, and Friedrich Engels. 1968. *Selected Works*. New York: International Publishers.

Mascia-Less, Frances, Patricia Sharpe, and Colleen Ballerino Cohen. 1989. "The Postmodernist Turn in Anthropology: Cautions from a Feminist Perspective." *Signs* 15:7–33.

Mayuga, Sylvia, and Alfred Yuson. 1980. "In the Wrong Waters." In *Philippines*. Created and designed by Hans Johannes Hoefer. Hong Kong: Apa Productions.

McClintock, Anne. 1994. "The Angel of Progress: Pitfalls of the Term 'Post-Colonialism.'" *Colonial Discourse and Post-Colonial Theory*. Eds. Patrick Williams and Laura Chrisman. New York: Columbia University Press. Pp. 291–304.

McWilliams, Carey. 1964. *Brothers Under the Skin*. Boston: Little, Brown.

_____. 1973. "Introduction." In *America Is in the Heart* by Carlos Bulosan. Seattle: University of Washington Press.

_____. 1997 [1935]. "Most Filipino Immigrants Do Not Want Repatriation." In *Asian Americans: Opposing Viewpoints*. Ed. William Dudley. San Diego, CA: Greenhaven.

Meillassoux, Claude. 1993. "Toward a Theory of the 'Social Corps.'" In *The Curtain Rises: Rethinking Culture, Ideology, and the State in Eastern Europe*. Eds. Hermine De Soto and David Anderson. Atlantic Highlands, NJ: Humanities Press.

Melendy, H. Brett. 1980. "Filipinos." In *Harvard Encyclopedia of American Ethnic Groups*. Cambridge, MA: Harvard University Press.

_____. 1981 [1977]. *Asians in America: Filipinos, Koreans, and East Indians*. New York: Hippocrene Books.

Memmi, Albert. 1965. *The Colonizer and the Colonized*. Boston: Beacon.

Meñez, Herminia Q. 1986–1987. "Agyu and the Skyworld: The Philippine Folk Epic and Multicultural Education." *AmerAsia Journal* 13.1:135–49.

Miles, Robert. 1986. "Labour Migration, Racism and Capital Accumulation in Western Europe Since 1945: An Overview." *Capital and Class* 28:49–86.

_____. 1989. Racism. London: Routledge.

Miller, Stuart Creighton. 1982. *"Benevolent Assimilation": The American Conquest of the Philippines 1899–1903.* New Haven: Yale University Press.

Morales, Royal F. 1974. *Makibaka: The Pilipino American Struggle.* Los Angeles: Mountainview Publishers.

Moy, James. 1996. "Fierce Visibility: Anglo-American Desire Constructing Asian Sexuality." In *Nationalism and Sexuality: Crises of Identity.* Eds. Yiorgos Kalogeras and Domna Pastourmatzi. Thessaloniki, Greece: Hellenic Association of American Studies and Aristotle University.

Myrdal, Gunnar. 1974. *An American Dilemma.* New York: McGraw-Hill.

Nakanishi, Don T. 1976. "Minorities and International Politics." In *Counterpoint.* Ed. Emma Gee. Los Angeles: UCLA. Pp. 81–85.

Navarro, Jovina, ed. 1974. *Diwang Pilipino.* Davis, CA: Asian American Studies, University of California, Davis.

Nee, Victor, and Jimy Sanders. 1985. "The Road to Parity: Determinants of the Socioeconomic Achievements of Asian Americans." *Ethnic and Racial Studies* 8.1 (January):75–93.

Negri, Antonio, and Michael Hardt. 1994. *Labor of Dionysus: A Critique of the State-Form.* Minneapolis: University of Minnesota Press.

Ngugi, Wa Thiong'o. 1981. *Writers in Politics.* London: Heinemann.

Nixon, Rob. 1995. "Refugees and Homecomings: Bessie Head and the End of Exile." In *Late Imperial Culture.* Eds. Roman de la Campa, E. Ann Kaplan, and Michael Sprinker. London: Verso. Pp. 149–65.

O'Brien, Edward J. 1933. "Introduction." In *Footnote to Youth by Jose Garcia Villa.* New York: Scribner.

Occeña, Bruce. 1985. "The Filipino Nationality in the U.S.: An Overview." *Line of March* (Fall):29–41.

O'Hare, William P., and Judy C. Felt. 1991. *Asian Americans: America's Fastest Growing Minority Group.* Washington DC: Population Reference Bureau.

Omatsu, Glenn. 1994. "In Memoriam Philip Vera Cruz." *AmerAsia Journal* 20.2: iii–v.

Omi, Michael, and Howard Winant. 1986. *Racial Formation in the United States.* New York: Routledge.

Pajaron, Ding. 1990. "Dogeaters Is a Sumptuous Feast." *Katipunan*:17, 20.

Palumbo-Liu, David. 1993. "Closure as Capitulation: The Ideology of Healing in Asian American Literature." Unpublished manuscript, 23 pages. (Revised and forthcoming as "Model Minority Discourse and the Course of Healing" in *Minority Discourse: Ideological Containment and Utopian/Heterotopian Potential,* ed. Abdul JanMohamed)

Paredes, Ruby, ed. 1988. *Philippine Colonial Democracy.* Monograph Series 32, Yale University Southeast Asia Studies. New Haven: Yale Center for International and Area Studies.

Parry, Benita. 1987. "Problems in Current Theories of Colonial Discourse." *Oxford Literary Review* 9.1–2:27–58.

Patel, Dinker. 1992. "Asian Americans: A Growing Force." In *Race and Ethnic Relations 92/93*. Ed. John Kromkowski. Guilford, CT: Dushkin. Pp. 109–13.

Peñaranda, Oscar, Serafin Syquia, and Sam Tagatac. 1975. "An Introduction to Filipino-American Literature." In *Aiiieeeee!* Eds. Frank Chin et al. New York: Anchor.

Pe-pua, Rogelia. 1989. *Sikolohiyang Pilipino: Teorya, Metodo at Gamit.* Quezon City: University of the Philippines Press.

Philippine Center for Immigrant Rights. 1985. *Filipinos in the USA.* New York: Author.

Pido, Antonio J. A. 1986. *The Pilipinos in America.* New York: Center for Immigration Studies.

Posadas, Barbara. 1986–1987. "At a Crossroad: Filipino American History and the Old-Timers' Generation." *AmerAsia Journal* 13.1:85–97.

Putzel, James. 1982. *A Captive Land.* New York: Monthly Review Press.

Quinsaat, Jesse, ed. 1976. *Letters in Exile.* Los Angeles: UCLA Asian American Studies Center.

Rabaya, Violet. 1971. "Filipino Immigration: The Creation of a New Social Problem." In *Roots: An Asian American Reader.* Eds. Amy Takichi et al. Los Angeles: UCLA Asian American Studies Center.

Rafael, Vicente, ed. 1989. *Discrepant Histories: Translocal Essays on Filipino Culture.* Philadelphia: Temple University Press.

Retamar, Roberto Fernandez. 1989. *Caliban and Other Essays.* Minneapolis: University of Minnesota Press.

Rex, John. 1983. "Race." In *Dictionary of Marxist Thought.* Ed. Tom Bottomore. Cambridge, MA: Harvard University Press.

Richardson, Jim. 1989. "Introduction." *The Philippines.* Oxford, UK: Clio Press.

Robinson, Cedric. 1994. "Ota Benga's Flight Through Geronimo's Eyes: Tales of Science and Multiculturalism." In *Multiculturalism: A Reader.* Ed. David Theo Goldberg. Oxford, UK: Blackwell.

Robles, Al. 1996. *Rappin' with Ten Thousand Carabaos in the Dark.* Los Angeles: UCLA Asian American Studies Center.

Roces, Alfredo, and Grace Roces. 1985. *Culture Shock! Philippines.* Singapore: Times Books International.

Rodil, B. R. 1993. *The Lumad and Moro of Mindanao. Minority Rights Group Intervention Report.* London: Minority Rights Group.

Ruoff, A., LaVonne Brown, and Jerry Ward Jr., eds. 1990. *Redefining American Literary History.* New York: Modern Language Association of America.

Rushdie, Salman. 1983. *Shame.* New York: Vintage.

Said, Edward. 1978. *Orientalism.* London: Routledge & Kegan Paul.

_____. 1990. "Reflections on Exile." In *Out There: Marginalization and Contemporary Culture.* Eds. Russell Ferguson et al. New York: New Museum of Contemporary Art.

_____. 1994. *Culture and Imperialism.* New York: Knopf.

Saldivar, Ramon. 1990. *Chicano Narrative: The Dialectic of Difference.* Madison: University of Wisconsin Press.

San Buenaventura, Steffi. 1996. "Filipino Folk Spirituality and Immigration: From Mutual Aid to Religion." *AmerAsia Journal* 22.1 (Spring):1–30.

San Juan, E. Jr. 1972. *Carlos Bulosan and the Imagination of the Class Struggle.* New York: Oriole Editions (originally published by the University of the Philippines Press).

_____. 1979. "Introduction." *AmerAsia Journal* [Special Bulosan issue] 6.6 (May):3–29.

_____. 1983. *Bulosan: An Introduction with Selections.* Manila: National Book Store.

_____. 1984. *Toward a People's Literature: Essays in the Dialectics of Praxis and Contradiction.* Quezon City: University of the Philippines Press.

_____. 1986. *Crisis in the Philippines.* Hadley, MA: Bergin & Garvey.

_____. 1988. *Only by Struggle.* Manila: Kalikasan Press.

_____. 1989a. "Pax Americana on the Boob Tube." *Solidaridad* (1st and 2nd quarters):65–66.

_____. 1989b. "Problems in the Marxist Project of Theorizing Race." *Rethinking Marxism* 2.2 (Summer):58–80.

_____. 1990. *From People to Nation: Essays in Cultural Politics.* Manila: Asian Social Institute.

_____. 1991a. "Beyond Identity Politics: The Predicament of the Asian American Writer in Late Capitalism." *American Literary History* (Fall):542–65.

_____. 1991b. "Mapping the Boundaries: The Filipino Writer in the U.S.A." *Journal of Ethnic Studies* 19.1 (Spring 1991):117–31.

_____. 1991c. *Writing and National Liberation.* Quezon City: University of the Philippines Press.

_____. 1992a. *Racial Formations/Critical Transformations.* Atlantic Highlands, NJ: Humanities Press.

_____. 1992b. *Reading the West/Writing the East.* New York: Peter Lang.

_____. 1992c. "Symbolizing the Asian Diaspora in the United States: A Return to the Primal Scene of Deracination." *Border/Lines* 24–25:23–29.

_____. 1994a. *Allegories of Resistance.* Quezon City: University of the Philippines Press.

_____. 1994b. "Configuring the Filipino Diaspora in the United States." *Diaspora* 3.2:117–32.

_____. 1995a. "From the 'Boondocks' to the 'Belly of the Beast': What We Can Learn from the Life-History of a Filipino Worker-Intellectual." *Mediations* 19.1 (Spring):76–91.

_____, ed. 1995b. *On Becoming Filipino: Selected Writings of Carlos Bulosan.* Philadelphia: Temple University Press.

_____. 1996a. *Hegemony and Strategies of Transgression.* Albany: State University of New York Press.

_____. 1996b. *The Philippine Temptation: Dialectics of Philippines–U.S. Literary Relations.* Philadelphia: Temple University Press.

_____. 1996c. "Postcolonial Theory and Philippine Reality: The Challenge of a Third World Culture to Global Capitalism." *Left Curve* 20:87–102.

_____. 1996d. "Searching for the Heart of 'America.'" In *Teaching American Ethnic Literatures.* Eds. John Maitino and David Peck. Albuquerque: University of New Mexico Press. Pp. 259–72.

_____. 1997. *Beyond Postcolonial Theory*. New York: St. Martin's.

Santos, Bienvenido. 1979. *Scent of Apples*. Seattle: University of Washington Press.

_____. 1982. "Words from a Writer in Exile." In *Asian Writers on Literature and Justice*. Ed. Leopoldo Yabes. Manila: Philippine Center of International PEN.

Saxton, Alexander. 1977. "Nathan Glazer, Daniel Moynihan and the Cult of Ethnicity." *AmerAsia Journal*, 4.2:141–50.

Schaefer, Richard T. 1996. *Racial and Ethnic Groups*. 6th ed. New York: HarperCollins College Publishers.

Scharlin, Craig, and Lilia V. Villanueva. 1992. *Philip Vera Cruz*. Eds. Glenn Omatsu and Augusto Espiritu. Los Angeles: UCLA Labor Center and UCLA Asian American Studies Center.

Schirmer, Daniel B. 1995. *Military Access: The Pentagon vs. The Philippine Constitution*. Boston: Friends of the Filipino People.

Scott, William Henry. 1982. *Cracks in the Parchment Curtain*. Quezon City, Philippines: New Day Publishers.

_____. 1993. *Of Igorots and Independence*. Baguio City, Philippines: ERA.

Sharma, Miriam. 1987. "Towards a Political Economy of Emigration from the Philippines: The 1906 to 1946 Ilocano Movement to Hawaii in Historical Perspective." *Philippine Sociological Review* 35 (July–December):15–33.

Simmel, Georg. 1977. "The Stranger." In *Race, Ethnicity, and Social Change*. Ed. John Stone. North Scituate, MA: Duxbury.

Sison, Jose Maria. 1986. *Philippine Crisis and Revolution*. Ten lectures delivered at the Asian Center, University of the Philippines, Quezon City, April-May.

Sklair, Leslie. 1991. *Sociology of the Global System*. Baltimore: Johns Hopkins University Press.

Smith, Joseph. 1976. *Portrait of a Cold Warrior*. New York: Ballantine.

Solberg, S. E. 1991 [1975]. "An Introduction to Filipino American Literature." In *Aiiieeeee!* Eds. Frank Chin et al. New York: Mentor Books.

Sollors, Werner. 1986. *Beyond Ethnicity*. New York: Oxford University Press.

Solomon, Mark. 1994. "Reflections on the Global Economy." *Dialogue and Initiative* 9 (Summer):28–32.

Somera, Rene. 1982. "Between Two Worlds: The Hawaii Ilocano Immigrant Experience." *The Diliman Review* (January–February):54–59.

Spinoza, Benedict [Baruch]. 1994. *A Spinoza Reader*. Ed. Edwin Curley. Princeton: Princeton University Press.

Spivak, Gayatri Chakravorty. 1988. "Can the Subaltern Speak?" *Marxism and the Interpretation of Culture*. Eds. C. Nelson and L. Grossberg. Urbana: University of Illinois Press.

_____. 1991. *The Post-Colonial Critic: Interviews, Strategies, Dialogues*. New York: Routledge.

Stanley, Peter. 1974. *A Nation in the Making: The Philippines and the United States, 1899–1921*. Cambridge, MA: Harvard University Press.

_____. 1985. "The Manongs of California." *Philippines-U.S. Free Press* (November):4, 7–8, 50.

_____, ed. 1984. *Re-Appraising an Empire: New Perspectives on Philippine-American History.* Cambridge, MA: Harvard University Press.

Stauffer, Robert B. 1985. *The Marcos Regime: Failure of Transnational Developmentalism and Hegemony-Building From Above and Outside.* Research Monograph No. 23. Sydney, Australia: Transnational Corporations Research Project.

_____.1987. "Review of Peter Stanley, Reappraising an Empire." *Journal of Asian and African Studies* 12.1–2:102–4.

_____. 1990. "Philippine Democracy: Contradictions of Third World Redemocratization." University of Hawaii: Philippine Studies Colloqium, May 4.

Stegner, Wallace. 1945. *One Nation.* Boston: Houghton Mifflin.

Steinberg, David Joel. 1982. *The Philippines: A Singular and a Plural Place.* Boulder: Westview.

Steinberg, Stephen. 1996. *Turning Back.* Boston: Beacon.

Stone, John. 1996. "Internal Colonialism." In *Ethnicity.* Eds. John Hutchinson and Anthony Smith. New York: Oxford University Press.

Sturtevant, David. 1976. *Popular Uprisings in the Philippines 1840–1940.* Ithaca, NY: Cornell University Press.

Suleri, Sara. 1995. "Woman Skin Deep: Feminism and the Postcolonial Condition." *The Post-Colonial Studies Reader.* Eds. Bill Ashcroft, Gareth Griffiths, and Helen Tiffin. London and New York: Routledge.

Sussman, Gerald. 1992. "What 'Hearts of Darkness' Left Out." *Guardian* (April 29):19.

Tajima, Renee. 1996. "Site-Seeing Through Asian America: On the Making of Fortune Cookies." *Mapping Multi-Culturalism.* Eds. Avery Gordon and Christopher Newfield. Minneapolis: University of Minnesota Press. Pp. 263–96.

Takaki, Roland. 1987. "Reflections on Racial Patterns in America." In *From Different Shores.* Ed. Roland Takaki. New York: Oxford University Press. Pp. 26–37.

_____. 1989. *Strangers from a Different Shore.* Boston: Little, Brown.

Tanada, Wigberto. 1994–1995. "Senator Tanada Addresses Security Issues." *Philippine Witness* 50:5, 9.

Tarr, Peter. 1989. "Learning to Love Imperialism." *The Nation* (June 5):779–84.

Taruc, Luis. 1953. *Born of the People.* New York: International Publishers.

Thernstrom, S. 1983. "Ethnic Pluralism: The U.S. Model." In *Minorities: Community and Identity.* Ed. C. Fried. Berlin: Springer-Verlag. Pp. 247–54.

Thrift, Nigel. 1996. *Spatial Formations.* London: Sage.

Tinker, Edward Larocque. 1970 [1924]. *Lafcadio Hearn's American Days.* Detroit, MI: Gale Research.

Todorov, Tzvetan. 1981. *Introduction to Poetics.* Minneapolis: University of Minnesota Press.

Trinh Minh-ha. 1989. *Woman, Native, Other: Writing Postcoloniality and Feminism.* Bloomington: Indiana University Press.

Tucker, Robert, ed. 1978. *The Marx-Engels Reader.* New York: Norton.

Turki, Fawaz. 1978. *Tel Zaatar Was the Hill of Thyme.* Washington, DC: Free Palestine Press.

Turner, Bryan S. 1994. *Orientalism, Postmodernism, and Globalism.* New York: Routledge.

Twain, Mark. 1952. "Thirty Thousand Killed a Million." *The Atlantic Monthly* (April):52–65.

U.S. Bureau of the Census. 1993. *1990 Census of the Population: Asians and Pacific Islanders in the United States.* Washington, DC: Government Printing Office.

Vallangca, Caridad Concepcion. 1987. *The Second Wave: Pinay & Pinoy.* (1945–1960). San Francisco: Strawberry Hill Press.

Vallangca, Roberto. 1977. *Pinoy: The First Wave.* San Francisco: Strawberry Hill Press.

Vallejo, Cesar. 1976. *Selected Poems.* New York: Penguin.

Van der Pijl, Kees. 1997. "The History of Class Struggle: From Original Accumulation to Neoliberalism." *Monthly Review* 49 (May):28–44.

Van Erven, Eugene. 1992. *The Playful Revolution.* Bloomington: University of Indiana Press.

Vera, Arleen de. 1994. "Without Parallel: The Local 7 Deportation Cases, 1949–1955," *AmerAsia Journal* 20.2:1–25.

Vera Cruz, Philip. 1992. *Philip Vera Cruz: A Personal History of Filipino Immigrants and the Farmworkers Movements.* Los Angeles: University of California, Los Angeles, Labor Center and Asian American Studies Center.

Vidal, Gore. 1986–1992. *The Decline and Fall of the American Empire.* Berkeley, CA: Odonian Press.

Villa, Jose Garcia. 1933. *Footnote to Youth.* New York: Scribner.

_____. 1942. *Have Come Am Here.* New York: Viking.

_____. 1949. *Volume Two.* New York: New Directions.

_____. 1958. *Selected Poems and New.* New York: McDowell Obolensky.

Villanueva, Marianne. 1991. *Ginseng and Other Tales from Manila.* Corvallis, OR: Calyx.

Wald, Alan. 1987. "Theorizing Cultural Difference: A Critique of the Ethnicity School." *MELUS* 14.2 (Summer):21–33.

Wallerstein, Immanuel. 1983. *Historical Capitalism.* London: Verso.

Wand, David Hsin-Fu, ed. 1974. *Asian American Heritage.* New York: Washington Square Press.

Weiss, Peter. 1973. *Trotsky in Exile.* New York: Pocket Books.

Wilden, Anthony, 1980. *Systems and Structure.* New York: Tavistock.

Willett, John. 1964. *Brecht on Theater.* New York: Hill & Wang.

Williams, Raymond. 1977. *Marxism and Literature.* New York: Oxford University Press.

_____. 1983. *Keywords.* New York: Oxford University Press.

Williams, Rhonda. 1995. "Consenting to Whiteness: Reflections on Race and Marxian Theories of Discrimination." In *Marxism in the Postmodern Age.* Ed. Antonio Callari, Stephen Cullenberg, and Carole Biewener. New York: Guilford.

Williams, William Appleman. 1962. *The Tragedy of American Diplomacy.* New York: Dell.

Wojciehowski, Dolora. 1972. "Petrarch's Temporal Exile and the Wounds of History." In *The Literature of Emigration and Exile.* Eds. James Whitlark and Wendell Aycock. Lubbock: Texas Tech University Press.

Wolf, Eric. 1982. *Europe and the People Without History.* Berkeley: University of California Press.

Wolff, Leon. 1961. *Little Brown Brother.* New York: Doubleday.

Yoneda, Karl. 1988. "Asian Pacific Workers and the U.S. Labor Movement." *Nature, Society, and Thought* 1.3:436–43.

Yovel, Yirmiyahu. 1989. *Spinoza and Other Heretics: The Marrano of Reason.* Princeton: Princeton University Press.

Zamora Linmark, R. 1995. *Rolling the R's.* New York: Kaya Production.

_____. 1997. "R. Zamora Linmark." *A. Magazine* (Spring):37–38.

Zinn, Howard. 1992. *The Twentieth Century.* New York: Harper & Row.

Index